P9-DMI-573

THE BEST OF Gourmet 2000

FROM THE EDITORS OF GOURMET

PHOTOGRAPHS BY ROMULO A. YANES

CONDÉ NAST BOOKS · RANDOM HOUSE, NEW YORK

Copyright © 1999
The Condé Nast Publications Inc.
All rights reserved under International and Pan-
American Copyright Conventions. Published in the
United States by Random House, Inc., New York,
and simultaneously in Canada by Random House
of Canada Limited, Toronto.

ISBN 0-375-50431-1
ISSN 1046-1760

Random House website address:
www.atrandom.com

Most of the recipes in this work were published previously in *Gourmet* Magazine.

Printed in the United States of America on acid-free paper

98765432
First Edition

Informative text in this book was written by
Diane Keitt, Caroline A. Schleifer, and Nancie
McDermott.

The text of this book was set in Times Roman by
Media Projects Incorporated. The four-color separations
were done by American Color, Applied Graphic
Technologies, and Quad/Graphics, Inc. The book was
printed and bound at R. R. Donnelley and Sons. Stock
is Citation Web Gloss, Westvāco.

Front jacket: Pomelo Salad (page 230)
Back jacket: Quail Eggs with Toasted Sesame Salt
(page 93); Baked Asparagus and Yellow Pepper
Frittata (page 140); Hot Cross Buns (page 106); and
Grapefruit Coolers (page 209).

Frontispiece: Grape Tart (page 192).

For Condé Nast Books
Lisa Faith Phillips, Vice President/General Manager
Tom Downing, Associate Direct Marketing Director
Deborah Williams, Operations Manager
Colleen P. Shire, Direct Marketing Manager
Angela Lee, Assistant Direct Marketing Manager
Meredith Peters, Direct Marketing Assistant
Margaret McCreary, Direct Marketing Assistant
Richard B. Elman, Production Manager

For *Gourmet* Books
Diane Keitt, Director
Caroline A. Schleifer, Editor
Ellen Morrissey, Associate Editor

For *Gourmet* Magazine
Ruth Reichl, Editor-in-Chief

Zanne Early Stewart, Executive Food Editor
Kemp Miles Minifie, Senior Food Editor
Alexis M. Touchet, Associate Food Editor
Lori Walther Powell, Food Editor
Elizabeth Vought, Food Editor
Katy Massam, Food Editor
Shelton Wiseman, Food Editor
Alix Palley, Food Editor
Ruth Cousineau, Food Editor

Romulo A. Yanes, Photographer
Marjorie H. Webb, Style Director
Nancy Purdum, Senior Style Editor

Produced in association with
Media Projects Incorporated
Carter Smith, Executive Editor
Anne B. Wright, Project Editor
John W. Kern, Project Consultant
Aaron R. Murray, Production Editor
Marilyn Flaig, Indexer
Karen Salsgiver, Design Consultant

THE BEST OF
Gourmet

ACKNOWLEDGMENTS

The editors of Gourmet Books would like to thank everyone who worked on this volume, especially Zanne Early Stewart, *Gourmet*'s Executive Food Editor, who acted as consultant, and Kemp Minifie, *Gourmet*'s Senior Food Editor, who tasted and critiqued all new recipes.

We also would like to give special thanks to Nancie McDermott, respected cookbook author and teacher of the regional cuisines of Thailand, who kept a keen eye on everyone's work as we developed our international section. Nancie wrote the insightful opener and primer on traditional Thai kitchens. An authentic Thai Dinner was developed by Alexis Touchet, and Elizabeth Vought and Lori Walther Powell created a collection of Thai snacks. Lori also styled her Pomelo Salad for the jacket. All Thai food was photographed by Romulo Yanes and prop-styled by Jeannie Oberholtzer. Photographs of Thailand from Nick Wheeler, Jim Babson, Timothy Shea, and Ruth MacKay-Shea and line drawings by Laura Hartman Maestro bring the people and countryside of this exquisite country to life.

The recipes that appear in our special section—Unusual Pastas and Grains—were developed by Alexis Touchet, Lori Walther Powell, Elizabeth Vought, and Alix Palley. Alexis Seabrook's clever border drawing gives this section a distinctive flair.

Over the years, *The Best of Gourmet* series has attracted a talented group of artists. This volume contains drawings by Jean Chandler, Suzanne Dunaway, Maurie Harrington, Vicky Gonis, Elisa Mambrino, Jeanne Meinke, Bob Palevitz, Agni Saucier, Jim Saucier, Alexis Seabrook, Harley Seabrook, and Meg Shields.

And finally, thanks to Karen Salsgiver for her wonderful sense of design; and to Anne Wright, John Kern, Aaron Murray, Cheryl Brown, Hobby McKenney Coudert, and Kathleen Duffy Freud, who carefully massaged the manuscript into final form.

. . .

CONTENTS

INTRODUCTION

As everyone knows, the key to *good living* is finding the balance between time spent at work and with family and friends. It's difficult to get it right, and yet the rewards are beyond measure. That is why *Gourmet* magazine is more intent than ever on offering plenty of exceptional everyday dishes that don't require much fuss. We believe in simplicity and shortcuts as long as taste is not compromised. For example, the heart of our Beyond Backyard Basics menu (page 61) is ratatouille with penne, an easy dish that masterfully layers the fresh flavors of vegetables from the summer garden. The finale, a luscious grape tart, is made with frozen puff pastry—a well-known timesaver—for buttery flakiness that pairs ideally with velvety-smooth pastry cream and crisp, juicy grapes. This collection offers 28 menus and more than 350 recipes. When time is tight, look for recipes that can be made in 45 minutes or less (indicated by a clock). If you're watching your waistline, head for recipes low in fat and calories (marked with a feather).

Every year *Gourmet*'s food editors travel extensively to study and sample the foods of talented chefs from around the world. During 1999, we explored Thailand, Australia, and Europe and returned with plenty of exciting ideas for new recipes to share with you. This year's Cuisines of the World section (page 210) features the exotic flavors of Thailand with a Traditional Thai Dinner for eight and a collection of Thai snacks. You may want to make the Thai jasmine rice to accompany another menu, or serve the grilled chicken wings with sweet garlic sauce as an hors d'oeuvre, or prepare an entire meal with these dishes. Whichever you choose, we're sure you'll return to these recipes again and again. And, to help you use some of the lesser-known foods found on today's ever-expanding supermarket shelves, we've included a special section on Unusual Pastas and Grains (page 240). Here you'll find 24 new recipes, many Eastern in origin, for udon noodles, bean thread noodles, Israeli couscous, rice noodles, Japanese rice, quinoa, grits, cornmeal, wheat berries, and more. They're a perfect way to shake up an ordinary meal.

Whether we're introducing or reintroducing you to the basics (Thanksgiving Primer, page 66) or encouraging you to scale new culinary heights (make your own wedding cake with blackberries and roses, page 182), the new *Gourmet* is committed to a sensible, straight-forward approach. Along the way, we'll be sure to keep practicality and "doability" uppermost in mind.

The Editors of Gourmet

• • •

THE MENU
COLLECTION

Throughout the 1990's, *Gourmet* entertaining became more relaxed. Menus often were pared down to three simple courses, and the recipes themselves became less complicated. Along with this simplification came a heightened awareness of the food itself. Respected chefs convinced us that everything tastes better when cooked with the purest, farm-fresh ingredients. During 1999, *Gourmet* magazine offered an array of menus—most are decidedly casual, all are prepared with ultimate flavor in mind.

These days, entertaining at home often means serving comforting dishes that everyone enjoys. The next time you crave honey-glazed spareribs, or collard greens and turnips with ham hock, or candied sweet potatoes, look no further than Southern Comforts, a feast of favorites that will draw your guests into the kitchen to see what's cooking. There's even A Weekend at Home breakfast featuring buttermilk waffles (with a bit of prosciutto) that will pamper your sweetheart in style.

And, because most of us prefer to dine *alfresco* when the weather is fine, here you'll find a host of parties to enjoy *in fresh air*. Begin with our Easter Brunch, a fabulous spread filled with the tastes of spring—baked asparagus frittata, cheddar scones with ham, hot cross buns, and more. Then, throughout the summer, heat up the grill for cookouts galore. Our Cooking with Friends menu will please both fish- and meat-lovers alike with grilled butterflied leg of lamb and grilled halibut, while A Weekend at the Shore will treat your guests to Dinner on the Deck with grilled lobsters in a luscious Southeast Asian dipping sauce. There's also A Sizzling Summer Fiesta backyard buffet filled with Latin American flavors (the chilled roasted red pepper soup is divine).

You'll even find an informal loft Wedding in the City that boasts exotic fare. Dishes like stuffed grape leaves with Merguez sausage, grilled Charmoula lamb chops, and beet and jícama on endive make this a union to remember. (For a smaller version of this delightful menu, turn to Without Ceremony: Wedding Food for an Intimate Dinner.)

Come explore the best of *Gourmet*'s newest menus—with lots of flavorful surprises.

• • •

A SKI HOUSE DINNER

Serves 6

SMOKED SALMON WITH
CILANTRO CREAM, p. 93

Louis Roederer Estate Brut Premier Champagne

• • •

ROASTED VEAL CHOPS WITH SHALLOTS,
TOMATOES, AND OLIVE JUS, p. 124

SOFT POLENTA, p. 124

Rocca di Montegrossi Chianti Classico '96

• • •

WARM CHOCOLATE RASPBERRY
PUDDING CAKE, p. 181

Courvoisier Cognac V.S.

Warm Chocolate Raspberry Pudding Cake

Roasted Veal Chops with Shallots,
Tomatoes, and Olive Jus; Soft Polenta

SOUTHERN COMFORTS

Serves 8 to 10

CRAB SPREAD WITH
BENNE-SEED WAFERS, P. 104

Estancia Pinnacles Monterey County Chardonnay '97

• • •

ROASTED HONEY-GLAZED SPARERIBS, P. 126

CANDIED SWEET-POTATO PURÉE, P. 163

COLLARD GREENS AND TURNIPS WITH
HAM HOCK AND PEPPER VINEGAR, P. 156

PICKLED BLACK-EYED PEAS, P. 165

BUTTERMILK SCALLION SKILLET
CORN BREAD, P. 108

Cline Cellars "Ancient Vines" Zinfandel '96

• • •

LEMON MOLASSES CHESS PIE, P. 189

TOASTED-COCONUT COOKIES, P. 187

BROWN-SUGAR PECAN ICE CREAM, P. 196

A WEEKEND AT HOME:
BREAKFAST

Serves 2

ALMOND COCONUT GRANOLA, P. 141

BUTTERMILK WAFFLES
WITH CRISP PROSCIUTTO, P. 141

Green-Grape Juice, p. 209

Coffee

Tea

A WEEKEND AT HOME:
LUNCH

Serves 6

SALMON AND LEEK PIE,
SOUR-CREAM CHILE SAUCE, P. 118

SPINACH AND ROASTED RED
PEPPER SALAD, P. 171

Echelon Central Coast Pinot Noir '97

• • •

CITRUS CHIFFON CAKE,
CITRUS SYRUP, P. 184

A Weekend at Home: Dinner

Serves 2

CUCUMBER CAVIAR CANAPÉS, P. 100

MUSTARD-SEED CHEDDAR STICKS, P. 91

Martinis, p. 208

• • •

ROASTED POUSSINS WITH
CUMIN AND LEMON, P. 131

ROASTED POTATO WEDGES, P. 161

STEAMED BROCCOLI, P. 156

Acacia Carneros Chardonnay '97

• • •

PASSION-FRUIT MERINGUES, P. 200

Château Lafaurie-Peyraguey Sauternes '95

COCKTAILS IN AN ARTIST'S LOFT

Serves 8 to 10

SHREDDED-CHICKEN WRAPS WITH AVOCADO,
CUCUMBER, AND CILANTRO, P. 86

TAPENADE GOAT-CHEESE CRACKERS, P. 102

CRAB MEAT AND BEET PURÉE ON
GRANNY SMITH APPLE, P. 98

GINGER-HOISIN BEEF AND SCALLIONS
ON CRISPY NOODLE CAKES, P. 99

SMOKED PEPPERED MACKEREL AND SOUR
CREAM ON HOMEMADE POTATO CHIPS, P. 102

Vodka Gimlets

Campari-and-Sodas

J. Rochioli Sauvignon Blanc '97

Meridien Vineyards Coastal Reserve Pinot Noir '96

• • •

CHOCOLATE CARAMEL DIAMONDS, P. 179

A Vegetarian
Italian Dinner

Serves 6

ARTICHOKE, OLIVE, AND
ROASTED PEPPER ANTIPASTO, P. 87

Bruno Giacosa Arneis di Roero '97

• • •

WILD MUSHROOM LASAGNE, P. 146

CABBAGE SALAD WITH
MUSTARD VINAIGRETTE, P. 172

Monte Antico Vino da Tavola '95

• • •

RED WINE–MACERATED WINTER FRUIT, P. 202

CASHEW ORANGE BISCOTTI, P. 186

Wild Mushroom Lasagne; Cabbage Salad with Mustard Vinaigrette

Red Wine-Macerated Winter Fruit; Cashew Orange Biscotti

EASTER BRUNCH

Serves 12

Grapefruit Coolers, p. 209

Laurent-Perrier Rosé Brut NV Champagne

QUAIL EGGS WITH
TOASTED SESAME SALT, P. 93

BAKED ASPARAGUS AND
YELLOW PEPPER FRITTATA, P. 140

CHEDDAR SCONES WITH HAM AND
HONEY-MUSTARD BUTTER, P. 108

SALMON CAKES WITH TARRAGON-CHIVE
DIPPING SAUCE, P. 117

HOT CROSS BUNS, P. 106

CELEBRATE SPRING

Serves 6

MUSHROOM, RADISH, AND BIBB LETTUCE
SALAD WITH AVOCADO DRESSING, P. 170

Weingut Bründlmayer Zöbinger
Heiligenstein Riesling '97

• • •

GREEN OLIVE, LEMON, AND
GARLIC-ROASTED LEG OF LAMB WITH
POTATOES AND PAN GRAVY, P. 129

BRAISED BABY ARTICHOKES
AND SHALLOTS, P. 154

Remelluri Rioja '95

• • •

GINGERSNAP CRUMBLE
ICE-CREAM TART WITH CHUNKY
PINEAPPLE SAUCE, P. 194

A Weekend at the Shore: Breakfast on the Beach

Serves 6

BAKED BLUEBERRY-PECAN FRENCH TOAST
WITH BLUEBERRY SYRUP, P. 142

Coffee

Orange Juice

A Weekend at the Shore:
Lunch Indoors

Serves 6

COMPOSED SALAD:
SAUTÉED CHICKEN BREASTS WITH CAPERS,
WHITE BEAN SALAD,
ASPARAGUS WITH LEMON VINAIGRETTE,
ROASTED PEPPERS WITH GARLIC, pp. 167—168

Domaine Couly-Dutheil Chinon "Les Gravières" '97

• • •

RHUBARB RICE PUDDING, p. 205

A WEEKEND AT THE SHORE: DINNER ON THE DECK

Serves 6

CURRY-MARINATED MUSSELS
ON THE HALF SHELL, P. 91

JÍCAMA-DATE CANAPÉS, P. 101

Trimbach Pinot Blanc '96

• • •

FARMERS MARKET GREEN SALAD
WITH FRIED SHALLOTS, P. 170

GRILLED LOBSTERS WITH SOUTHEAST
ASIAN DIPPING SAUCE, P. 119

SAUTÉED PEAS AND SMALL POTATOES, P. 160

GRILLED PARSLEY-BUTTER BREAD, P. 110

Edmunds St. John "Alban-Durell" Viognier '97

• • •

STAR ANISE AND CORIANDER
SPICE CAKE, P. 181

LIME-VANILLA FROZEN YOGURT, P. 195

Star Anise and Coriander Spice Cake; Lime-Vanilla Frozen Yogurt

Grilled Lobster with Southeast Asian Dipping Sauce; Sautéed
Peas and Small Potatoes; Grilled Parsley-Butter Bread

COOKING WITH FRIENDS
TONI ROSS AND JEFF SALAWAY

Serves 8

FETA AND MARINATED NIÇOISE OLIVES
WITH GRILLED PITAS, P. 89

CUCUMBER SPEARS

• • •

GRILLED BUTTERFLIED LEG OF LAMB WITH
LEMON, HERBS, AND GARLIC, P. 128

Pellegrini Alexander Valley "Old Vines" Carignane '97

GRILLED HALIBUT STEAKS, P. 116

Pieropan Soave Classico Superiore Vigneto La Rocca '96

FENNEL TSATSIKI, P. 174

GOLDEN POTATO WEDGES, P. 162

ROASTED PEPPERS STUFFED WITH CHERRY
TOMATOES, ONION, AND BASIL, P. 161

BABY GREENS WITH OLIVE OIL, P. 170

• • •

PLUM PINE-NUT TART, P. 192

Feta and Marinated Niçoise Olives with Grilled Pitas. Opposite/clockwise from top left: Roasted Peppers Stuffed with Cherry Tomatoes, Onion, and Basil; Grilled Halibut Steaks; Grilled Butterflied Leg of Lamb; plated lamb, peppers, baby greens, and potato wedges

A VINEYARD DINNER

Serves 6

HERBED SUMMER SUCCOTASH ON
GARLIC CROÛTES, P. 98

Rodney Strong Charlotte's Home Vineyard
Sauvignon Blanc '98

• • •

ROUGET AND SHRIMP WITH
LEMON SAUCE, P. 116

ZUCCHINI POTATO LEMON-THYME MASH, P. 117

Joseph Drouhin Chablis '97

• • •

FIG, APRICOT, AND RASPBERRY BRÛLÉE, P. 199

VANILLA-BEAN SUGAR COOKIES, P. 188

Hermann J. Wiemer
Johannisberg Riesling Late Harvest '95

A Sizzling Summer Fiesta

Serves 8

Caipirinhas, p. 208

• • •

CHILLED ROASTED RED PEPPER SOUP, p. 112

Casa Lapostolle Sauvignon Blanc '97

• • •

AVOCADO AND SWEET ONION SALAD, p. 173

CORN PANCAKES, p. 107

GRILLED STEAK, p. 122

CHIMICHURRI SAUCE, p. 176

GRILLED STRIPED BASS, p. 115

Don Miguel Gascón Malbec '97

• • •

GRILLED PINEAPPLE, p. 201

RUM DULCE DE LECHE, p. 202

Grilled Steak; Chimichurri Sauce; Avocado and Sweet Onion Salad;
Corn Pancakes

Grilled Pineapple; Rum Dulce de Leche

A WEDDING IN THE CITY

Serves 50

DRIED APRICOTS WITH GOAT CHEESE
AND PISTACHIOS. P. 86

SMOKED CAVIAR AND HUMMUS
ON PITA TOASTS. P. 100

STUFFED GRAPE LEAVES
WITH MERGUEZ SAUSAGE. P. 90

Alban Vineyards Central Coast Viognier '98

• • •

GRILLED CHARMOULA LAMB CHOPS. P. 127

SPICY LEMON-MARINATED SHRIMP. P. 121

ISRAELI COUSCOUS WITH ROASTED BUTTERNUT
SQUASH AND PRESERVED LEMON. P. 144

BROILED EGGPLANT WITH
CILANTRO VINAIGRETTE. P. 157

BEET AND JÍCAMA ON ENDIVE
WITH GARLIC YOGURT DRESSING. P. 172

ALFONSO OLIVES

Boutari Nemea '96

• • •

WEDDING CAKE WITH BLACKBERRIES
AND ROSES. P. 182

Gancia Asti Spumante

GAME PLAN

• • •

For those planning to serve the entire wedding menu,
here's a strategy for breaking up the work.

One month ahead:
• bake cake layers and freeze

Six days ahead:
• make filling for grape leaves
• make syrup for cake

Five days ahead:
• stuff grape leaves and cook
• make spice mixture for
  lamb chops

Three days ahead:
• make marinated shrimp
• make cream-cheese frosting
• drain yogurt for dressing

Two days ahead:
• make hummus for
  hors d'oeuvres
• marinate lamb chops
• toast pita triangles for
  hummus hors d'oeuvres
• make yogurt dressing
  for endive

One day ahead:
• thaw cake layers
• grill lamb chops
• prep for couscous
• cook eggplant
• prep for endive with
  beets and jícama
• assemble and crumb-coat
  cake tiers

Day of wedding:
• assemble and decorate cake
• make vinaigrette for eggplant
• assemble couscous
• assemble dried-apricot
  hors d'oeuvres
• assemble hummus
  hors d'oeuvres
• reheat lamb
• assemble endive with
  beets and jícama

WITHOUT CEREMONY: WEDDING FOOD FOR AN INTIMATE DINNER

Serves 6

SPICY LEMON-MARINATED SHRIMP, P. 94

GRILLED CHARMOULA LAMB CHOPS, P. 128

ISRAELI COUSCOUS WITH ROASTED
BUTTERNUT SQUASH AND
PRESERVED LEMON, P. 145

BROILED EGGPLANT WITH
CILANTRO VINAIGRETTE, P. 158

Boutari Nemea '96

• • •

BLOSSOM-TOPPED CUPCAKES, P. 178

BEYOND BACKYARD BASICS

Serves 6

RATATOUILLE WITH PENNE, P. 150

RED-LEAF LETTUCE WITH
SHALLOT VINAIGRETTE, P. 170

BANON CHEESE AND BAGUETTES, P. 252

Rioja Crianza of CUNE '96

• • •

GRAPE TART, P. 192

A Vegetarian Thanksgiving with Anna Thomas

Serves 8

TAMALITOS, P. 96

ROASTED GREEN BEANS, P. 87

• • •

SQUASH AND SWEET-POTATO
SOUP WITH CHIPOTLE SAUCE, P. 113

ROASTED WILD MUSHROOMS IN
RED-WINE REDUCTION, P. 160

SAGE, ONION, AND WILD-RICE
RISOTTO CAKES, P. 152

CRANBERRY GINGER SAUCE, P. 175

JÍCAMA AND CILANTRO RELISH, P. 176

• • •

PUMPKIN FLAN WITH
PUMPKIN-SEED PRALINE, P. 204

APPLE AND PRUNE TART, P. 188

Assembling Tamalitos

Risotto Cake; Roasted Wild Mushrooms in Red-Wine Reduction;
Cranberry Ginger Sauce; Jícama and Cilantro Relish. Opposite:
Pumpkin Flan with Pumpkin-Seed Praline; Squash and Sweet-
Potato Soup with Chipotle Sauce; Apple and Prune Tart

Thanksgiving Primer

Serves 8

ROAST TURKEY WITH HERBED BREAD
STUFFING AND GIBLET GRAVY, P. 138

CRANBERRY SAUCE, P. 175

CREAMY MASHED POTATOES, P. 163 OR
PARSLEYED STEAMED POTATOES, P. 161

CANDIED SWEET POTATOES, P. 163

BUTTERED BRUSSELS SPROUTS, P. 156

PARKER HOUSE ROLLS, P. 106

Chalk Hill Sonoma County Chardonnay '97

Domaine Carneros Pinot Noir '97

• • •

PUMPKIN PIE, P. 190

PECAN TART, P. 191

Ramos-Pinto Quinta do Bom Retiro
20-Year-Old Tawny Port

GAME PLAN

• • •

Here's how to organize your time and break up the work.

Three days ahead:
• You can get a jump start on making stock for gravy by substituting a package of chicken wings or turkey parts for the giblets if you haven't picked up your turkey yet or if the giblets are trapped inside your still-frozen bird
• Make cranberry sauce

Two days ahead:
• Make pastry dough for pie and tart

One day ahead:
• Make stock
• Make stuffing
• Make rolls
• Make sweet potatoes
• Make desserts

Thanksgiving Day:
• Stuff turkey and roast
• Whip cream for desserts and chill
• Make mashed or steamed potatoes
• Reheat sweet potatoes and rolls
• Cook green vegetable
• Take advantage of the fact that the turkey needs to stand at least 30 minutes before carving and use the time— and oven space—to bake any uncooked stuffing and make gravy

Candied Sweet Potatoes; Herbed Bread Stuffing; Buttered Brussels Sprouts.
Opposite: Roast Turkey and all the trimmings

A Gingerbread
Christmas Party

Serves 8 adults plus 10 children

OLD-FASHIONED HAM

LIME, APRICOT, AND SOY-SAUCE
CHICKEN WINGS, P. 133

MACARONI AND CHEESE WITH GARLIC BREAD
CRUMBS—PLAIN AND CHIPOTLE, P. 148

APPLE AND CELERY SALAD
WITH PEANUTS, P. 172

CARROT STICKS

Bassermann-Jordan Forster Jesuitengarten Kabinett '98

Georges Duboeuf Beaujolais Nouveau '99

• • •

MINI BROWNIE CUPCAKES, P. 180

HANUKKAH
WITH ROZANNE GOLD

Serves 6

SEARED SMOKED SALMON WITH
CUCUMBER PRESSÉ, P. 94

Gamla Sauvignon Blanc '96

• • •

RIB-EYE ROAST, GRAVLAKS STYLE, P. 122

THE GOLD FAMILY LATKES, P. 162

APPLE-CRANBERRY SAUCE, P. 162

SWEET-GARLIC FRENCHED GREEN BEANS, P. 155

Yarden Oregon Merlot '96

• • •

CHOCOLATE MOUSSE SPONGE, P. 180

BAKED SABRA ORANGES WITH
ORANGE SORBET, P. 199

CHOCOLATE SESAME CUPS, P. 188

Gan Eden Late Harvest Gewürztraminer '96

Clockwise from top left: Rib-eye Roast; Baked Sabra Oranges with Orange Sorbet; Plated roast, Apple-Cranberry Sauce, The Gold Family Latkes, and Sweet-Garlic Frenched Green Beans; Chocolate-Sesame Cups. Opposite: Chocolate Mousse Sponge

New Year's Eve Cocktail Party

Serves 20

Times Square Cocktail, p. 208

Cosmopolitan Champagne Cocktail, p. 207

"FISH AND CHIPS", P. 100

SALT-AND-PEPPER EDAMAME, P. 88

JERK PORK AND RED PEPPER MAYO ON
BLACK-EYED-PEA CAKES, P. 92

SEARED FOIE GRAS AND LINGONBERRY JAM
ON BRIOCHE TOASTS, P. 101

PANKO SCALLOPS WITH
GREEN CHILE CHUTNEY, P. 97

SPICY-SWEET KUMQUATS, P. 91

KOREAN BARBECUED BEEF, P. 89

Above: Times Square Cocktail and Panko Scallop with Green Chile
Chutney. Opposite/clockwise from top left: Salt-and-Pepper
Edamame; Cosmopolitan Champagne Cocktail and Jerk Pork and
Red Pepper Mayo on Black-Eyed-Pea Cake; "Fish and Chips"

Low Fat & Delicious:
A Hearty Dinner

Serves 4

ROASTED SPICED SHRIMP ON
WILTED SPINACH, P. 95

• • •

BUFFALO STEAK AND ONION CONFIT
ON GARLIC TOASTS, P. 123

ROASTED BEETS WITH GARLIC-BEET
PURÉE, P. 155

• • •

POPPY-SEED ANGEL FOOD CAKES
WITH LEMON SYRUP, P. 177

LOW FAT & DELICIOUS:
FLAVORS OF INDIA

Serves 4

Each serving about 581 calories and 10 grams fat

CUMIN PEA SOUP, P. 111

• • •

TANDOORI-SPICED CHICKEN BREASTS, P. 132

CARROT SALAD WITH LIME AND
CILANTRO, P. 173

BASMATI RICE AND MUSTARD-SEED PILAF, P. 151

• • •

MANGO IN GINGER-MINT SYRUP, P. 198

Low Fat & Delicious:
Midsummer Light

Serves 4

Each serving about 637 calories and 11 grams fat

GAZPACHO, P. 111

• • •

GRILLED SCALLOPS, ZUCCHINI, AND
SCALLIONS WITH WHITE BEANS, P. 120

• • •

PLUMS WITH ORANGE AND MINT, P. 202

GINGER ALMOND BISCOTTI
ICE-CREAM SANDWICHES, P. 195

A RECIPE COMPENDIUM

W hat are you in the mood for? Turkey cheddar sandwiches with honey mustard? Or garlicky lentil soup? Or perhaps something more exotic, like bean-thread noodles with beef and Asian pear? Or maybe simply a crunchy tuna salad? This collection of *Gourmet*'s best recipes from 1999 offers over 350 choices for everything from intriguing hors d'oeuvres to luscious desserts, and everything in-between. Without exception, all recipes were tested to perfection in *Gourmet*'s test kitchens with only the finest, freshest ingredients.

In addition to all the recipes that are pictured in our Menu Collection, this compendium includes a wide selection of dishes from *Gourmet*'s monthly food columns. In keeping with the busy lifestyle that most of us have today, nearly half of the recipes found here can be made in 45 minutes or less. Who would guess that recipes like scallion, mushroom, and shrimp custards; or pork chops with sweet curried onions; or hot banana crème brulée could be prepared so quickly? (Quick recipes are indicated by a clock symbol ☾ throughout the book and in the index.)

Throughout the year favorite foods were featured in special columns. Many are included here, such as luscious chicken wing recipes—deviled chicken wings; grilled Indian-style chicken wings with carrot-cumin yogurt sauce; and grilled chicken wings with two Thai sauces; prized pasta dishes—*pappardelle* in lemon cream sauce with asparagus and smoked salmon (photo opposite); and *gemelli* with garlic, herbs, and *bocconcini* mozzarella; and heavenly offerings made with Meyer lemons—Moroccan chicken with preserved Meyer lemons and green olives; and Meyer lemon "jam."

And, for those times when you are keeping an eye on your waistline a healthy sprinkling of low-fat dishes, such as gazpacho; cumin pea soup; arugula, fennel, and parmesan salad; squid risotto; even tasty treats like grapefruit tarragon sorbet, and ginger almond *biscotti*, are at hand. (Lighter recipes are marked with a feather symbol ☙ throughout the book and in the index.)

So, what *are* you in the mood for? The choices are plentiful, and whimsy is permitted.

APPETIZERS

DRIED APRICOTS WITH GOAT CHEESE AND PISTACHIOS ◑

Makes 150

To ensure you get moist, beautiful-looking apricots, avoid those sold in boxes and bags that you can't see through. If you buy Turkish apricots, keep in mind that they're usually sold pitted but whole and, unlike most California apricots, will need to be halved horizontally.

150 dried apricot halves (2 lb)
1½ cups fresh orange juice
1½ cups shelled pistachios, half of
   them toasted
1 lb soft mild goat cheese, chilled

Toss apricots with juice and let stand, tossing occasionally, 20 minutes.

Chop all pistachios, preferably by hand, and season with salt. Drain apricots, cut sides up, on paper towels. Top each with a small chunk of cheese and sprinkle with nuts.

Cooks' note:
• You can assemble these 1 day ahead and chill them, covered, but they can't be stacked and will take up a lot of refrigerator space.

SHREDDED-CHICKEN WRAPS WITH AVOCADO, CUCUMBER, AND CILANTRO

Makes about 32

1 small onion
2 skinless whole chicken legs (about 1 lb)
2 tablespoons unsalted butter
1 (14- to 16-oz) can whole tomatoes
½ cup water
¼ teaspoon cayenne, or to taste
1 teaspoon ground cumin
¾ teaspoon salt
1 English cucumber
2 tablespoons fresh lime juice, or to taste
1 firm-ripe California avocado
4 (12-inch) flour tortillas
2 cups fresh cilantro sprigs

Chop onion. In a 2-quart heavy saucepan cook onion and chicken legs in butter over moderate heat, stirring, 5 minutes. Drain tomatoes and measure 1 cup packed, reserving remainder for another use. Stir tomatoes into chicken mixture with water, cayenne to taste, and cumin and simmer, covered, 1 hour. Working over pan, pull meat off bones with tongs, returning it to pan, and discard bones. Simmer chicken mixture, uncovered, until most liquid is evaporated, about 20 minutes. Stir in salt and cool chicken mixture.

Halve cucumber lengthwise and crosswise and seed. Cut pieces lengthwise into very thin strips. In a bowl toss cucumber with 1 tablespoon lime juice and season with salt and pepper. Halve, peel, and pit avocado. Cut avocado into ¼-inch-thick slices. Toss avocado with remaining lime juice and season with salt and pepper.

Cut 1 inch off 1 edge of each tortilla. On a work surface arrange 1 tortilla with cut edge farthest from you and smear a small piece of avocado lengthwise along cut edge of tortilla (this will help the "wrap" hold together). Spread about one fourth chicken mixture across lower fourth of tortilla about 1 inch from bottom.

Top chicken mixture with ½ cup cilantro sprigs. Top cilantro with 4 or 5 avocado slices and top avocado with about one fourth cucumber. Beginning with bottom edge, tightly roll up tortilla and arrange seam side down on work surface. Make 3 more wraps with remaining tortillas, chicken, cilantro, avocado, and cucumber.

Cut wraps on a slight diagonal into ⅜-inch-thick slices and serve chilled or at room temperature.

Cooks' notes:
• Chicken mixture may be made 1 day ahead and cooled completely before being chilled, covered. Bring to room temperature before proceeding.
• Wraps may be made 6 hours ahead and chilled, individually wrapped in plastic wrap.

PHOTO ON PAGE 24

ARTICHOKE, OLIVE, AND ROASTED PEPPER ANTIPASTO ⊙

Serves 6 (first course)
For an especially fast dish, use store-bought roasted peppers.

3 red bell peppers
3 yellow bell peppers
2 garlic cloves
2 (14-oz) cans whole artichoke hearts
⅔ cup packed fresh flat-leaf parsley
1 tablespoon extra-virgin olive oil
1 tablespoon unsalted butter
2 tablespoons fresh lemon juice
⅔ cup brine-cured black olives

Accompaniment: crusty Italian bread

Quick-roast and peel bell peppers (procedure follows). Cut roasted peppers into ¾-inch-wide strips. Mince garlic. Rinse and drain artichoke hearts. Pat artichokes dry and cut through stem ends into quarters. Chop parsley.

In a 12-inch heavy skillet cook garlic in oil and butter over moderate heat, stirring, until fragrant. Add artichokes and cook, stirring, until heated through, about 3 minutes. Stir in roasted peppers, parsley, remaining ingredients, and salt and pepper to taste until combined.

Serve antipasto at room temperature with bread.

PHOTO ON PAGE 26

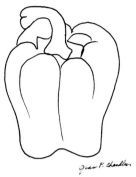

TO QUICK-ROAST AND PEEL PEPPERS ⊙

Broiler method:
Preheat broiler.

Quarter peppers lengthwise, discarding stems, seeds, and ribs. Put peppers, skin sides up, on rack of a broiler pan and broil them about 2 inches from heat until skins are blistered and charred, 8 to 12 minutes.

Gas stove method:
Lay peppers on their sides on racks of burners (preferably 1 to a burner) and turn flames on high. Char peppers, turning them with tongs, until skins are blackened, 5 to 8 minutes. (If peppers are small, spear through stem ends with a long-handled fork and rest on burner racks.)

Transfer peppers roasted by either method to a bowl and let stand, covered with plastic wrap, until cool enough to handle. Peel peppers and cut off tops, discarding seeds and ribs if necessary.

Cooks' note:
• Peppers may be roasted 2 days ahead and chilled, covered.

ROASTED GREEN BEANS ⊙+

Serves 8 to 10

3 lb *haricots verts* or other thin green beans
1½ tablespoons olive oil

Preheat oven to 375°F.

Toss beans with oil and salt to taste. Roast in 2 large shallow baking pans in upper and lower thirds of oven, switching position of pans halfway and stirring occasionally, until spotted here and there with dark brown and thinner beans are crisp, 45 to 55 minutes total (depending on size of beans). Season with salt.

Serve beans immediately as finger food.

CRAB POT STICKERS WITH SESAME-GINGER DIPPING SAUCE ☺

Serves 2

For dipping sauce
2 tablespoons soy sauce
1 tablespoon Dijon mustard
1 tablespoon honey
¼ teaspoon Asian sesame oil
¼ teaspoon grated peeled fresh ginger
2½ teaspoons water

1 scallion
6 oz jumbo lump crab meat
1 tablespoon sesame seeds
1 large egg white
1 teaspoon grated peeled fresh ginger
12 won ton or *gyoza* wrappers,
   thawed if frozen
Cornstarch for dusting plate
1 tablespoon vegetable oil

Make dipping sauce:
In a small bowl whisk together all dipping sauce ingredients.

Chop scallion and pick over crab meat to remove any bits of shell and cartilage. Break up larger pieces of crab meat.

In a dry small heavy skillet toast sesame seeds with salt to taste over moderate heat, stirring frequently, until golden, about 2 minutes. Transfer seeds to a medium bowl and cool slightly. Add egg white and ginger to seeds and lightly beat. Gently stir in crab and scallion and season with salt and pepper.

Put 6 won ton wrappers on a dry surface, keeping remaining wrappers in package, and lightly brush edges with water. Mound about 1 tablespoon filling in center of each wrapper. Gather edge of each wrapper up and around filling and form a waist with wrapper (filling should be exposed and level with top of wrapper). Lightly dust a plate with cornstarch and arrange pot stickers in one layer. Make 6 more pot stickers with remaining filling in same manner.

In a large nonstick skillet heat vegetable oil over moderately high heat until hot but not smoking and fry pot stickers, flat sides down, until undersides are golden, about 1 minute. Add ¼ cup water down side of skillet. Cover skillet and steam crab pot stickers over moderately low heat until cooked through, about 2 minutes. Remove lid and cook pot stickers until any water is evaporated.

Serve pot stickers with dipping sauce.

SALT-AND-PEPPER EDAMAME ☺+
(SOYBEANS IN THE POD)

Serves 20 (hors d'oeuvres)
Edamame are fun to eat—the slightly fuzzy bright-green pods tickle your lips as you gently suck the beans into your mouth. Provide bowls for the empty pods.

½ cup kosher salt
2 tablespoons Sichuan peppercorns (sources on
   page 252)
2 tablespoons pink peppercorns (sources on
   page 252)
4 (1-lb) bags frozen edamame (soybeans in the pod)
   (sources on page 252)

Toast salt in a dry, small, heavy skillet over moderate heat, stirring, until salt turns light tan, about 7 minutes. Transfer salt to a bowl. Toast Sichuan peppercorns in skillet over moderate heat, stirring, until fragrant, about 2 minutes. Transfer toasted peppercorns to a sheet of wax paper to cool. Using paper as a funnel, pour toasted peppercorns into an electric coffee/spice grinder or a mortar. Add pink peppercorns and pulse or pound with a pestle until finely ground. Pour through a coarse sieve into bowl of salt and stir together.

Cook *edamame* in 4 batches in salted boiling water until tender, about 4 minutes, and immediately transfer with a slotted spoon to a bowl of ice and cold water to stop cooking. Return water to a boil between batches. Drain in a colander and pat dry.

Toss *edamame* with some peppered salt to taste and serve with remainder on the side.

Cooks' notes:
· Peppered salt may be made 1 week ahead and kept in an
  airtight container at cool room temperature.
· *Edamame* may be cooked 1 day ahead and chilled, covered.
  Bring to room temperature before tossing with peppered salt.

PHOTO ON PAGE 77

KOREAN BARBECUED BEEF

Makes 60 hors d'oeuvres

For marinade
½ cup soy sauce
¼ cup rice vinegar (not seasoned)
⅓ cup chopped scallion
2 tablespoons sugar
2 tablespoons minced garlic
2 tablespoons minced peeled fresh ginger
1 tablespoon Asian sesame oil
1½ teaspoons Asian chili sauce
   (sources on page 252)

1¾ lb skirt steak
2 small red apples such as Gala
1 firm-ripe mango, peeled and pitted
2 tablespoons fresh lime juice
1 teaspoon Asian chili sauce, or to taste
60 (3- to 4-inch-long) Bibb lettuce leaves
Toasted sesame seeds

Make marinade:
Stir together marinade ingredients and reserve one fourth of marinade for sauce.

Marinate steak, then broil:
Put steak and remaining three fourths of marinade in a glass dish, turning steak to coat, and marinate at room temperature, turning once, 30 minutes. While steak is marinating, cut apples and mango into 1- by ¼-inch sticks. Toss together with juice and chili sauce and season with salt.

Preheat broiler.

Broil steak on rack of a broiler pan 2 to 3 inches from heat until slightly charred, 2 to 3 minutes on each side for medium meat. Let steak stand 5 minutes. Cut steak crosswise into ¼-inch-thick slices, then halve slices crosswise. Toss beef in reserved marinade with salt and pepper to taste and divide among lettuce leaves. Top with fruit and sesame seeds.

Cooks' note:
• Fruit mixture may be made 1 day ahead and chilled, covered.

FETA AND MARINATED NIÇOISE OLIVES WITH GRILLED PITAS ◑+

Serves 8

For marinated olives
1 lemon
1 garlic clove
1 (6-inch) fresh rosemary sprig
2 (3-inch) fresh thyme sprigs
2 bay leaves (preferably Turkish)
¼ teaspoon cracked or coarsely ground black pepper
⅓ cup extra-virgin olive oil
1 cup Niçoise olives (about 6 oz)

2 (½-lb) pieces feta
8 to 12 (6-inch) pitas
About 2 tablespoons olive oil

Accompaniment: Japanese or English cucumber
   spears

Make marinated olives:
With a vegetable peeler remove 4 wide strips zest from lemon. Thinly slice garlic. Break rosemary and thyme into 1-inch pieces and halve bay leaves. In a small airtight container stir together all marinated-olive ingredients. Marinate olives, covered and chilled, at least 2 hours.

Prepare grill.

Put feta on a platter and pour olives and marinade over it. Lightly brush pitas with oil and season with salt and pepper. Grill pitas on a rack set 5 to 6 inches over glowing coals about 1 minute on each side. (Alternatively, grill pitas in a hot well-seasoned ridged grill pan over moderately high heat.)

Serve pitas warm with feta and olives. Serve cucumber spears on the side.

Cooks' note:
• Marinated olives keep, covered and chilled, up to 1 month.

PHOTO ON PAGE 46

STUFFED GRAPE LEAVES WITH MERGUEZ SAUSAGE

Makes 150

While this recipe isn't terribly difficult, it is labor-intensive. We recommend you break it up into a couple of steps: Make the filling, then enlist a friend or two to help you do the rolling the following day.

3½ (1-lb) jars brine-packed Greek or California
    grape leaves
3 large lemons
4 cups water
1 teaspoon salt
2 cups long-grain rice
1½ lb *merguez* (sources on page 252) or
    hot Italian sausage
3 cups finely chopped red onion
10 tablespoons olive oil
1 cup pine nuts, toasted
½ cup chopped fresh dill
½ cup chopped fresh flat-leaf parsley
1 cup dried currants
4 (14½-oz) cans chicken broth

Prepare leaves:

Unfurl stacks of grape leaves into a large bowl of water (leaves should remain stacked) and gently agitate without separating leaves. Blanch stacks in batches in a large saucepan of boiling water 3 minutes. Transfer to a colander and refresh under cold running water.

Make filling:

Finely grate zest from lemons and squeeze ½ cup lemon juice.

Bring water with salt to a boil in a large saucepan and stir in rice. Cook rice, covered, over moderately low heat until water is absorbed, 17 to 20 minutes, and transfer to a large bowl.

Remove sausage from casings and cook in a large nonstick skillet over moderate heat, stirring to break up lumps, until no longer pink. Cool to room temperature and crumble into ¼-inch pieces.

Cook onion with 3 tablespoons oil in a 12-inch heavy skillet over moderate heat, stirring, until soft but not browned and stir into rice with zest, ¼ cup lemon juice, sausage, nuts, dill, parsley, currants, and salt and pepper to taste.

Fill and roll grape leaves:

Arrange 1 grape leaf, smooth side down, on a kitchen towel. Trim stem flush with leaf (if leaf is extra large, trim to about 5½ inches wide), saving any trimmings. Spoon 1 tablespoon filling onto leaf near stem end and tightly roll up filling in leaf, folding in sides and squeezing roll to pack filling. (Roll should be about 3½ inches long.) Make more rolls in same manner.

Cook grape leaves:

Heat broth just to a simmer and keep warm, covered. Line bottom of a large heavy pot with leaf trimmings and any remaining whole leaves and arrange rolls, seam sides down, close together in layers over leaves, seasoning each layer with salt. Drizzle with 4 tablespoons oil and remaining ¼ cup lemon juice and cover with an inverted heatproof plate slightly smaller than pan, pressing down gently.

Add just enough broth to reach rim of plate and bring to a boil. Cook rolls at a bare simmer, covered with plate and lid, 50 minutes (stuffed leaves should be tender, but filling should not be mushy). Remove from heat and transfer rolls with tongs to large trays to cool, brushing with remaining 3 tablespoons oil. Cover with plastic wrap and chill until cool.

Cooks' notes:
• You can make filling 1 day before rolling.
• Stuffed grape leaves keep, chilled, in an airtight container 5 days.

SPICY-SWEET KUMQUATS ☺+

Makes 60 hors d'oeuvres

6 tablespoons granulated sugar
1½ tablespoons chili powder
4 teaspoons powdered egg whites (sources on
  page 252)
¼ cup warm water
60 kumquats (preferably thin-skinned)

Stir together sugar and chili powder. Whisk egg whites with water until dissolved. Working with 1 kumquat at a time, dip 1 side in whites, letting excess drip off, then dip in sugar mixture. Transfer to a rack to dry, coated side up.

Cooks' note:
• Coat kumquats 3 days ahead and keep, between layers of wax paper, in an airtight container at room temperature.

CURRY-MARINATED MUSSELS ON THE HALF SHELL

Makes about 40 to 50

¾ teaspoon Thai red or yellow curry paste
  (sources on page 252)
¼ teaspoon curry powder
2 tablespoons white-wine vinegar
5 tablespoons olive oil
2 lb mussels (preferably cultivated)
2 shallots
1 carrot
1 celery rib
½ red bell pepper
¼ cup water
¼ cup packed fresh cilantro

In a large bowl stir together curry paste, curry powder, vinegar, and 4 tablespoons oil. Scrub mussels and remove beards. Mince shallots and cut carrot, celery, and bell pepper into ¼-inch dice. In a 12-inch skillet heat remaining tablespoon oil over moderately high heat until hot but not smoking and sauté vegetables, stirring and adding salt to taste, until slightly softened but not browned. Add vegetables to curry mixture. In skillet steam mussels in ¼ cup water, covered, over moderately high heat, 3 to 8 minutes, checking occasionally after 3 minutes and transferring them as they open to another bowl. Discard any unopened mussels.

Remove mussels from shells and add to curry-vegetable mixture, gently tossing to coat. Wash and reserve half of each mussel shell. Marinate mussels, covered and chilled, at least 2 hours and up to 1 day.

Just before serving, chop cilantro and stir into mussels. Fill each reserved shell with a mussel and some curried vegetables.

PHOTO ON PAGE 41

MUSTARD-SEED CHEDDAR STICKS

Makes about 45

¾ stick unsalted butter
¾ cup all-purpose flour
1 tablespoon kosher salt
⅛ teaspoon cayenne
1 cup grated sharp white Cheddar (about 4 oz)
2 teaspoons mustard seeds

Preheat oven to 400°F and line a large baking sheet with parchment paper.

Cut butter into bits and in a food processor pulse with flour, 1 teaspoon salt, and cayenne until mixture resembles coarse meal. Add Cheddar and pulse until mixture forms a dough. Form dough into a disk. Chill dough, wrapped in plastic wrap, until firm, at least 30 minutes, and up to 2 days.

On a lightly floured surface with a lightly floured rolling pin roll out dough into a 16- by 4-inch rectangle (about ¼ inch thick). Trim edges of rectangle and lightly brush rectangle with water. Sprinkle rectangle with mustard seeds and remaining 2 teaspoons salt. Gently roll rolling pin over dough to make mustard seeds and salt adhere.

With a sharp long knife cut rectangle crosswise into roughly ⅓-inch-wide sticks. Transfer sticks with a spatula to baking sheet and arrange about ¾ inch apart. Bake sticks in middle of oven until golden, about 10 minutes, and transfer to a rack to cool.

Cooks' note:
• Cheddar sticks may be kept in an airtight container at cool room temperature 1 week, or frozen 1 month.

CARAMELIZED ONION AND GOAT CHEESE TARTS ◔

Serves 2 (first course)

1 large onion
1 tablespoon unsalted butter
¼ cup water
½ teaspoon chopped fresh thyme
1 puff pastry sheet (from a 17¼-oz package frozen
   puff pastry sheets), thawed
1 oz soft mild goat cheese, at room temperature

Garnish: fresh thyme sprigs

Preheat oven to 450°F and butter a baking sheet.

Cut onion into very thin slices. In a heavy skillet heat butter over moderately high heat until foam subsides and sauté onion, stirring occasionally, until golden. Add water and deglaze skillet, scraping up any brown bits and cooking until water is evaporated. Stir in thyme and cook mixture until onion is deep golden.

While onion is cooking, cutting lengthwise along a fold line, cut off one third of pastry sheet, about 10 by 3 inches, and reserve remaining pastry for another use. Halve pastry strip crosswise and transfer pieces to baking sheet. Prick pastry all over with a fork and bake in middle of oven until deep golden, about 12 minutes. Transfer a pastry piece with a spatula to each of 2 plates and immediately press down centers to form an indentation for goat cheese and onion. Spread goat cheese in middle of pastry pieces and top with caramelized onion.

Garnish tarts with fresh thyme sprigs and serve immediately.

JERK PORK AND RED PEPPER MAYO ON BLACK-EYED-PEA CAKES

Makes about 60 hors d'oeuvres

As any southerner will tell you, eating black-eyed peas at New Year's will ensure good luck. For a simpler (and meatless) version of this hors d'oeuvre, omit the pork and serve these tender little cakes topped with just the red pepper mayo.

4 (15½-oz) cans black-eyed peas, rinsed and
   drained (about 6½ cups)
3 red bell peppers, finely chopped
3 tablespoons unsalted butter
4 large garlic cloves, minced
1¼ cups fresh bread crumbs
½ cup finely chopped fresh cilantro
2 large eggs, lightly beaten
2 tablespoons ground cumin
1½ tablespoons kosher salt
1½ cups yellow cornmeal plus additional
   for dusting
1 cup plus 3 tablespoons vegetable oil
1 cup mayonnaise

Accompaniment: jerk pork (recipe follows)

Mash half of peas in a bowl with a fork and stir in remaining peas.

Cook red peppers in butter in a large nonstick skillet over moderate heat, stirring, until barely softened. Add garlic and cook, stirring, 1 minute more. Transfer one third of pepper mixture to a bowl and cool. Set aside for red pepper mayo.

Stir remaining pepper mixture into peas with bread crumbs, cilantro, eggs, cumin, and salt. Scoop 1 table-spoon mixture into palm of your hand (mixture will be soft and moist) and form into a roughly 1-inch-wide patty. Put it on a tray and form more patties in same manner, arranging in 1 layer on tray. Dip patties, 1 at a time, into cornmeal, turning gently to coat, and transfer to a tray lined with wax paper and dusted with cornmeal. Chill patties, covered, at least 2 hours and up to 8.

Preheat oven to 400°F.

Heat 3 tablespoons oil in a 12-inch nonstick skillet over moderate heat until hot but not smoking, then cook cakes, 12 at a time, until golden, about 3 minutes on each side. Put cakes as cooked in 1 layer in a large shallow baking pan. Between batches, carefully wipe skillet clean with paper towels and add more oil.

Stir mayonnaise into reserved red pepper mixture and season with salt and pepper. Reheat cakes in middle of oven until hot, about 5 minutes, and top with red pepper mayo and jerk pork.

Cooks' notes:
• Cakes may be cooked 1 day ahead, then chilled, covered. Bring to room temperature before reheating.
• Red pepper mayo may be made 1 day ahead and chilled, covered.

PHOTO ON PAGE 77

JERK PORK ○+

Makes enough to top about 60 hors d'oeuvres

For marinade
½ cup chopped scallion
4 *serrano* or jalapeño chiles, chopped with seeds, or
    ½ Scotch bonnet chile, chopped without seeds
1 tablespoon soy sauce
1 tablespoon fresh lime juice
2 teaspoons ground allspice
1 garlic clove, chopped
1 teaspoon kosher salt
½ teaspoon sugar
½ teaspoon freshly ground black pepper
½ teaspoon dried thyme
¼ teaspoon cinnamon
¼ teaspoon ground ginger
⅛ teaspoon freshly grated nutmeg

1 lb boneless pork loin, cut crosswise into
    1-inch-thick slices
2 teaspoons vegetable oil plus extra for brushing
1 tablespoon chopped scallion (optional)

Make marinade:
Purée marinade ingredients in a small food processor or a blender and transfer to a sealable plastic bag.
Marinate pork, then grill:
Put pork in bag, turning to coat, and seal bag. Marinate pork, chilled, turning occasionally, 8 hours.

Brush a well-seasoned cast-iron ridged grill pan lightly with some oil and heat over moderately high heat until hot but not smoking. Grill pork, seasoned with salt, in batches over moderate heat, turning occasionally, until cooked through, about 9 minutes on each side. (Discard any remaining marinade in bag.) Transfer pork to a plate to cool slightly. With your fingers, shred warm pork into a bowl and toss with oil, scallion, and salt to taste. Keep warm, covered.

Cooks' note:
• Jerk pork may be grilled and shredded 1 day ahead and cooled completely before being chilled, covered. Reheat, covered, in a 400°F oven until hot and season with salt and pepper.

QUAIL EGGS WITH TOASTED-SESAME SALT ○

Serves 12 (as part of a brunch menu)

¾ cup sesame seeds
1 teaspoon kosher salt
48 quail eggs or 12 chicken eggs

Preheat oven to 350°F.

In a baking pan spread seeds evenly and toast, stirring once halfway through toasting, until deep golden, about 12 minutes. Cool seeds and in a food processor pulse with salt until coarsely ground.

In a saucepan cover eggs with cold water by 1 inch and bring just to a boil. Remove pan from heat and let eggs stand, covered, 7 minutes for quail eggs or 17 minutes for chicken eggs. Drain water from pan and run cold water over eggs, cracking shells against side of pan. Peel eggs and quarter chicken eggs if using.

Serve eggs with salt.

Cooks' note:
• Sesame salt may be made 2 weeks ahead and kept, covered, at room temperature.

PHOTO ON PAGE 31

SMOKED SALMON WITH CILANTRO CREAM ○

Serves 6

1 cup packed fresh cilantro
1 (8-oz) container sour cream
1 tablespoon fresh lime juice
1 teaspoon ground coriander seeds
1 lb sliced smoked salmon

Accompaniment: slices of pumpernickel or
    whole-wheat bread
Garnish: lime halves

Finely chop cilantro and in a small bowl stir together with sour cream, lime juice, coriander seeds, and salt and pepper to taste.

Arrange salmon on a platter and serve with cilantro cream and bread. Garnish salmon with lime halves.

PHOTO ON PAGE 13

SEARED SMOKED SALMON WITH CUCUMBER PRESSÉ ☺+

Serves 6

1 large English cucumber, peeled and
   very thinly sliced
1 tablespoon kosher salt
2 tablespoons lemon olive oil
1-lb piece center-cut smoked salmon, skinned
   and cut crosswise into 6 strips

Toss cucumber with kosher salt and put in a colander set over a bowl. Weight cucumber with an inverted plate topped with a 2-pound weight and chill 1 hour.

Rinse cucumbers under cold running water and drain. Squeeze small handfuls to extract as much water as possible and toss together with ½ tablespoon oil and salt and pepper to taste.

Heat remaining 1½ tablespoons oil in a large nonstick skillet over moderately high heat until hot but not smoking, then sear smoked salmon until golden, about 2 minutes total.

Serve salmon on a bed of cucumber.

Cooks' notes:
- For a striped effect, remove alternate strips from cucumber skin with a vegetable peeler before slicing.
- Do not use pure lemon oil, as it can flame in skillet.

PHOTO ON PAGE 73

SPICY LEMON-MARINATED SHRIMP ☺+

Serves 6

In our wedding menu (page 55), these marinated shrimp are a main course dish. Here, served in smaller portions on pesticide-free lemon leaves, they make an easy hors d'oeuvre.

1 large lemon
1½ teaspoons coriander seeds
3 tablespoons white-wine vinegar
1 tablespoon olive oil
1 tablespoon water
1 tablespoon sugar
1½ teaspoons dried Aleppo or New Mexican chile
   flakes (sources on page 252) or a rounded
   ¼ teaspoon dried hot red pepper flakes
1 tablespoon plus 2½ teaspoons kosher salt

2 tablespoons pickling spices
1 lb large shrimp, shelled and deveined

Remove zest from lemon with a vegetable peeler and remove white pith from zest strips with a sharp knife. Squeeze 3 tablespoons juice. Finely grind coriander in an electric coffee/spice grinder. Whisk together zest, juice, coriander, vinegar, oil, water, sugar, chile flakes, and 2½ teaspoons kosher salt in a large bowl until sugar and salt are dissolved.

Bring a 3- to 4-quart pot of water to a boil with pickling spices and remaining tablespoon salt and cook shrimp 1½ minutes, or until just cooked through. Transfer shrimp with a slotted spoon to marinade, tossing to coat well.

Cool shrimp slightly and transfer with marinade to a large sealable plastic bag. Marinate, chilled, turning bag occasionally, at least 8 hours.

Drain shrimp before serving.

Cooks' note:
- You can marinate the shrimp up to 3 days.

PHOTO ON PAGE 58

SCALLION, MUSHROOM, AND SHRIMP CUSTARDS ☺

Serves 4 (first course)

These custards are inspired by chawan mushi, the Japanese egg custard made with dashi broth (a stock of dried kelp and dried bonito flakes). We've used chicken broth for simplicity, but any broth or stock that you have on hand will work fine. Steaming the custards gives them a delicate texture, which is enhanced by the spare use of solid ingredients (the shrimp, scallion, and mushrooms).

3 large eggs
1½ cups chicken broth
2 teaspoons *mirin* (Japanese sweetened rice wine)
   (sources on page 252)
1 teaspoon soy sauce (preferably Kikkoman)
1 teaspoon freshly grated lemon zest
4 medium shrimp
1 scallion
1 large mushroom

In a bowl with a fork beat eggs until combined well. Skim any fat from broth and add broth with *mirin*, soy

sauce, and zest to eggs, stirring to combine well. Pour custard through a fine sieve into another bowl.

Peel shrimp and devein if desired. Diagonally cut white and pale-green parts of scallion into thin slices and thinly slice mushroom.

Divide shrimp, scallion, mushroom, and custard among four ⅔-cup custard cups or ramekins and cover each tightly with foil. Arrange cups or ramekins in a steamer over boiling water and steam custards, covered, over high heat 2 minutes.

Reduce heat to moderate and steam custards, covered, until set, about 10 minutes more.

Serve custards immediately.

SHRIMP DUMPLINGS ◐

Serves 2

½ lb shrimp (about 8 large)
½ cup drained canned water chestnuts
2 scallions
1 large egg white
1 tablespoon grated peeled fresh ginger
3 tablespoons soy sauce (preferably Kikkoman)
14 won ton wrappers, thawed if frozen
½ teaspoon sugar
2 tablespoons vegetable oil
¾ cup boiling-hot water

Peel shrimp and, if desired, devein. In a food processor purée 3 shrimp. Rinse and drain water chestnuts. Finely chop water chestnuts and remaining shrimp. Finely chop scallion greens, reserving white parts for another use. Lightly beat egg white and put 1 tablespoon in a bowl. Stir in puréed and chopped shrimp, water chestnuts, about two thirds each of scallion greens and ginger, and 1 tablespoon soy sauce.

Put 7 won ton wrappers on a dry surface, keeping remaining wrappers in package, and lightly brush edges with water. Mound about 1 tablespoon filling in center of each wrapper. Fold each wrapper over filling to form a triangle. Press down around filling to force out excess air and seal edges well. Make additional dumplings with remaining wrappers and filling in same manner.

Stir together sugar and remaining scallion greens, ginger, and soy sauce to make dipping sauce.

In a 12-inch nonstick skillet heat vegetable oil over moderately high heat until hot but not smoking and brown dumplings on both sides, about 3 minutes total. Add boiling-hot water and cook, covered, 5 minutes.

Serve dumplings with sauce.

ROASTED SPICED SHRIMP ON WILTED SPINACH ◐

Serves 4 (first course)

6 large shrimp
⅛ teaspoon chili powder
⅛ teaspoon salt
½ lb spinach (about 1 bunch)
2 scallions
1 teaspoon fresh lime juice
2 tablespoons water
1 teaspoon grated peeled fresh ginger
½ teaspoon sesame oil

Accompaniment: lime wedges

Preheat oven to 450°F.

Leaving shells intact, pull legs off shrimp and with a sharp knife halve shrimp lengthwise. Arrange shrimp, shell sides down, in 1 layer in a shallow baking pan. In a small bowl stir together chili powder and salt and sprinkle evenly over shrimp.

Discard stems from spinach and diagonally cut scallions into ¼-inch-thick slices. Drizzle shrimp with lime juice and roast in middle of oven until just cooked through, about 5 minutes.

In a large nonstick skillet bring water with ginger to a simmer over moderate heat and add spinach. Cook spinach, stirring, until slightly wilted, about 20 seconds. Remove skillet from heat and immediately stir in scallions and oil until combined well. Season spinach with salt and pepper.

Mound spinach in center of each of 4 plates and arrange shrimp halves around it. Serve shrimp and spinach with lime wedges.

Cooks' note:
• Shrimp may be prepared for roasting 3 hours ahead (before drizzling with lime juice) and chilled, covered.

🍃 each serving about 23 calories and less than 1 gram fat

PHOTO ON PAGE 78

TAMALITOS

Makes 36

Corn is the essential flavor here, so be sure yours is sweet and fresh by tasting each ear. In the absence of fresh corn you can use frozen, but you should taste that, too.

About 6 dozen dried corn husks (6 oz)
   (sources on page 252)
3 cups fresh or thawed frozen corn kernels
1½ cups light vegetable stock (recipe follows)
   or broth
½ cup milk
2 or 3 fresh *poblano* chiles (sources on page 252)
1 large red bell pepper or 4 pieces bottled Italian
   roasted red peppers, rinsed and drained
3 cups *masa harina* (dry corn *masa*; 10 oz)
   (sources on page 252)
1 tablespoon baking powder
1½ teaspoons salt
2¼ sticks unsalted butter, softened
½ cup thinly sliced scallion

Prepare husks:

Soak corn husks in a large bowl of hot water, weighting with an inverted heavy plate to keep submerged, turning husks occasionally, until soft, about 30 minutes. Rinse husks under running water, separating them (and discarding torn, tough, or badly discolored husks). Pile best husks on a plate and cover with a damp kitchen towel. Tear some of the thickest husks into ½-inch-wide strips to use as ties. (Keep ties damp as well.)

Prepare filling:

Simmer corn in stock, uncovered, stirring occasionally, 10 minutes. Stir in milk and purée in a blender until smooth. Transfer to a bowl and cool completely, about 25 minutes.

Preheat broiler.

Put chiles and, if using, fresh bell pepper on a rack of a broiler pan and broil about 2 inches from heat, turning them, until skins are blistered and charred, 8 to 12 minutes. Transfer to a bowl and let stand, covered with plastic wrap, until cool enough to handle. Peel peppers and remove veins if desired. Cut tops from peppers and discard with seeds. Separately chop chiles and fresh or bottled bell pepper.

Sift *masa harina* with baking powder and salt into a bowl. Beat butter in a large bowl with an electric mixer until smooth and fluffy. Alternately beat in corn purée and *masa harina* mixture, ½ cup at a time, beating until mixture forms a fluffy and moist but fairly stiff dough. Divide filling in half and stir chiles into one half and bell pepper and scallion into the other. Season both fillings with salt.

Assemble tamalitos:

Put 1 husk on a work surface, pointy end facing you, and, spreading it flat, mound 2 tablespoons filling (about the size of an egg) in center. Bring pointy end of husk up and over mound of filling and fold sides of husk over filling, overlapping. Now gather the protruding end of husk and tie it with a corn-husk strip. (This purse will expand slightly as the *tamalito* is steamed.) Assemble remaining *tamalitos* in same manner.

Stack *tamalitos*, in a crosshatch pattern so steam can move freely around them, in a large steamer basket. (*Tamalitos* can also be steamed in batches.) Set steamer over boiling water in a deep heavy pot, without *tamalitos* touching water, and cover with a folded kitchen towel. (Towel absorbs condensation so *tamalitos* don't get soggy.) Steam *tamalitos*, covered with lid, adding more boiling water as necessary, until filling is tender but no longer mushy, about 45 minutes. (If any part is still gummy, steam 10 to 15 minutes more.)

Cooks' notes:
· *Tamalitos* can be steamed 1 day ahead, cooled completely, and chilled, covered. Just before serving, bring *tamalitos* to room temperature and steam until hot, at least 10 minutes.
· Set a coin in the bottom of your pot so you'll know if all the water has evaporated. If you can no longer hear the coin bouncing around, you need to add more water.

PHOTO ON PAGE 63

LIGHT VEGETABLE STOCK

Makes about 4½ quarts

7 qt water
10 large carrots, sliced
4 large celery ribs, sliced
4 large onions, coarsely chopped
2 unpeeled heads of garlic, halved horizontally
Peels of 2 large potatoes
2 medium turnips, coarsely chopped
24 fresh cilantro sprigs

8 fresh flat-leaf parsley sprigs
2 bay leaves
1 tablespoon salt
2 teaspoons dried thyme
2 teaspoons whole black peppercorns

Bring water to a boil with remaining ingredients in a 10- to 12-quart pot and boil gently 1 hour, or until vegetables are completely soft.

Pour stock through a colander into a large bowl. Strain stock again, through a fine sieve into another large bowl.

Cooks' note:
• Stock may be made 4 days ahead, cooled, uncovered, and chilled, covered. It keeps frozen 1 month.

PANKO SCALLOPS WITH GREEN CHILE CHUTNEY

Makes 60 hors d'oeuvres

For chutney
2 cups packed fresh cilantro, chopped
½ cup chopped scallion
¼ cup sweetened flaked coconut
2 to 3 *serrano* or jalapeño chiles, chopped with seeds
3 tablespoons vegetable oil
1½ tablespoons finely grated peeled fresh ginger
2½ tablespoons fresh lime juice, or to taste
2 tablespoons water

60 small sea scallops (about 3½ lb)
2 large eggs
¼ cup milk
3 cups *panko* (Japanese bread crumbs) or coarse dry
    bread crumbs (sources on page 252)
1 cup vegetable oil

Make chutney:
Purée chutney ingredients in a blender, stirring occasionally to assist blending, and transfer to a bowl. Season chutney with salt and pepper and chill, covered, until ready to use.

Make scallops:
Remove muscle from scallops if still attached. Pat scallops dry and season with salt and pepper. Whisk together eggs and milk in a shallow bowl. Put *panko* in another shallow bowl. Dip scallops, 1 at a time, in egg mixture and then in *panko*, turning to coat, and transfer to a tray.

Preheat oven to 400°F.

Heat 3 tablespoons oil in a 12-inch nonstick skillet over moderate heat until hot but not smoking, then cook scallops, 12 at a time, until just cooked through and golden brown (adjust heat if necessary), about 1½ minutes on each side. Put scallops as cooked in 1 layer on a rack set in a shallow baking pan. Between batches, carefully wipe skillet clean with paper towels and add more oil. Bake scallops in middle of oven until just heated through, about 3 minutes.

Serve scallops topped with chutney.

Cooks' notes:
• Chutney may be made 3 days ahead and chilled, covered. Before serving, season with salt and pepper.
• Scallops may be coated with *panko* 4 hours ahead and chilled, covered. Panfry them 1 hour ahead and keep at room temperature. Bake right before serving.

PHOTO ON PAGE 76

HERBED SUMMER SUCCOTASH ON GARLIC CROÛTES

Serves 6 (first course)

In this recipe we used fresh baby lima beans (the frozen ones are excellent, too), but you can substitute any other fresh young shell beans such as fava or cranberry beans.

¼ lb bacon (about 4 slices)
1 lb fresh shell beans in pod or 1 cup frozen
  baby lima beans
¾ lb cherry tomatoes (about 1½ pints)
4 ears corn
1 small Vidalia onion or other sweet onion
1 large garlic clove
1½ tablespoons olive oil
1 tablespoon Sherry vinegar
¼ cup packed small fresh basil leaves
¼ cup packed small fresh arugula leaves

Accompaniment: garlic *croûtes* (recipe follows)

In a skillet cook bacon over moderate heat until crisp. Drain bacon on paper towels and crumble. Pour off all but 1 tablespoon fat from skillet and set skillet aside.

Shell fresh beans if using. In a small saucepan of boiling salted water cook beans, covered, over moderate heat, stirring occasionally, until just tender, about 5 minutes. In a sieve drain beans and rinse under cold running water to stop cooking.

Cut larger cherry tomatoes in half. Working over a bowl to catch the juices, cut corn kernels from cobs. Chop onion and mince garlic.

Add oil to bacon fat in skillet and cook onion over moderate heat, stirring, until softened. Add garlic and cook, stirring, 1 minute. Add tomatoes, corn, and vinegar and cook, stirring, until tomatoes just begin to lose their shape. Remove skillet from heat and gently stir in beans and half of bacon. Cool succotash to room temperature and gently stir in basil, arugula, and salt and pepper to taste.

Serve succotash spooned over garlic *croûtes* and sprinkled evenly with remaining bacon.

GARLIC CROÛTES ◔

Makes 6

Great flavor resulted when we made these croûtes in a ridged grill pan, but a broiler will get the job done.

1 garlic clove
1 round loaf crusty bread
2 tablespoons extra-virgin olive oil
Fine sea salt

Halve garlic. Cut six ⅓-inch-thick slices from middle of loaf and brush bread with oil. Lightly oil a well-seasoned ridged grill pan and heat over moderately high heat until hot but not smoking. Grill bread until golden brown on both sides. Immediately rub bread on 1 side with cut side of garlic and sprinkle with salt.

TUNA IN AVOCADO HALVES ◔

Serves 2 (first course)

1 (6-oz) can tuna in olive oil (not drained)
2 tablespoons balsamic vinegar
1 California avocado

Drain oil from tuna can into a small bowl and whisk in vinegar and salt and pepper to taste. In a bowl combine tuna and half of dressing, keeping tuna in large chunks. Halve and pit avocado and season with salt and pepper. Fill avocado halves with tuna and drizzle with remaining dressing.

CANAPÉS

CRAB MEAT AND BEET PURÉE ON GRANNY SMITH APPLE

Makes about 32

1 medium beet (about ⅓ lb)
½ lb jumbo lump crab meat
1½ tablespoons finely chopped fresh chives
1½ teaspoons fresh lemon juice
1½ tablespoons sour cream

1 teaspoon balsamic vinegar
1 large Granny Smith apple

Preheat oven to 450°F.

Trim beet, leaving about 1 inch of stem attached, and wrap tightly in foil. In a small baking pan roast beet in middle of oven until tender, about 1 hour.

Pick over crab meat to remove any bits of shell and cartilage. Slightly break up large pieces of crab and in a small bowl stir together with chives, lemon juice, 1 tablespoon sour cream, and salt and pepper to taste.

Unwrap beet carefully. When beet is just cool enough to handle, slip off skin and stem and cut beet into a few pieces. While beet is still warm, using a mortar and pestle mash beet until smooth. In a small bowl stir together mashed beet, vinegar, remaining ½ tablespoon sour cream, and salt and pepper to taste.

Just before serving, quarter apple through stem end and core. Cut apple quarters crosswise into ¼-inch-thick slices. Top each apple slice with ¼ teaspoon beet purée and some crab mixture.

Cooks' notes:
- Crab mixture may be made 6 hours ahead and chilled, covered.
- Beet purée may be made 1 day ahead and chilled, covered.
- Assemble just before serving or the apple will discolor.

PHOTO ON PAGE 25

GINGER-HOISIN BEEF AND SCALLIONS ON CRISPY NOODLE CAKES

Makes about 32

¼ lb rice noodles (rice vermicelli)
    (sources on page 252)
8 thin scallions
2 tablespoons grated peeled fresh ginger
About ½ cup vegetable oil
1 (1-lb) piece beef tenderloin
¼ cup fresh lime juice
¼ cup hoisin sauce
2 tablespoons soy sauce (preferably Kikkoman)

Fill a 4-quart kettle three fourths full with water and bring to a boil. Cook noodles in boiling water until tender, about 3 minutes, and drain in a colander. Finely chop white and pale-green parts of scallions, reserving dark-green parts. In a bowl toss noodles with chopped scallions and 1 tablespoon each of ginger and oil until combined well.

To cook noodle "cakes," in a large nonstick skillet heat enough oil to cover bottom of skillet over moderate heat until hot but not smoking. Drop some noodles by heaping tablespoons (see note, below), evenly spaced, into skillet and with a fork spread to form 1½-inch circles. Cook noodle cakes until golden and crisp, about 2 minutes on each side. With tongs transfer noodle cakes as cooked to paper towels to drain. Make more cakes in same manner, adding more oil to skillet as needed.

Pat tenderloin dry and halve lengthwise. Cut each piece in half lengthwise to form 2 long strips (4 long strips total). In a bowl whisk together lime juice, hoisin and soy sauces, and remaining tablespoon ginger. Put beef and hoisin mixture into a sealable heavy-duty plastic bag. Marinate beef, covered and chilled, turning bag over once or twice, at least 1 hour and up to 6.

Preheat oven to 450°F.

Remove beef from bag and transfer marinade to a small saucepan. Simmer marinade 2 minutes and cool completely.

In a heavy skillet heat ½ tablespoon oil over moderately high heat until just smoking and brown beef on all sides, about 3 minutes total for each piece. Transfer beef to a small shallow roasting pan and cook in middle of oven 10 to 12 minutes for medium-rare. Transfer beef to a cutting board and let stand 20 minutes.

While beef is standing, cut reserved scallion greens into 1½-inch-long thin julienne strips. Chill scallion greens, wrapped in a dampened paper towel, at least 10 minutes and, in a sealable plastic bag, up to 1 day.

Cut beef into ¼-inch-thick slices and top each noodle cake with a slice. Top beef slices with about ¼ teaspoon sauce and a few scallion greens.

Cooks' notes:
- To form the noodle cakes, measure them out by taking a few strands of noodles and loosely squiggling them into a tablespoon. Once you get the hang of the amount needed, you can eyeball it.
- Noodle cakes may be made 1 day ahead and kept in an airtight container at room temperature.
- Ginger-hoisin sauce may be made 1 day ahead and chilled, covered.
- Beef may be cooked 1 day ahead and chilled, covered.

PHOTO ON PAGE 25

SMOKED CAVIAR AND HUMMUS ON PITA TOASTS

Makes 160

Using a pastry bag to pipe the hummus onto the toasts saved us a lot of time. You can make your own pastry bag with a heavy-duty plastic bag. Just spoon the hummus into the bag and squeeze it into one corner. Then snip off the corner to make a small hole and begin piping.

10 (5- to 6-inch) pita pockets
¾ cup olive oil
2 teaspoons paprika
For hummus
4 teaspoons cumin seeds, toasted
2 (15½-oz) cans chick-peas, rinsed
1 garlic clove, coarsely chopped
⅓ cup chopped fresh flat-leaf parsley
½ cup well-stirred *tahini* (Middle Eastern
   sesame paste)
¼ cup fresh lemon juice
1½ teaspoons salt
⅓ to ½ cup water

1 (11½-oz) jar smoked whitefish caviar (sources on
   page 252)

Garnish: 160 small fresh flat-leaf parsley leaves

Toast pitas:
Preheat oven to 350°F.
Halve pitas horizontally and stir together oil and paprika. Brush rough sides of pitas with paprika oil and season with salt. Cut each pita round into 8 wedges and bake in single layers on a large baking sheet in middle of oven 10 minutes, or until crisp.
Make hummus:
Finely grind cumin seeds in an electric coffee/spice grinder. Purée chick-peas in a food processor with cumin, garlic, parsley, *tahini*, lemon juice, and salt and add enough water to make smooth.
Assemble hors d'oeuvres:
Put hummus in a pastry bag fitted with a ⅜-inch plain tip. Pipe a scant ½ teaspoon onto each pita toast and top with ¼ teaspoon caviar.

Cooks' notes:
• Pita toasts may be made 2 days ahead, cooled, and kept in sealable plastic bags at room temperature.

• Hummus can be made (without lemon juice so parsley remains green) 2 days ahead and chilled, covered. Stir in lemon juice just before assembling.

PHOTO ON PAGE 55

CUCUMBER CAVIAR CANAPÉS

Serves 2

We used osetra caviar for this hors d'oeuvre, but feel free to substitute your favorite. Any leftover caviar can be used to brighten up a number of dishes, from scrambled eggs to pasta.

¼ English cucumber
About 3 tablespoons sour cream
About 1.75 oz caviar (sources on page 252)

Diagonally cut cucumber into eight ⅛-inch-thick slices. Serve cucumber slices topped with sour cream and caviar.

"FISH AND CHIPS"

Makes 80 hors d'oeuvres

⅔ cup crème fraîche (5 oz)
1½ teaspoons finely grated fresh lemon zest,
   or to taste
1 teaspoon finely chopped fresh chives
¼ cup olive oil
4 large russet (baking) potatoes
6 oz caviar (preferably osetra)
   (sources on page 252)

Special equipment:
Mandoline or other manual slicer
1½- to 2-inch star cutter

Preheat oven to 375°F.
Stir together crème fraîche, zest, chives, and salt to taste. Chill topping until ready to use.
Brush 2 large baking sheets generously with some oil. Cut potatoes crosswise on a slight diagonal into ⅛-inch-thick slices with *mandoline*. Cut out 80 potato stars with cutter and arrange in 1 layer on baking sheets. Brush tops with more oil and season with salt.
Bake potato stars in batches in middle of oven until golden and crisp, about 10 minutes (stars may curl).

Immediately transfer stars carefully with a metal spatula to paper towels to drain and cool (stars will continue to crisp as they cool).

Serve stars topped with crème fraîche and caviar.

Cooks' notes:
- Crème fraîche topping may be made 2 days ahead and chilled, covered.
- Stars may be made 2 days ahead and kept, between paper towels, in an airtight container at room temperature.

PHOTO ON PAGE 77

SEARED FOIE GRAS AND LINGONBERRY JAM ON BRIOCHE TOASTS

Makes 60 hors d'oeuvres

3 large brioche or challah loaves, crusts removed
5 tablespoons unsalted butter
¾ cup plus 3 tablespoons olive oil
2 teaspoons freshly ground black pepper, or to taste
2 teaspoons fresh lemon juice
1½ cups lingonberry jam or spread
1 lb fresh foie gras or cleaned chicken livers
    (sources on page 252)

Cut brioche into ¾-inch-thick slices, then into 60 (1½-inch) cubes. Heat 1 tablespoon butter with 2 tablespoons oil in a 12-inch nonstick skillet over moderate heat until foam subsides. Cook brioche cubes, 12 at a time, until golden brown on top and bottom, about 3 minutes total. Transfer brioche as cooked to a rack to cool and sprinkle with salt to taste. Between batches, carefully wipe skillet clean with paper towels and add more butter and oil.

Stir pepper and juice into jam. Chill jam, covered, until ready to use.

Preheat oven to 400°F.

Cut foie gras into 1- by ½-inch pieces and season with salt and pepper. Heat 1 tablespoon oil in a 12-inch nonstick skillet over moderately high heat until hot but not smoking. Reduce heat to moderate and cook foie gras, about 20 pieces at a time, until golden brown on both sides, about 1½ minutes total. Transfer foie gras as cooked to a shallow baking pan with a spatula and arrange in 1 layer. Between batches, carefully wipe skillet clean.

Reheat foie gras as needed in middle of oven 2 minutes, or until just hot, before assembling hors d'oeuvres. Just before serving, top toasts with lingonberry jam, then foie gras.

Cooks' notes:
- Lingonberry jam topping may be made 2 days ahead and chilled, covered.
- Toasts may be made 1 day ahead and cooled completely before being stored in an airtight container at room temperature. If toasts get soft, recrisp them on a baking sheet in middle of a 400°F oven.
- If using chicken livers, separate lobes and pat dry. Season with salt and pepper. Cook the livers, whole, until cooked through, about 4 minutes total. Cut the livers into pieces after they are cooked.

JÍCAMA-DATE CANAPÉS ☺

Makes about 45

1 large *jícama* (about 1¼ lb)
1 cup packed dried pitted dates (about ½ lb)
3 tablespoons fresh lime juice
2 tablespoons minced scallion
2 tablespoons chopped fresh mint

Garnish: small fresh mint leaves

Peel *jícama* and cut enough into ¼-inch dice to measure ½ cup. In a food processor pulse dates to a paste and transfer to a bowl. Stir diced *jícama*, lime juice, scallion, and mint into dates and season with salt. Cut remaining *jícama* into ¼-inch-thick slices and cut each slice into as many 1½-inch triangles as possible. Top *jícama* triangles with some date mixture and garnish with small mint leaves.

Cooks' notes:
- Date mixture may be made 1 day ahead and chilled, covered.
- *Jícama* triangles may be made 1 day ahead, wrapped in damp paper towels, and chilled in a sealable plastic bag.

PHOTO ON PAGE 41

SMOKED PEPPERED MACKEREL AND SOUR CREAM ON HOMEMADE POTATO CHIPS

Makes about 32

Store-bought potato chips, heated to crisp and refresh, would make this a very quick hors d'oeuvre.

3 tablespoons vegetable oil
2 medium Yukon Gold or other boiling potatoes
3 tablespoons sour cream
1 (8-oz) package smoked peppered mackerel
    (sources on page 252)

Preheat oven to 375°F and generously brush 2 large baking sheets with some oil.

With a *mandoline* or other hand-held slicer cut 1 potato crosswise into ⅛-inch-thick slices. Immediately arrange slices in one layer on 1 baking sheet and brush tops with some oil. Sprinkle slices with salt to taste.

Bake slices in middle of oven until golden, 10 to 15 minutes, and with a metal spatula immediately transfer to a rack to cool completely. Make more potato chips with remaining potato.

Top each potato chip with ¼ teaspoon sour cream and a small piece of mackerel.

Cooks' note:
• Potato chips may be made 3 days ahead and kept in an airtight container at room temperature.

PEPERONATA ON GOAT CHEESE TOASTS ☉

Serves 2

This peperonata would also be delicious tossed with pasta and the small balls of mozzarella called bocconcini—and as a condiment on sandwiches.

1 baguette (preferably sourdough)
3 tablespoons olive oil
2 garlic cloves
1 red bell pepper
1 plum tomato
2 tablespoons finely chopped shallot
¼ teaspoon dried hot red pepper flakes
1½ tablespoons balsamic vinegar, or to taste
2 oz soft mild goat cheese, softened

Garnish: small fresh basil leaves

Preheat broiler.

Diagonally cut eight ¼-inch-thick slices from baguette with a serrated knife and arrange in one layer on a baking sheet. Brush tops of bread slices with 1 tablespoon oil and sprinkle with salt. Broil bread about 4 inches from heat, turning once, until golden, about 2 minutes. Cool toasts on a rack.

Halve garlic cloves and finely chop bell pepper. Seed tomato and finely chop.

In a small heavy saucepan cook garlic in remaining 2 tablespoons oil over moderate heat, stirring, until just golden. Discard garlic. Add bell pepper, tomato, shallot, and red pepper flakes and cook, stirring occasionally, until bell pepper is softened. Stir in vinegar and cook, stirring, until liquid is evaporated, about 5 minutes. Transfer *peperonata* to a bowl and cool to room temperature. Season *peperonata* with salt and pepper.

Spread toasts with goat cheese. Top cheese with *peperonata* and garnish with basil.

TAPENADE GOAT-CHEESE CRACKERS

Makes about 120

1½ cups all-purpose flour
¼ teaspoon salt
1¼ sticks cold unsalted butter
1 (11-oz) log soft mild goat cheese
About 1 cup *tapenade* (recipe follows)

In a food processor or in a large bowl with a pastry blender pulse or blend flour and salt. Cut butter into small pieces. Add butter to flour mixture and pulse or blend until mixture resembles coarse meal. Measure ⅓ cup goat cheese, reserving remainder at room temperature, and break into small pieces. Add cheese to flour mixture and pulse or blend until mixture just begins to form a dough. Halve dough and roll out each half between sheets of parchment paper into a 12- by 10-inch rectangle (about ⅛ inch thick). Chill rectangles in parchment on baking sheets until firm, about 30 minutes.

Preheat oven to 375°F.

Transfer 1 rectangle of dough on baking sheet to a work surface and remove top sheet of parchment paper. Working quickly (use a ruler as a guide), cut rectangle into 1¼-inch squares without separating squares. (If the dough becomes too soft to work with, freeze or chill on parchment and baking sheet until firm.)

Bake crackers on parchment and baking sheet in middle of oven until golden, 15 to 20 minutes. Cool crackers on parchment on a rack. (Crackers will continue to crisp as they cool.) Cut and bake more crackers with remaining rectangle of dough. With a spatula carefully remove crackers from parchment.

Spread crackers with reserved goat cheese and top with *tapenade*.

Cooks' note:
• Crackers may be made 5 days ahead and kept in an airtight container at room temperature.

PHOTO ON PAGE 25

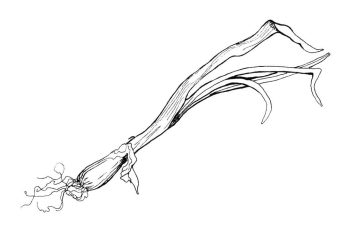

TAPENADE

Makes about 1 cup

2 cups Kalamata or other brine-cured black olives
    (about 16 oz)
¼ cup extra-virgin olive oil
¼ cup packed fresh flat-leaf parsley

In a colander rinse olives. Working with several olives at a time and using flat side of a large heavy knife, press olives to crush them, and remove pits. In a food processor pulse olives with oil until coarsely chopped. Chop parsley and stir into *tapenade*.

Cooks' note:
• *Tapenade* may be made 3 days ahead (before adding parsley), chilled in an airtight container.

AVOCADO AND TOMATILLO DIP

Makes about 3½ cups

¾ lb fresh tomatillos
4 large garlic cloves
3 California avocados
½ cup chopped fresh cilantro
1½ tablespoons fresh lime juice, or to taste
4 tablespoons finely chopped red onion

Accompaniment: tortilla chips

Remove husks and rinse tomatillos under warm water to remove stickiness. Heat a well-seasoned cast-iron skillet or griddle over moderately high heat until hot but not smoking and lightly brown tomatillos and garlic in spots all over (do not let burn). Transfer tomatillos and garlic to a plate and cool them to room temperature.

In a food processor purée tomatillos and garlic until smooth. Halve and pit avocados and scoop flesh into tomatillo mixture. Pulse until coarsely chopped. Stir in cilantro, lime juice, 3 tablespoons onion, and salt and pepper to taste. Garnish dip with remaining tablespoon chopped onion and serve with tortilla chips.

BLUE CHEESE AND SCALLION DIP

Serves 4 (makes about ⅔ cup)

2 oz blue cheese, crumbled
½ cup sour cream
3 tablespoons chopped scallion greens

Accompaniment: thick-cut potato chips or
    raw cauliflower

Gently stir together cheese, sour cream, and most of scallion, leaving cheese chunky. Garnish with remaining scallion.

CHIPOTLE DIP ◔

Makes about 1½ cups

This recipe calls for chipotle chiles, which are actually dried, smoked jalapeños. They can be bought packed in adobo, a sauce made from ground chiles, herbs, tomatoes, and vinegar.

2 scallions
2 to 3 small canned *chipotle* chiles in *adobo* plus
  ¼ teaspoon *adobo* sauce (sources on page 252)
1 cup mayonnaise
½ cup sour cream
1 teaspoon fresh lemon juice

Accompaniments: bell pepper strips, chips,
  or crackers

Finely chop scallions. Wearing protective gloves, mince enough *chipotles* to a paste to measure 1½ tablespoons. In a bowl whisk together all ingredients with salt to taste.

Cooks' note:
• Dip may be kept, covered and chilled, 3 days.

CRAB SPREAD WITH BENNE-SEED WAFERS

Makes about 4 cups

6 small scallions
1 garlic clove
1 lb jumbo lump crab meat
8 oz cream cheese, softened
⅓ cup sour cream
1 tablespoon drained bottled horseradish
2 teaspoons fresh lemon juice, or to taste
1 teaspoon Dijon mustard
1 teaspoon Worcestershire sauce, or to taste
½ teaspoon salt
¼ teaspoon cayenne

Accompaniment: benne-seed wafers (recipe follows)
  or other crackers

Finely chop scallions and mince garlic. Pick over crab meat to remove any bits of shell and cartilage. In a bowl stir together cream cheese and sour cream until smooth and stir in all ingredients except the crab until combined well. Stir in crab until just combined. Chill crab spread, covered, at least 8 hours and up to 1 day to develop flavors.

Serve crab spread with benne-seed wafers or other crackers.

PHOTO ON PAGE 16

BENNE-SEED WAFERS

Makes about 60

Because of their high oil content, sesame seeds begin to turn rancid very easily. For this recipe it is important that they be very fresh. Taste the seeds after you purchase them, and if they are a little "off" take them back.

⅓ cup very fresh sesame (benne) seeds
1 cup all-purpose flour
½ teaspoon baking powder
½ teaspoon table salt
¼ cup cold lard or vegetable shortening
¼ cup whole milk
Coarse salt for sprinkling wafers

Preheat oven to 350°F.

In a shallow baking pan spread seeds evenly and toast in middle of oven, stirring occasionally, until golden, about 8 minutes. Cool seeds.

Into a bowl sift together flour, baking powder, and table salt. With your fingertips or a pastry blender blend in lard or shortening until mixture resembles coarse meal. Add seeds and milk, stirring until a soft dough is formed. Divide dough in half. Keeping remaining piece of dough wrapped in plastic wrap, roll out 1 piece between sheets of plastic wrap to ⅛ inch thick (about an 8½-inch square) and remove top sheet of plastic wrap. With a sharp knife cut dough into 1½-inch squares, reserving scraps. Peel squares off plastic wrap and arrange about ½ inch apart on ungreased baking sheets. Roll out and cut remaining piece of dough in same manner. Reroll reserved scraps and cut in same manner.

Bake wafers in batches in middle of oven until pale golden, 12 to 15 minutes. Sprinkle wafers with coarse salt and transfer to a rack to cool.

Cooks' note:
• Wafers may be made 1 week ahead and kept in an airtight container at cool room temperature.

ROASTED EGGPLANT AND GARLIC DIP

Makes about 2 cups

2 small heads garlic
1 eggplant (1 lb)
¼ cup extra-virgin olive oil
1 teaspoon red-wine vinegar, or to taste

Accompaniment: pita toasts

Preheat oven to 425°F.

Separate garlic cloves without peeling and tightly wrap together in foil. Prick eggplant with a fork. In a shallow baking pan roast garlic and eggplant in middle of oven until very tender, about 30 minutes for garlic and about 45 minutes for eggplant.

Unwrap garlic and peel, transferring garlic to a food processor. Scrape flesh from eggplant into food processor, discarding skin. Purée mixture until smooth and, with motor running, add oil and vinegar until combined well. Season dip with salt and pepper and serve with pita toasts.

FETA PINE-NUT DIP ☺

Makes about 2 cups

½ cup pine nuts
½ red bell pepper
½ cup packed fresh flat-leaf parsley
6 oz feta
¼ teaspoon minced garlic
1 cup plain yogurt

Accompaniment: pita toasts or bagel chips

Preheat oven to 350°F.

In a shallow baking pan toast pine nuts, stirring occasionally, until golden, about 7 minutes, and transfer to a plate to cool. Separately chop nuts, bell pepper, and parsley and combine in a bowl.

Crumble feta into a food processor and pulse until it resembles coarse meal. Stir feta into nut mixture with garlic, yogurt, and salt and pepper to taste. Serve dip with pita toasts or bagel chips.

JERUSALEM ARTICHOKE CHIPS WITH LEMON THYME DIP ☺

Serves 2

¼ cup mayonnaise
1 teaspoon finely grated fresh lemon zest
1 teaspoon fresh lemon juice
1 teaspoon chopped fresh thyme leaves
4 cups vegetable oil
½ lb Jerusalem artichokes (sometimes called
    Sun Chokes)

Stir together mayonnaise, zest, lemon juice, thyme, and salt and pepper to taste.

In a 4-quart heavy kettle heat oil over moderate heat until a deep-fat thermometer registers 325°F.

While oil is heating, cut unpeeled artichokes lengthwise into ⅛-inch-thick slices. Fry them in 2 batches in oil 1½ minutes (artichokes will not color) and transfer to paper towels to drain.

Heat oil to 350°F. Return artichokes in 2 batches to oil and fry, stirring occasionally, until golden and crisp, about 5 minutes. Transfer chips with a slotted spoon to clean paper towels to drain and season with salt.

Serve chips with dip.

SMOKED-TROUT HORSERADISH DIP ☺

Makes about 2 cups

½ lb smoked trout
¾ cup mayonnaise
½ cup sour cream
3 tablespoons chopped fresh dill
2 tablespoons drained bottled horseradish,
    or to taste

Accompaniment: pumpernickel toasts

Discard skin and bones from trout and break into pieces. In a food processor pulse trout until finely chopped. Stir in remaining ingredients and salt and pepper to taste. Serve dip with pumpernickel toasts.

BREADS

PARKER HOUSE ROLLS

Makes 20

3 tablespoons warm water (105–110°F)
3 tablespoons sugar
¼-oz package active dry yeast (2½ teaspoons)
1 stick unsalted butter
1 cup whole milk
2 cups bread flour
1½ teaspoons salt
1½ to 2 cups all-purpose flour

Stir together warm water, 1 tablespoon sugar, and yeast in a small bowl and let stand until foamy, about 5 minutes.

Melt ¾ stick butter in a small saucepan. Add milk and heat to lukewarm. Stir together yeast mixture, remaining 2 tablespoons sugar, butter mixture, bread flour, and salt in a bowl with a wooden spoon until combined well, then stir in enough all-purpose flour to make a slightly sticky dough that forms a ball.

Butter a large bowl. Knead dough on a lightly floured surface, kneading in more all-purpose flour if dough is too sticky, 10 minutes, or until smooth and elastic but still slightly sticky. Form into a ball and put in buttered bowl. Turn to coat with butter, then let rise in bowl, covered with plastic wrap, in a warm place 1 hour, or until doubled in bulk.

Butter a 13- by 9-inch baking pan. Divide dough into 20 equal pieces and roll into balls. Arrange evenly in 4 rows of 5 in pan and let rise, covered loosely, in a warm place 45 minutes, or until almost doubled in bulk. Make a deep crease down center of each row of rolls using length of a floured chopstick or side of a ruler. Let rolls rise, covered loosely, 15 minutes.

Preheat oven to 375°F.

Melt remaining 2 tablespoons butter and cool slightly. Brush tops of rolls with butter and bake in middle of oven until golden, 20 to 25 minutes. Let rolls cool in pan on a rack 5 minutes. Turn out rolls onto rack and cool to warm.

Cooks' note:
• You can make rolls 1 day ahead and keep, wrapped well in foil, at room temperature. Reheat in foil in a preheated 375°F oven 15 to 20 minutes.

PHOTO ON PAGE 66

HOT CROSS BUNS

Makes 24

These special sweet buns, marked with a symbolic cross, are a fixture on many Easter tables. They are delicious plain; with fresh fruit (we loved them with the first strawberries of the season); or split, toasted, and spread with butter and jam.

1 cup warm milk (105°–115°F)
2 (¼-oz) packages active dry yeast
   (5 teaspoons)
½ cup plus 1 teaspoon granulated sugar
4 cups all-purpose flour
1½ teaspoons ground allspice
½ teaspoon cinnamon
1 teaspoon salt
1¼ sticks cold unsalted butter
2 large eggs
1 large egg yolk
½ cup dried currants
⅓ cup golden raisins
2 teaspoons finely grated fresh orange zest
2 teaspoons finely grated fresh lemon zest
3 tablespoons superfine granulated sugar
Pastry dough (page 190)

In a small bowl stir together milk, yeast, and 1 teaspoon granulated sugar. Let mixture stand 5 minutes, or until foamy.

Into a large bowl sift together flour, allspice, cinnamon, salt, and remaining ½ cup granulated sugar. Cut butter into bits and with your fingertips or a pastry blender blend into flour mixture until mixture resembles coarse meal. Lightly beat 1 whole egg with egg yolk. Make a well in center of flour mixture and pour in yeast and egg mixtures, currants, raisins, and zests. Stir mixture until a dough is formed. Transfer dough to a floured surface and with floured hands knead until smooth and elastic, about 10 minutes. Transfer dough to an oiled large bowl and turn to coat. Let dough rise, covered with plastic wrap, in a warm place until doubled in bulk, about 1½ hours.

Butter 2 large baking sheets.

On a floured surface with floured hands knead dough briefly and form into two 12-inch-long logs. Cut each log crosswise into 12 equal pieces. Form each piece into a ball and arrange about 1½ inches apart on baking sheets. Let buns rise, covered, in a warm place until doubled in bulk, about 45 minutes.

Preheat oven to 400°F.

While buns are rising, lightly beat remaining egg with superfine sugar to make an egg glaze. On a lightly floured surface with a floured rolling pin roll out pastry dough into a 20- by 6-inch rectangle (about ⅛ inch thick). With a sharp knife cut rectangle crosswise into ⅛-inch-wide strips.

Brush buns with egg glaze and arrange 2 pastry strips over center of each bun to form a cross. Trim ends of pastry strips flush with bottoms of buns. Bake buns in upper and lower thirds of oven, switching position of sheets halfway through baking, until golden, about 12 minutes. Transfer buns to a rack to cool slightly. Serve buns warm or at room temperature.

Cooks' note:
• Buns may be made 1 week ahead and frozen, wrapped in foil and put in a sealable plastic bag. Thaw buns and reheat before serving.

PHOTO ON PAGE 30

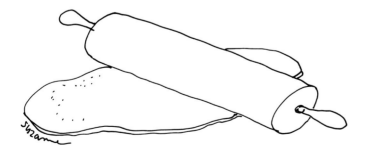

CORN PANCAKES

Makes about 30

The crisp-crusted corn cakes of Colombia and Venezuela called arepas were the inspiration for these delicious sauce soppers. In their native habitats they can be found as thin as crêpes or as thick as scones; savory or sweet; plain or stuffed; fried, baked, or even grilled.

5 ears corn
3 tablespoons unsalted butter
3 large eggs
¾ cup whole milk
¼ lb fresh mozzarella
¾ cup all-purpose flour
¾ cup fine yellow cornmeal
1½ tablespoons kosher salt
1 teaspoon freshly ground black pepper
About ¼ cup vegetable oil

Cut enough kernels from cobs to measure 2½ cups. In a food processor pulse corn until coarsely chopped and slightly wet. Melt butter and cool. In a bowl whisk together butter, eggs, and milk. Coarsely grate mozzarella and in a large bowl stir together with corn, flour, cornmeal, salt, and pepper. Whisk in egg mixture until combined.

In a 12-inch nonstick skillet heat 1 tablespoon oil over moderate heat until hot but not smoking. Working in batches, drop ⅛-cup measures of batter into skillet to form pancakes about 2 inches in diameter (do not spread or flatten pancakes) and cook until edges begin to set and undersides are golden brown, about 1½ minutes. Flip pancakes and cook until undersides are golden brown and pancakes are cooked through. Add more oil to skillet as necessary between batches.

Cooks' note:
• Pancakes may be made 1 day ahead and chilled, covered. Reheat pancakes in middle of a 350°F oven until hot, about 15 minutes.

PHOTO ON PAGE 52

BUTTERMILK SCALLION SKILLET CORN BREAD ☺

Serves 8 to 10

1 stick unsalted butter
6 scallions
2 cups stone-ground yellow cornmeal
1½ cups all-purpose flour
4 teaspoons sugar
1 tablespoon baking powder
1 teaspoon baking soda
2 teaspoons salt
1 tablespoon vegetable shortening or
   rendered bacon fat
4 large eggs
2 cups well-shaken buttermilk

Preheat oven to 425°F.

Melt butter and cool. Finely chop scallions. Into a bowl sift together cornmeal, flour, sugar, baking powder, baking soda, and salt.

Heat a dry well-seasoned 10-inch cast-iron skillet in middle of oven 10 minutes. Put shortening or bacon fat in skillet and heat 5 minutes. Swirl skillet to coat.

While skillet is heating, make batter:

Separate eggs. In a large bowl with an electric mixer beat yolks until pale and beat in butter and buttermilk. In a bowl with cleaned beaters beat whites until they just hold stiff peaks. Stir flour mixture into yolk mixture and fold in whites and scallions gently but thoroughly.

Pour batter into hot skillet and, working quickly, spread evenly. Bake corn bread in middle of oven until a tester comes out clean, 20 to 25 minutes.

Cooks' notes:
• It's important here that your cast-iron skillet is well seasoned and thoroughly preheated—you want the batter to sizzle when you pour it in.
• Corn bread may be made 4 hours ahead and kept, loosely covered, at room temperature.

PHOTO ON PAGE 16

CHEDDAR SCONES WITH HAM AND HONEY-MUSTARD BUTTER

Makes about 24

For scones
4 cups all-purpose flour
2 tablespoons baking powder
1½ teaspoons salt
1 stick cold unsalted butter
6 oz coarsely grated extra-sharp Cheddar
   (about 1½ cups)
1 cup whole milk
⅔ cup heavy cream

1 stick unsalted butter, softened
3 tablespoons coarse-grained mustard
3 tablespoons honey
6 large soft-leaf lettuce leaves such as Bibb
½ lb very thinly sliced cooked ham (preferably
   Black Forest)

Preheat oven to 425°F. Butter a large baking sheet.
Make scones:

Into a large bowl sift together flour, baking powder, and salt. Cut butter into small bits and with your fingertips or a pastry blender blend into flour mixture until mixture resembles coarse meal. With a fork stir in Cheddar. Add milk and cream, stirring until just combined. Transfer mixture to a floured surface and with floured hands knead until it forms a dough. Roll out dough into a 12-inch round (about ½ inch thick). Using a 2-inch fluted round cutter cut out scones and arrange about ½ inch apart on baking sheet. Gather and gently reroll scraps. Cut out more scones and arrange on baking sheet.

Bake scones in middle of oven until pale golden, about 12 minutes, and transfer to a rack to cool.

In a small bowl stir together butter, mustard, and honey. Tear each lettuce leaf into 4 pieces. Split scones and spread each split side with honey-mustard butter. Make sandwiches with scones, lettuce, and folded slices of ham.

Cooks' note:
• Scones may be made 1 day ahead and kept in an airtight container at cool room temperature.

PHOTO ON PAGE 30

GINGER DATE MUFFINS

Makes 12

1¼ cups all-purpose flour
1 teaspoon ground ginger
½ teaspoon baking powder
¼ teaspoon baking soda
¼ teaspoon salt
1 large egg
6 tablespoons unsulfured molasses
1¾ cups packed pitted dates (about 10 oz)
1½ sticks unsalted butter, softened
6 tablespoons packed dark brown sugar

Preheat oven to 400°F. Butter 12 (⅓-cup) muffin cups.
Into a bowl sift together flour, ginger, baking powder, baking soda, and salt. In a small bowl whisk together egg and molasses until combined. Coarsely chop dates. In a large bowl with an electric mixer beat together butter and sugar until light and fluffy. Beat in flour and egg mixtures until just combined and stir in dates. Divide batter among muffin cups and bake in middle of oven until a tester comes out clean, about 15 minutes (muffins will not dome).

MIX-IN MUFFINS

Makes 12

Becoming a muffin master is easy. Flavor the basic muffin batter below by adding, for example:
•a chopped banana and ¾ cup semisweet chocolate chips
•1 cup toasted almonds, ¾ cup dried cranberries, and
  ¼ teaspoon almond extract
•1 cup chopped drained canned pineapple and 1 cup sweetened
  flaked coconut
•1 cup chopped dried apricots and 1 tablespoon poppy seeds

1½ cups all-purpose flour
⅓ cup sugar
1½ teaspoons baking powder
¼ teaspoon baking soda
¼ teaspoon salt
1 stick unsalted butter
1 cup sour cream
1 large egg
1 teaspoon vanilla

Preheat oven to 400°F. Butter 12 (⅓-cup) muffin cups.
Into a bowl sift together flour, sugar, baking powder, baking soda, and salt. Melt butter and in a small bowl whisk together with sour cream, egg, and vanilla. Stir butter mixture (and desired additional ingredients; see note, above) into flour mixture until just combined. Divide batter among muffin cups and bake in middle of oven until golden and a tester comes out clean, about 20 minutes.

PUMPKIN-SEED CHEDDAR CORN MUFFINS

Makes 12

1½ cups grated sharp Cheddar (about 6 oz)
¾ cup hulled green pumpkin seeds (sources
  on page 252)
1 cup all-purpose flour
¾ cup yellow cornmeal
1 tablespoon baking powder
1½ teaspoons salt
2 pickled jalapeño chiles
¾ stick unsalted butter
1 cup whole milk
1 large egg

Preheat oven to 400°F. Butter 12 (⅓-cup) muffin cups.
Reserve ½ cup Cheddar and ¼ cup pumpkin seeds. Coarsely chop remaining ½ cup pumpkin seeds. Into a bowl sift together flour, cornmeal, baking powder, and salt and stir in remaining cup Cheddar and chopped pumpkin seeds. Wearing protective gloves, seed and mince jalapeños. Melt butter and in a small bowl whisk together with jalapeños, milk, and egg. Stir butter mixture into flour mixture until just combined. Divide batter among muffin cups and sprinkle with reserved Cheddar and pumpkin seeds. Bake muffins in middle of oven until golden and a tester comes out clean, about 20 minutes.

SCALLION GOAT CHEESE MUFFINS ☺

Makes 12

1 cup whole milk
¼ lb soft mild goat cheese
1½ cups all-purpose flour
1 tablespoon baking powder
1½ teaspoons sugar
½ teaspoon salt
¾ stick unsalted butter
1 large egg
1 bunch scallions

Preheat oven to 400°F. Butter 12 (⅓-cup) muffin cups.

In a small bowl stir together 2 tablespoons milk and goat cheese until combined. Into a bowl sift together flour, baking powder, sugar, and salt. Melt butter and in another small bowl whisk together with remaining milk and egg. Finely chop enough scallions to measure 1 cup. Stir butter mixture and scallions into flour mixture until just combined. Divide half of batter evenly among muffin cups and top each with about 2 teaspoons goat cheese filling. Divide remaining batter over filling. Bake muffins in middle of oven until golden and a tester comes out clean, about 20 minutes.

SPICY CAJUN TOASTS ☺

Makes about 6

½ loaf Italian or French bread
½ stick unsalted butter
1 tablespoon Cajun or Creole seasoning
¾ teaspoon salt

Preheat oven to 375°F.

Cut bread lengthwise into ¼-inch-thick slices. Melt butter and stir in seasoning and salt. Brush spice butter on 1 side of slices and transfer to a baking sheet. Bake slices, buttered sides up, in middle of oven until golden, 8 to 10 minutes.

Cooks' note:
• Toasts keep in an airtight container at room temperature 3 days.

GRILLED PARSLEY-BUTTER BREAD ☺

Serves 6

1 stick unsalted butter, softened
½ cup packed fresh flat-leaf parsley
1 (24-inch) baguette or loaf of Italian bread

In a blender pulse butter and parsley until parsley is finely chopped. Season butter with salt and pepper.

Prepare grill.

Halve bread lengthwise and spread cut sides with parsley butter. On a rack set 5 to 6 inches over glowing coals grill bread, cut sides up, covered, 2 minutes, or until parsley butter melts into bread. Turn bread over and grill until just toasted, 1 to 2 minutes. Cut bread crosswise into 2½-inch-thick slices.

Cooks' note:
• Parsley butter may be made 2 days ahead and chilled, covered. Bring to room temperature before proceeding.

PHOTO ON PAGE 42

SOUPS

CHICKEN RICE SOUP

Makes about 4 quarts

1 large onion
3 large celery ribs
3 medium carrots
1 (3½-lb) chicken
3 qt water
1 cup long-grain brown rice
⅓ cup packed fresh flat-leaf parsley
1 teaspoon salt

Coarsely chop onion and cut celery and carrots crosswise into ¼-inch-thick slices. Remove giblets from chicken and reserve for another use.

In a 5-quart kettle combine all ingredients and bring to a boil. Simmer soup, covered, 1 hour, and if necessary skim fat. Transfer chicken to a colander and when cool enough to handle discard skin and bones. Coarsely shred meat and return to soup. Season soup with salt and pepper and reheat if necessary.

GAZPACHO ◎+

Makes about 5 cups

1 English cucumber (about 13 inches long)
1 (¼-lb) piece *jícama*
1 small red bell pepper
1 celery rib
1 small garlic clove
2 cups V8 or tomato juice
2 tablespoons fresh lemon juice, or to taste
1½ teaspoons Worcestershire sauce, or to taste

Garnish: chopped fresh chives

Cut cucumber in half lengthwise and cut each half lengthwise into 3 spears. Cut spears crosswise into ¼-inch-thick pieces and transfer to a large bowl. Peel

jícama and cut enough into ¼-inch dice to measure 1 cup. Cut bell pepper and celery into ¼-inch dice and add with diced *jícama* to cucumber. Mince garlic and toss with cucumber mixture. Stir in remaining ingredients and season with salt and pepper.

In a blender purée half of soup until smooth and return to bowl, stirring to combine. Chill soup, covered, until cold, at least 1 hour and up to 2 days.

Season soup and serve garnished with chives.

☙ each serving about 59 calories and less than 1 gram fat

PHOTO ON PAGE 82

CUMIN PEA SOUP ◎

Makes about 3 cups, serving 4

2 teaspoons cumin seeds
1 small onion
¾ cup chicken broth
1½ cups water
1 (10-oz) package frozen peas
1 teaspoon kosher salt

In a dry small heavy skillet toast cumin seeds over moderate heat, shaking skillet frequently, until a shade darker and fragrant, 3 to 5 minutes, and cool. With a mortar and pestle or in an electric coffee/spice grinder finely grind seeds.

Finely chop onion and in a 2-quart saucepan simmer onion in broth and water until soft. Add peas, half of cumin, and half of salt and simmer, uncovered, until peas are tender, about 5 minutes. In a blender purée soup in 2 batches until smooth (use caution when blending hot liquids) and transfer to another saucepan.

In a small bowl stir together remaining cumin and salt to use as garnish.

☙ each serving about 73 calories and 1 gram fat

PHOTO ON PAGE 80

GARLICKY LENTIL SOUP ☺

Makes about 3 cups

8 large garlic cloves
4 cups cold water
⅔ cup lentils (preferably French green lentils)
1 tablespoon chopped fresh thyme
2 tablespoons chopped fresh flat-leaf parsley
1½ to 2 teaspoons salt

Accompaniments: extra-virgin olive oil and
    red-wine vinegar to taste

Slice garlic. In a 2-quart saucepan bring cold water to a boil with garlic, lentils, and thyme and simmer until lentils are tender, about 25 minutes. In a blender coarsely purée mixture (use caution when blending hot liquids) and return to pan. Stir in parsley, salt, and pepper to taste and bring soup to a simmer.
Serve soup drizzled with oil and vinegar.

CHILLED ROASTED RED PEPPER SOUP

Makes about 9 cups

7 red bell peppers (2¾ lb)
1 medium onion
1 small boiling potato

2 tablespoons olive oil
1 teaspoon ground cumin
3½ cups water
2 cups chicken broth
1 medium tomato

Accompaniment: lime wedges

Quick-roast and peel peppers (procedure page 87).
Chop onion. Peel potato and cut into ¼-inch dice. In a 5-quart heavy kettle heat oil over moderately high heat until hot but not smoking and sauté onion, potato, and cumin, stirring, 5 minutes. Add roasted peppers, water, and broth and simmer, covered, 20 minutes, or until vegetables are very tender.
While soup is cooking, peel and seed tomato.
Purée soup in batches with tomato in a blender (use caution when blending hot liquids), transferring to a bowl, and season with salt and pepper. Cool soup. Chill soup, covered, at least 4 hours. Adjust seasoning.
Serve soup with lime wedges.

Cooks' note:
• Soup may be made 2 days ahead and chilled, covered.

PHOTO ON PAGE 50

SEAFOOD IN SAFFRON BROTH ☺

Serves 2 (main course)

½ fennel bulb (sometimes called anise)
1 small onion
1 large plum tomato
1 large garlic clove
½ lb mussels (preferably cultivated)
¼ lb large shrimp (about 7)
1 (½-lb) piece skinless scrod or halibut
¼ teaspoon crumbled saffron threads
½ cup dry white wine
1½ tablespoons olive oil
3 cups fish stock or low-salt chicken broth

Garnish: lemon wedges
Accompaniment: crusty bread

Trim fennel stalks flush with bulb, discarding stalks. Finely chop fennel and onion. Seed tomato and finely chop. Mince garlic. Scrub mussels well and remove beards. Shell shrimp and devein. Cut scrod into 1-inch pieces. Stir saffron into wine.

In a 4-quart kettle cook fennel and onion in oil over moderate heat, stirring, until slightly softened, about 5 minutes. Add garlic and cook, stirring, 1 minute. Add wine mixture and simmer until reduced to about 1 tablespoon, about 3 minutes. Add mussels and ½ cup stock and simmer, covered, stirring occasionally, until most mussels are opened, about 2 minutes. Add shrimp, scrod, tomato, and remaining 2½ cups stock and cook at a bare simmer until fish is just cooked through, about 2 minutes. (Discard any unopened mussels.) Season mixture with salt and pepper.

Divide seafood between 2 bowls and ladle broth over it. Garnish seafood with lemon wedges and serve with crusty bread.

SQUASH AND SWEET-POTATO SOUP WITH CHIPOTLE SAUCE

Makes about 12 cups

3 lb butternut squash (1 large), halved lengthwise
    and seeds discarded
1 tablespoon olive oil
2 lb sweet potatoes (2 large)
1 large onion, chopped
White part of 1 leek, chopped
2 teaspoons chopped peeled fresh ginger
8 to 10 cups light vegetable stock (page 96)
    or broth
White pepper to taste
2 to 3 tablespoons fresh lemon juice,
    or to taste
1 tablespoon honey (optional)
Chipotle sauce (recipe follows)

Preheat oven to 400°F.

Brush cut sides of squash with ½ teaspoon oil and arrange, cut sides down, in a shallow baking pan. Prick sweet potatoes all over with a fork and roast with squash until very tender, about 50 minutes for squash and about 1¼ hours for sweet potatoes.

Cool vegetables and scoop flesh from squash into a bowl. Peel sweet potatoes and add to squash.

Cook onion in remaining 2½ teaspoons oil with salt

to taste in a 6-quart heavy pot over moderately high heat, stirring occasionally, until golden brown, about 10 minutes. Stir in squash and sweet potato, leek, ginger, and 8 cups stock and simmer, uncovered, stirring occasionally, 30 minutes.

Purée mixture in batches in a blender (use caution when blending hot liquids), transferring to a clean pot. Bring to a simmer and, if too thick, add more stock. Season with salt and white pepper. Finish with lemon juice and, if desired, honey.

Serve soup drizzled with some *chipotle* sauce or swirl sauce in to make a pattern.

Cooks' note:
· Soup may be made 2 days ahead, cooled completely, and chilled, covered. Reheat before serving.

PHOTO ON PAGE 65

CHIPOTLE SAUCE

Makes about 1 cup

2 dried *ancho* chiles (1 oz) (sources on
    page 252)
1 dried *chipotle* chile (sources on page 252)
2 cups water
1 small yellow onion, coarsely chopped
2 garlic cloves
1 tablespoon cumin seeds, toasted

Discard stems from chiles and remove seeds. Rinse chiles under cold running water. Bring chiles with water to a simmer in a nonreactive 1½-quart saucepan. Add onion, garlic, and a pinch of salt, then simmer, uncovered, stirring occasionally (add more water if necessary to cover chiles), until softened, about 30 minutes.

While chiles are cooking, finely grind cumin with a mortar and pestle or in an electric coffee/spice grinder.

Transfer chiles and vegetables with a slotted spoon to a blender and purée with ground cumin and ¼ cup chile water (save remaining chile water) until smooth. (Sauce should be thick but not stiff; add more chile water, 1 tablespoon at a time, if necessary.) Season with salt.

Cooks' note:
· Sauce may be made 3 days ahead, cooled completely, and chilled, covered. Reheat before serving.

POMO PAPPA AL POMODORA

TOMATO AND BREAD SOUP

Makes about 7 cups

1 medium onion
2 garlic cloves
3 tablespoons olive oil
1 (28- to 32-oz) can organic tomatoes
½ loaf day-old rustic Italian bread
3½ cups chicken broth

Finely chop onion and mince garlic. In a 4-quart heavy kettle heat oil over moderately high heat until hot but not smoking and sauté onion and garlic, stirring, until softened. Drain tomatoes, reserving juice, and chop. Stir tomatoes and reserved juice into onion mixture and simmer, stirring occasionally, 15 minutes.

While tomato mixture is simmering, discard crust from bread and cut enough bread into 1-inch cubes to measure 2 cups. Add bread and broth to tomato mixture and simmer, stirring occasionally, until bread has absorbed liquid and soup is thick, about 40 minutes. Season soup with salt and pepper.

LETTUCE SOUP

Makes about 5 cups

2 medium heads Boston lettuce
  (about ¾ lb total)
3 cups chicken broth
1 cup water
2 tablespoons unsalted butter
Freshly grated nutmeg to taste

Stack lettuce leaves and cut into thin shreds. In a 3-quart saucepan gently simmer lettuce, broth, and water, covered, 40 minutes. In a blender purée soup in 2 batches with butter, nutmeg, and salt and pepper to taste until smooth (use caution when blending hot liquids), transferring as blended to another saucepan. Heat soup over moderately high heat until hot.

FISH AND SHELLFISH

FISH

GRILLED STRIPED BASS

Serves 8 (as part of a buffet)

3 (2- to 3-lb) cleaned whole striped bass

Accompaniment: chimichurri sauce (page 176)

Prepare grill. Pat fish dry and season generously inside and out with salt and pepper. Grill fish on a well-oiled rack set 5 to 6 inches over glowing coals 8 to 10 minutes on each side, or until just cooked through in thickest part.

Serve fish with sauce.

PHOTO ON PAGE 51

GARLIC-ROASTED STRIPED BASS

Serves 4

2 (1¼-lb) whole striped bass or red snapper
   (head and tail intact), cleaned
3 tablespoons olive oil
4 garlic cloves
1 lemon, halved

Preheat oven to 500°F and put a large shallow baking pan in middle of oven.

Cut 3 deep slits (down to bone) crosswise on each side of fish and put fish on a tray. Rub fish inside and out with 2 tablespoons oil. Cut a garlic clove in half and rub all over skin of fish. Thinly slice all garlic and insert into slits and inside fish. Squeeze lemon juice over both sides of fish and season with salt and pepper.

Quickly brush hot baking pan with remaining tablespoon oil and transfer fish to pan (the pan should be hot enough to sizzle). Roast fish in middle of oven until just cooked through, 18 to 20 minutes.

To serve, remove top fillet from each fish by cutting through skin along top edge of backbone and along belly. Carefully slide a large metal spatula between backbone and fillet and invert onto a platter. Pull out backbone, starting from tail end, and discard. Transfer bottom fillets to platter.

CATFISH FILLETS WITH EGYPTIAN TAHINI SAUCE

Serves 2

1 garlic clove
¼ cup well-stirred *tahini* (Middle Eastern
   sesame paste)
⅓ cup water
1½ tablespoons fresh lemon juice
¼ teaspoon ground cumin
¼ teaspoon salt
2 teaspoons coriander seeds
2 (6-oz) catfish fillets
1 tablespoon olive oil
2 tablespoons coarsely chopped fresh
   flat-leaf parsley

Coarsely chop garlic and in a blender purée with *tahini*, water, lemon juice, cumin, and salt until smooth.

Using the flat side of a large knife coarsely crush coriander seeds. Pat catfish dry and season with salt and pepper. In a 10-inch nonstick skillet heat oil over moderately high heat until hot but not smoking and sauté fish 2 minutes. Turn fish over, sprinkling crushed coriander around it, and sauté 2 minutes more, or until just cooked through.

Divide *tahini* sauce between 2 plates and top with fish, crushed coriander and oil from skillet, and parsley.

GRILLED HALIBUT STEAKS ◐+

Serves 8

2 teaspoons fennel seeds
2 large garlic cloves
1 lemon
1 teaspoon kosher salt
2 tablespoons olive oil
4 (1-inch-thick) halibut steaks (about ¾ lb each)

Accompaniment: fennel *tsatsiki* (page 174)

Prepare grill.

In a dry small skillet toast fennel seeds over moderate heat, shaking skillet, until fragrant and a shade darker. In an electric coffee/spice grinder grind seeds. Mince garlic. Squeeze juice from lemon into a small bowl and stir in fennel, garlic, salt, and oil. Put halibut in a large dish and pour marinade over it, turning fish to coat. Marinate halibut, covered and chilled, at least 10 minutes and up to 1 hour.

Grill halibut on a lightly oiled rack set 5 to 6 inches over glowing coals until just cooked through, about 5 minutes on each side. (Alternatively, halibut can be grilled in a hot oiled well-seasoned ridged grill pan over moderate heat.)

Serve halibut with *tsatsiki.*

PHOTO ON PAGE 47

ROUGET AND SHRIMP WITH LEMON SAUCE

Serves 6

Rouget, or red mullet, is renowned in the Mediterranean for its delicate flavor. It is increasingly available here in the U.S. (Incidentally, the fish is not a true mullet but is a member of another piscine family.)

1 lb large shrimp (18 to 22)
12 (1-oz) *rouget* fillets or 6 small red snapper
 fillets with skin
2 large shallots
½ stick unsalted butter
¼ cup dry white wine
1 cup chicken broth
2 tablespoons fresh lemon juice
6 tablespoons olive oil plus additional
3 small zucchini (preferably assorted green and
 yellow; each about 4 inches long)

Accompaniment: zucchini potato lemon-thyme mash
 (recipe follows)

Peel shrimp and, if desired, devein. With tweezers remove any bones from fish fillets.

Preheat oven to 300°F.

Finely chop shallots. Cut butter into tablespoons. In a small saucepan boil wine, broth, lemon juice, and shallots until liquid is reduced by about half. Whisk in 2 tablespoons oil and simmer until emulsified, about 2 minutes. Remove pan from heat and whisk in butter 1 piece at a time, adding each new piece before previous one is incorporated. Keep sauce warm, covered. (It should not get hot enough to separate.)

Halve zucchini lengthwise and cut crosswise into ½-inch-thick pieces. In a small saucepan of boiling salted water cook zucchini until just tender, about 1 minute, and drain in a sieve. In a bowl toss zucchini with 1 tablespoon sauce and keep warm, covered.

Pat fish fillets dry and season with salt and pepper. In a large nonstick skillet heat 2 tablespoons oil over moderately high heat until hot but not smoking and in batches sear fish, skin sides down, until golden brown, about 2 minutes. Turn fish over and cook until just cooked through, about 2 minutes more for *rouget* and about 4 minutes more for snapper. (Add more oil if necessary between batches.) Transfer fish as cooked to a baking pan and keep warm, covered, in middle of oven.

Wipe skillet clean and heat 2 tablespoons oil over moderately high heat until hot but not smoking. Sauté shrimp, stirring occasionally, until golden brown and just cooked through, about 4 minutes.

Mound mash in center of each of 6 plates and top with fish. Arrange shrimp and zucchini evenly around mash and drizzle sauce over all.

PHOTO ON PAGE 49

ZUCCHINI POTATO LEMON-THYME MASH

Serves 6

1¾ lb zucchini
1½ lb boiling potatoes such as
    Yukon Gold
2 teaspoons finely chopped fresh lemon thyme
3 tablespoons unsalted butter

Cut zucchini crosswise into 1-inch-thick slices. In a large saucepan cover potatoes with salted cold water by 2 inches and simmer, covered, until tender, about 35 minutes. Transfer potatoes to a colander and reserve cooking water. When potatoes are cool enough to handle, peel and put in a large bowl. Add lemon thyme, butter, and salt and pepper to taste and with a potato masher coarsely mash. Keep mash warm, covered.

Bring cooking water to a boil and simmer zucchini until tender, about 8 minutes. Drain zucchini well in colander and coarsely mash into potatoes.

Cooks' note:
• Mash may be made 1 day ahead and cooled completely before being chilled, covered. Reheat mash before serving.

PHOTO ON PAGE 49

SALMON CAKES WITH TARRAGON-CHIVE DIPPING SAUCE

Makes about 36

1½ lb skinless boneless salmon fillet
1 large egg
½ cup fine fresh bread crumbs
1 tablespoon Dijon mustard
1 teaspoon freshly grated lime zest
½ teaspoon salt
⅛ teaspoon freshly ground black pepper

Garnish: lime wedges
Accompaniment: tarragon-chive dipping sauce
    (recipe follows)

Pat salmon dry and with a sharp knife cut into roughly ⅓-inch cubes. In a medium bowl lightly beat egg and gently stir in salmon and remaining ingredients until just combined.

Heat a 12-inch nonstick skillet over moderate heat and, working in batches, drop 2-tablespoon measures of salmon mixture about 1 inch apart into skillet. Cook cakes until undersides are golden, about 1 minute. Turn cakes over and cook until just cooked through, about 1 minute more. Transfer cakes as cooked to a platter.

Garnish cakes with lime wedges and serve with dipping sauce.

Cooks' note:
• Salmon cakes may be made 1 day ahead and chilled, covered. Bring to room temperature before serving.

PHOTO ON PAGE 30

TARRAGON-CHIVE DIPPING SAUCE ◌

Makes about 2 cups

⅔ cup mayonnaise
⅓ cup fresh tarragon
1⅓ cups sour cream
3 tablespoons finely chopped fresh chives
1 teaspoon fresh lime juice

Garnish: ½-inch lengths of fresh chives

In a food processor pulse together mayonnaise, tarragon, and ⅓ cup sour cream until smooth. Transfer mixture to a bowl and stir in remaining cup sour cream, chives, lime juice, and salt and pepper to taste.

Garnish dip with chives.

SALMON AND LEEK PIE

Serves 6

4 large leeks
2 tablespoons unsalted butter
2¼ lb skinless boneless salmon fillet
¼ cup chopped fresh dill
1 teaspoon freshly grated lime zest
1½ teaspoons kosher salt
¼ teaspoon freshly ground black pepper
1 large egg
1 tablespoon water
1 (17¼-oz) package frozen puff pastry sheets,
   thawed

Accompaniment: sour-cream chile sauce
   (recipe follows)

Cut white and pale-green parts of leeks crosswise into ½-inch-thick slices. In a bowl of cold water wash leeks well and lift from water into a colander to drain. Pat leeks dry. In a large skillet cook leeks in butter over moderate heat, stirring, until tender, about 12 minutes, and cool. Cut salmon into roughly ¾-inch pieces and in a bowl toss with leeks, dill, zest, salt, and pepper until combined well.

In a small bowl whisk together egg and water to make an egg wash. On a lightly floured surface with a lightly floured rolling pin roll 1 puff pastry sheet into a 10-inch square and the other into a 12-inch square. Transfer 10-inch pastry square to a floured large baking sheet and mound salmon filling in center, forming a round 8 inches in diameter. Brush edges of pastry evenly with some egg wash. Carefully drape remaining pastry square over salmon and gently press edges together to seal. With a sharp knife trim edges of pastry to form a 10-inch round. Crimp edges and cut 4 steam vents on top of crust. Brush crust evenly with some remaining egg wash. Chill pie, loosely covered, at least 1 hour and up to 3.

Preheat oven to 400°F.

Bake pie in middle of oven until pastry is golden brown, about 30 minutes.

Serve pie warm or at room temperature with sauce.

PHOTO ON PAGE 20

SOUR-CREAM CHILE SAUCE ☉

Makes about 2 cups

1 red bell pepper
1 fresh red or green hot chile
1 (16-oz) container sour cream (about 2 cups)

Quick-roast and peel bell pepper (procedure page 118) and cut into 1-inch-thick strips. Wearing protective gloves, seed and mince enough of chile to measure 1 teaspoon. In a blender blend roasted pepper, chile, and sour cream until very smooth and season with salt and black pepper.

Cooks' note:
• Sauce may be made 2 days ahead and chilled, covered.

SHELLFISH

BOILED LOBSTERS WITH TARRAGON BUTTER ☉

Serves 2

2 (1¼- to 1½-lb) live lobsters
1 shallot
½ stick unsalted butter
1 tablespoon chopped fresh tarragon
1 tablespoon white-wine vinegar

Fill a 6-quart pot three fourths full with salted water and bring to a boil. Plunge lobsters headfirst into water and boil, covered, 7 to 8 minutes. Transfer lobsters with tongs to a colander and drain head down to remove excess liquid.

Finely chop shallot. In a small saucepan melt butter with shallot, tarragon, white-wine vinegar, and salt and pepper to taste.

Arrange lobsters on a platter and using kitchen shears remove thin, hard membrane from underside of each tail by cutting just inside outer edge of shell.

Spoon some tarragon butter over each lobster tail and serve remainder on the side.

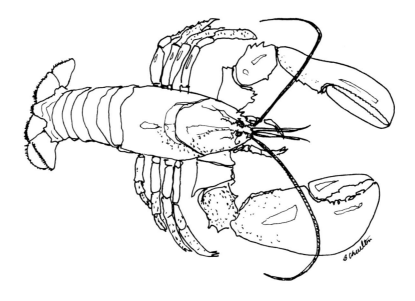

GRILLED LOBSTERS WITH SOUTHEAST ASIAN DIPPING SAUCE ◑+

Serves 6

Cooking lobsters is often perceived as a last-minute frenzy. The following recipe lets you progress through menu-planning worry free: The lobsters can be parboiled in the morning and kept chilled until you're ready to grill them at dinnertime.

To satisfy any die-hard lobster-and-butter traditionalists at your table, you might want to serve some clarified butter along with the dipping sauce.

3 garlic cloves
⅓ cup Asian fish sauce (sources on page 252)
⅓ cup fresh lime juice
⅓ cup packed brown sugar
3 tablespoons water
1½ teaspoons Asian chili paste (sources on page 252)
6 (1¼-lb) live lobsters
¼ cup packed fresh cilantro
¼ cup packed fresh mint

Garnish: lime halves

Bring an 8-quart kettle three fourths full with water to a boil.

Mince garlic and in a bowl stir together with fish sauce, lime juice, brown sugar, water, and chili paste.

Plunge 2 lobsters headfirst into boiling water and cook 3 minutes (lobsters will be only partially cooked). Transfer lobsters with tongs to a colander to drain and cool. Return water to a boil and cook remaining 4 lobsters in same manner.

When lobsters are cool enough to handle, twist off tails and break off claws at body of each lobster, discarding bodies. With kitchen shears halve tails (including shells) lengthwise. (Do not remove tail or claw meat from shells.)

Prepare grill.

Chop cilantro and mint and stir into dipping sauce. Measure out ¼ cup dipping sauce to use for basting lobster tails. Grill claws on a rack set 5 to 6 inches over glowing coals, covered, turning them occasionally, until liquid bubbles at open ends, about 5 minutes, and transfer to a serving platter.

Arrange tails on grill, cut sides up, and brush with basting sauce. Grill tails, covered, basting occasionally, 6 minutes, or until meat is opaque.

Serve lobster with dipping sauce and lime halves.

Cooks' notes:
- Before herbs are added, dipping sauce may be made 1 day ahead and chilled, covered.
- Lobsters can be boiled 1 day ahead and chilled, covered. Keep boiled lobsters chilled until ready to grill.

PHOTO ON PAGE 40

GRILLED SCALLOPS, ZUCCHINI, AND SCALLIONS WITH WHITE BEANS

Serves 4

8 (10-inch) wooden skewers
1 (15½-oz) can small white beans
½ cup fresh cilantro sprigs
1 lemon
1 teaspoon Dijon mustard
8 large scallions
2 medium zucchini
2 teaspoons kosher salt
1½ teaspoons ground cumin
24 large sea scallops (about 1¼ lb)
2 teaspoons olive oil

Garnish: fresh cilantro sprigs

Prepare grill. Soak wooden skewers in warm water 30 minutes.

In a colander rinse and drain beans. Chop cilantro. Squeeze 2 tablespoons juice from lemon. In a bowl toss together beans, cilantro, lemon juice, mustard, and salt and pepper to taste.

In a saucepan of boiling salted water blanch scallions until barely tender, about 4 minutes. Transfer scallions with tongs to paper towels to drain and season with salt and pepper. Cut zucchini lengthwise into ¼-inch-thick slices using a *mandoline* or other manual slicer and season with salt and pepper.

In a bowl combine kosher salt, cumin, and pepper to taste. Remove tough muscle from side of each scallop if necessary and pat scallops dry. Toss scallops in cumin mixture to coat. Hold 2 skewers parallel to each other and about ½ inch apart. Thread 6 scallops onto skewers so flat sides can lie flat on grill. (Each scallop should be pierced by both skewers. This prevents scallops from spinning when turning them over on grill.) Thread remaining scallops onto remaining skewers in same manner. Brush scallops with oil.

Grill scallions and zucchini on a lightly oiled rack set 5 to 6 inches over glowing coals until zucchini is tender and scallions are golden, about 1 minute on each side. Grill scallops, turning occasionally, until just cooked through, about 4 minutes on each side.

Toss zucchini with beans and serve topped with scallions and scallops and garnished with cilantro.

Cooks' note:
• Scallions and zucchini can be cooked—not on skewers—in a large nonstick skillet. Lightly brush skillet with oil and heat over moderately high heat until hot before cooking them, separately.

🍃 each serving about 338 calories and 4 grams fat

PHOTO ON PAGE 83

SHRIMP AND BROCCOLINI STIR-FRY ☺

Serves 2

If you have regular broccoli on hand, you could use the florets as a substitute for the Broccolini (a cross between broccoli and Chinese kale), though the flavor will be somewhat different. Round out this stir-fry with cooked white rice.

2 tablespoons vegetable oil
¾ lb large shrimp (15), peeled and deveined
1½ teaspoons grated peeled fresh ginger
1 teaspoon minced garlic
1 bunch Broccolini (8 oz), cut into
    ¼-inch-thick diagonal slices
½ cup water
3 tablespoons hoisin sauce
3 tablespoons soy sauce
½ teaspoon dried hot red pepper flakes

Heat 1 tablespoon oil in a large nonstick skillet over moderately high heat until hot but not smoking, then cook shrimp until golden and almost cooked through, about 1 minute on each side. Transfer shrimp to a dish. Heat remaining tablespoon oil in skillet over moderately high heat until hot but not smoking, then sauté ginger and garlic, stirring, until golden. Add Broccolini, water, hoisin, soy sauce, and red pepper flakes and cook, stirring occasionally, until Broccolini is just tender, about 5 minutes. Stir in shrimp and cook until just heated through.

SPICY LEMON-MARINATED SHRIMP

Serves 50

Terms like large and jumbo can vary among fishmongers. In this recipe we used what are known universally as "U 16/20s" (16 to 20 of them make a pound).

Dried Aleppo chile flakes are from the Aleppo province of northern Syria. Their earthy, robust flavor—with more richness than heat—is famous throughout the Middle East.

8 large lemons
¼ cup coriander seeds
1½ cups white-wine vinegar
½ cup olive oil
½ cup water
½ cup sugar
¼ cup dried Aleppo or New Mexican chile
    flakes (sources on page 252) or 1 tablespoon
    dried hot red pepper flakes
8 tablespoons kosher salt
¼ cup pickling spices
10 lb large (U 16/20) shrimp, shelled
    and deveined

Remove zest from lemons with a vegetable peeler and remove any white pith from zest strips with a sharp knife. Squeeze 1½ cups lemon juice. Finely grind coriander seeds in an electric coffee/spice grinder. Whisk together zest, juice, coriander, vinegar, oil, water, sugar, chile flakes, and 6 tablespoons kosher salt in a large bowl until sugar and salt are dissolved.

Bring an 8-quart pot of water to a boil with pickling spices and remaining 2 tablespoons salt and cook shrimp, 2 pounds at a time, 1½ minutes, or until just cooked through. Return water to a boil between batches. Transfer cooked shrimp with a slotted spoon to a colander to drain and add warm shrimp to marinade, tossing to coat.

Cool shrimp slightly and divide among about 8 large sealable plastic bags with marinade. Stack bags in a large roasting pan, keeping shrimp in single layers. Marinate shrimp, chilled, turning bags occasionally, at least 8 hours. Drain shrimp before serving.

Cooks' note:
• You can marinate the shrimp up to 3 days.

PHOTO ON PAGE 55

MEAT

GRILLED STEAK

Serves 8 (as part of a buffet)

When accompanied by the delicious tang of chimichurri sauce, all this steak needs is to be seasoned with salt and pepper.

8 T-bone steaks (each about 1 inch thick)

Accompaniment: chimichurri sauce (page 176)

Prepare grill. Pat steaks dry and season generously with salt and pepper. Grill steaks on a well-oiled rack set 5 to 6 inches over glowing coals 4 minutes each side for medium-rare. Transfer steaks as cooked to a platter and let stand 10 minutes. Serve steaks with sauce.

PHOTO ON PAGE 50

RIB-EYE ROAST, GRAVLAKS STYLE ◑+

Serves 6

A wonderfully salty exterior and a hint of dill make this easy-to-prepare roast one of the best we've tasted. We leave the dill mixture on top, as we like the texture it adds; but the flavor is strong, so you might want to scrape it all off before serving.

3½-lb boneless beef rib-eye roast, rolled and tied
¼ cup kosher salt
3 tablespoons sugar
1 teaspoon coarsely ground black pepper
1 cup chopped fresh dill

Pat beef dry with paper towels. Stir together salt, sugar, and pepper and rub all over beef. Pat dill over salt mixture and wrap beef tightly in plastic wrap. Put in a small roasting pan and weight with a baking sheet topped with a 4-pound weight. Chill beef 18 hours.
Preheat oven to 400°F.

Unwrap beef and let stand at room temperature 30 minutes. Scrape dill and salt mixture from bottom and sides. Roast beef in middle of oven until an instant-read thermometer inserted 2 inches into center registers 130°F for medium-rare, about 1¼ hours, then let stand 5 minutes.

PHOTO ON PAGE 74

SIRLOIN TIP STEAKS WITH HORSERADISH BUTTER SAUCE ◑

Serves 4

Tip steak has less marbling than other cuts of beef. It should be cooked rare to medium-rare for maximum flavor and juiciness.

2 (1-inch-thick) sirloin tip steaks (2 lb total)
1 tablespoon vegetable oil
½ stick unsalted butter
3½ tablespoons drained bottled horseradish
1 teaspoon Worcestershire sauce

Pat steaks dry and season with salt and pepper. Heat oil in a well-seasoned large cast-iron skillet over moderately high heat until hot but not smoking, then cook steaks 6 minutes on each side for medium-rare. Transfer steaks to plates. Remove skillet from heat and immediately add butter and horseradish, stirring and scraping up any brown bits. Stir in Worcestershire sauce and spoon sauce over steaks.

SALT-FRIED RIB-EYE STEAKS ◑

Serves 4

2 (1¼-inch-thick) rib-eye steaks
   (about 1¾ lb total)
4 teaspoons kosher salt

Pat steaks dry. Sprinkle salt evenly in bottom of a well-seasoned 10-inch cast-iron skillet. Heat skillet over moderately high heat until faint wisps of smoke are visible and fry steaks, shaking skillet after 1 or 2 minutes to loosen them from bottom, 6 minutes. Turn steaks over and fry 5 minutes more for medium-rare. Transfer steaks to a board and let stand 5 minutes before slicing.

SAUTÉED SKIRT STEAK IN SPICY TOMATO SAUCE ◌

Serves 2

This recipe was inspired by a dish prepared at New York City's Café Habana.

1 small onion
1 (14- to 15-oz) can whole tomatoes in purée
1 fresh *serrano* or jalapeño chile
¾ lb skirt steak
1 tablespoon vegetable oil

Preheat oven to 250°F.

Halve onion and thinly slice. Drain tomatoes, reserving purée, and finely chop. Wearing protective gloves, seed chile if desired for a milder sauce and finely chop. Cut steak crosswise into 4 pieces. Pat steak dry and season with salt.

Heat a dry 12-inch heavy skillet over moderately high heat until hot and add oil. Sauté steak about 2 minutes on each side for medium-rare and transfer to a baking dish. Keep steak warm in oven.

To skillet add onions with tomatoes, reserved purée, chile, and salt to taste and simmer, stirring occasionally, until thickened slightly and onion is crisp-tender, about 5 minutes. Stir in any juices that have accumulated on baking dish from steak. Serve steak with sauce.

BUFFALO AND VEAL

BUFFALO STEAK AND ONION CONFIT ON GARLIC TOASTS

Serves 4

For onion confit
1 lb onions (about 3 medium)
1 teaspoon olive oil
½ cup beef broth

6 tablespoons balsamic vinegar
1 tablespoon packed brown sugar
1 whole star anise (sources on page 252)

2 (8-oz) boneless buffalo strip loin steaks
   (sources on page 252)
1 teaspoon olive oil
1 garlic clove
4 (½-inch-thick) slices nonfat country-style bread

Accompaniment: roasted beets with garlic-beet purée
   (page 155)

Make onion confit:

Halve onions and cut each half lengthwise into 6 wedges. In a 2-quart heavy saucepan heat oil over moderately high heat until hot but not smoking and sauté onions, stirring, until edges are golden brown, about 2 minutes. Stir in remaining *confit* ingredients and simmer, covered, until onions are tender, about 20 minutes. Remove lid and simmer, stirring occasionally, until liquid is slightly thickened and syrupy, about 10 minutes more. Discard star anise. Keep *confit* warm, covered.

Preheat oven to 450°F.

Trim fat from steaks and cut each steak into 4 equal pieces. Pat steak dry and season with salt and pepper.

In a large nonstick skillet heat oil over moderately high heat until hot but not smoking and brown steak on both sides, about 3 minutes total. Transfer steak to a roasting pan and roast in middle of oven about 5 minutes for medium-rare. Let steak stand 5 minutes.

While steak is roasting, halve garlic clove. On a baking sheet in oven with steaks or in a toaster toast bread until golden brown. Immediately rub toasted bread with cut sides of garlic.

Serve steak and onion *confit* on toasts with roasted beet wedges and garlic-beet purée.

☞ each serving, including roasted beets and purée, about 400 calories and 4.6 grams fat

PHOTO ON PAGE 79

ROASTED VEAL CHOPS WITH SHALLOTS, TOMATOES, AND OLIVE JUS

Serves 6

6 garlic cloves
2 teaspoons salt
3 tablespoons chopped fresh rosemary
3 tablespoons chopped fresh thyme
1½ teaspoons freshly ground black pepper
5 tablespoons olive oil
6 (1¼-inch-thick) veal rib chops (12 to 14 oz each),
    frenched if desired
9 large shallots (about ¾ lb)
9 plum tomatoes (about 1¼ lb)
¼ teaspoon sugar
½ cup drained Kalamata olives
1½ cups dry white wine
1½ cups chicken broth
2 tablespoons unsalted butter

Accompaniment: soft polenta (recipe follows)

Mince garlic and mash with salt. In a small bowl stir together garlic paste, herbs, pepper, and 3 tablespoons oil. Pat veal chops dry. Reserve 1 tablespoon herb mixture for sauce and rub remainder evenly onto chops.

Preheat oven to 425°F.

Quarter shallots and tomatoes lengthwise and in a bowl toss with 1 tablespoon oil, sugar, and salt and pepper to taste. Arrange tomatoes, cut sides up, in one layer in a shallow baking pan with shallots and roast in upper third of oven 20 minutes. Halve and pit olives.

While vegetables are roasting, in a 12-inch nonstick skillet heat remaining tablespoon oil over moderately high heat until hot but not smoking and sear chops in batches until golden brown, about 3 minutes on each side. Transfer chops as seared to another shallow baking pan (do not wash skillet).

Reduce temperature to 375°F. Transfer shallots and tomatoes to lower third of oven and put chops in upper third of oven. Roast vegetables until tender and caramelized, about 20 minutes. Roast chops until an instant-read thermometer inserted horizontally into chops registers 160°F for medium, 20 to 25 minutes.

While chops and vegetables are roasting, pour wine into skillet with reserved herb mixture and boil, scraping up brown bits, 1 minute. Boil mixture until reduced to about ¼ cup, about 5 minutes. Add broth and boil mixture until reduced to about ¾ cup, about 5 minutes.

When chops are cooked, pour any meat juices from baking pan into wine mixture and bring *jus* to a boil. Cut butter into pieces and add with olives to *jus*. Swirl skillet to incorporate butter and boil until *jus* is slightly thickened. Season *jus* with salt and pepper.

Serve chops over polenta with shallots and tomatoes, drizzled with olive *jus*.

Cooks' notes:
• Veal chops from a butcher are usually about 1¼ inches thick and weigh 12 to 14 oz each. The supermarket variety of chop is thinner and smaller, ranging from 8 to 10 oz each, and would only need to be roasted 12 to 15 minutes in this recipe.
• Veal chops can be rubbed with herb mixture 1 day ahead and chilled, covered. Chill reserved herb mixture, covered.

PHOTO ON PAGE 14

SOFT POLENTA

Makes about 5 cups

The following recipe is based on Marcella Hazan's "no-stirring" method from her book Essentials of Classic Italian Cooking.

6 cups water
2 teaspoons salt
2 Turkish bay leaves or ½ California bay leaf
1½ cups cornmeal

In a 4-quart heavy saucepan bring water to a boil with salt and bay leaves and gradually whisk in cornmeal in a thin stream. Cook mixture over moderate heat, whisking, 2 minutes and cover pan. Simmer polenta, covered, over low heat, stirring for 1 minute after every 10 minutes of cooking, 45 minutes total. Remove pan from heat and discard bay leaves.

Cooks' note:
• The veal chops in the preceding recipe may be seared and roasted while the polenta is simmering.

PHOTO ON PAGE 14

PORK

CHIPOTLE-HONEY-GLAZED PORK ⊙

Serves 4

3 canned *chipotle* chiles in *adobo* (sources on
   page 252) (¼ cup total)
3 garlic cloves, coarsely chopped
3 tablespoons honey
1½ lb pork tenderloin

Preheat oven to 450°F.

Purée *chipotles* in *adobo* with garlic and honey in a
blender until smooth. Pat pork dry and season with salt.
Put pork on a foil-lined baking sheet and spread with
chile glaze to coat well. Roast in middle of oven until an
instant-read thermometer registers 155°F, about 20 minutes. Let stand 5 minutes on a cutting board before
cutting into thin slices.

MILK-BRAISED PORK

Serves 4 to 6

*In this simple recipe, an adaptation of Italian cooking legend
Marcella Hazan's Bolognese-style pork loin braised in milk, the
meat acquires a delicate texture and flavor and the milk slowly
evolves into a rich sauce of golden curds.*

1 (2½-lb) piece boneless pork shoulder
2 tablespoons vegetable oil
2 cups whole milk

Pat pork dry and season with salt and pepper. In a 4-
quart heavy kettle heat oil over moderately high heat
until hot but not smoking and brown pork on all sides,
about 5 minutes total. Carefully add milk and cook
pork, covered, at a bare simmer 2 hours. Continue to
cook pork, partially covered, at a bare simmer until very
tender, about 1 hour. Transfer pork to a cutting board
and let stand 5 minutes. Season cooking liquid generously with salt and pepper and boil until slightly
thickened, about 2 minutes.

Thinly slice pork and transfer to a platter. Skim fat
from cooking liquid and spoon liquid over pork.

PORK CHOPS WITH SWEET CURRIED ONION ⊙

Serves 2

¼ cup water
1 tablespoon apricot jam
1 large red onion
1½ tablespoons vegetable oil
1½ teaspoons curry powder
4 (½-inch-thick) rib pork chops
   (about 1 lb total)

Accompaniment: apple and celery salad
   (page 171)

In a small bowl stir together water and jam. Halve
onion and thinly slice. In a 12-inch nonstick skillet heat
1 tablespoon oil over moderate heat until hot but not
smoking and cook onion with curry powder, stirring,
until softened. Stir onions into jam mixture and season
with salt and pepper.

Pat pork chops dry and season with salt and pepper.
In skillet heat remaining ½ tablespoon oil over moderately high heat until hot but not smoking and sauté
chops until golden brown and cooked through, about 1½
minutes on each side. Add curried onion to pan and
cook, stirring, 1 minute.

Serve chops with salad.

ROASTED HONEY-GLAZED SPARERIBS

Serves 8 to 10

For marinade
4 garlic cloves
1 cup packed light brown sugar
1⅓ cups honey
¼ cup cider vinegar
¼ cup Worcestershire sauce
1½ tablespoons salt
2 teaspoons ground ginger
2 teaspoons Tabasco

4 untrimmed racks pork spareribs (3½ lb each)

Make marinade:

With flat side of a large knife smash garlic. In a small saucepan heat brown sugar, honey, and vinegar over moderate heat, stirring, until sugar is dissolved. Remove pan from heat and stir in garlic and remaining marinade ingredients until combined well. Cool marinade to room temperature.

Fold up spareribs and fit into two 1-gallon heavy-duty sealable plastic bags. Divide marinade between bags and seal bags, pressing out excess air. Marinate ribs in bags in a large roasting pan, chilled, turning them once, 1 day.

Preheat oven to 350°F.

Open bags and, holding ribs in bags, pour marinade into a saucepan. Discard garlic. Simmer marinade until reduced to about 1½ cups. Pour 1 cup marinade into a bowl and reserve as sauce for serving with ribs (remainder will be used for basting ribs).

Arrange ribs, overlapping slightly, in 2 large roasting pans and roast in upper and lower thirds of oven 30 minutes. With tongs turn ribs over so they will brown evenly. Roast ribs 30 minutes more and with tongs turn them over.

Switch position of pans in oven and baste ribs with some of remaining marinade in saucepan. Roast ribs 30 minutes and with tongs turn them over. Brush ribs with remaining marinade in saucepan and roast 30 minutes more, or until meat is very tender.

Transfer ribs to a cutting board and cut apart between bones. Serve ribs with reserved sauce.

PHOTO ON PAGE 16

HAM STEAK WITH CARAMELIZED APPLE STACKS ◔

Serves 2

1 large firm red apple such as Braeburn, Gala,
    Rome Beauty, or Fuji
2 tablespoons unsalted butter
2 (¼-inch-thick) baked ham slices, quartered
1 large shallot, finely chopped
2 teaspoons cider vinegar
½ cup apple juice
1½ tablespoons whole-grain mustard
½ tablespoon Dijon mustard, or to taste
Pinch of ground cloves

Preheat oven to 250°F.

Core whole apple (without peeling) and cut into 8 (¼-inch-thick) rounds.

Heat 1 tablespoon butter in a 12-inch nonstick skillet over moderately high heat, then sauté ham, turning once, until browned, 5 to 6 minutes total. Transfer ham to a heatproof dish and keep warm, loosely covered with foil, in oven. Add remaining tablespoon butter to skillet and sauté apple slices, turning once, until golden and tender, 4 minutes total. Top each piece of ham with an apple slice and continue layering, using all of ham and apple slices, to make 2 stacks. Keep warm in oven.

Add shallot to skillet and sauté over moderately high heat, stirring, until golden. Add vinegar and cook, stirring, 10 seconds, or until absorbed by shallots. Add apple juice and boil until reduced by half. Add mustards and cloves and boil until mixture is slightly thickened and syrupy. Serve stacks with sauce.

LAMB

RACK OF LAMB WITH GREEN PEPPERCORN
SAUCE ○

Serves 4

2 frenched racks of lamb (sources on page 252)
  (each about 1½ lb)
1 medium shallot
3 tablespoons drained green peppercorns
  in brine (sources on page 252)
½ stick unsalted butter
¾ cup dry red wine

Preheat oven to 450°F.

In a roasting pan season lamb with salt and arrange
rib sides down. Roast lamb in middle of oven until a
thermometer inserted 2 inches into center of a rack registers 130°F, about 25 minutes, for medium-rare.

While lamb is roasting, mince shallot and with flat
side of a large knife crush peppercorns. In a small
saucepan cook shallot in 1 tablespoon butter over moderate heat, stirring occasionally, until softened. Add
peppercorns and red wine and simmer until liquid is
reduced to about ⅓ cup.

Transfer lamb to a cutting board and let stand 10
minutes. Skim fat from roasting pan and add red-wine
mixture to pan, stirring and scraping up any browned
bits. In saucepan simmer sauce until reduced to about ¼
cup. Whisk in remaining 3 tablespoons butter until
incorporated and season sauce with salt if necessary.

Cut lamb into chops and pour sauce over them.

GRILLED CHARMOULA LAMB CHOPS

Serves 50

*Whether you are serving 50 (this recipe) or 6 (see recipe on
page 128) ask your butcher to french the lamb chops to the
eye (trim them of all fat and scrape the rib bone clean). This
not only makes for a nice presentation but also makes it
much easier for guests to pick them up.*

*Charmoula is a fragrant, spicy Moroccan marinade and
sauce often used with fish and seafood.*

3 (3-inch) cinnamon sticks
¼ cup coriander seeds
¼ cup cumin seeds
1 teaspoon whole cloves
½ cup paprika (not hot)
1½ teaspoons cayenne
1 cup olive oil
¼ cup finely chopped garlic
  (1 large head)
100 lamb rib chops, frenched to the eye
  (about 17 lb frenched)
4 cups chopped fresh cilantro
  (4 large bunches)

Break cinnamon sticks into 1-inch pieces and finely
grind in batches in an electric coffee/spice grinder with
coriander, cumin, and cloves. Stir together with paprika
and cayenne.

Stir together ¼ cup oil and 1 tablespoon garlic in a
large bowl and add 25 lamb chops, tossing to coat.
Season with salt and toss with ¼ cup spice mixture and
1 cup cilantro to coat. Transfer coated lamb to sealable
plastic bags and coat remaining meat in same manner.
Marinate, chilled, at least 2 hours.

Prepare grill.

Season lamb with salt and grill in batches on an oiled
rack about 4 minutes on one side, then 2 minutes on the
other for medium-rare. (Alternatively, broil lamb under
a preheated broiler 2 to 3 inches from heat.) Serve lamb
warm or at room temperature.

Cooks' notes:
· Spice mixture may be made up to 1 week ahead and kept,
  covered, at room temperature.
· Lamb chops may be marinated up to 1 day and/or grilled (or
  broiled) 1 day ahead and chilled, covered. Reheat the chops
  in batches, in single layers in shallow baking pans, in a 425°F
  oven 8 minutes, or until chops are heated through.

PHOTO ON PAGE 56

GRILLED CHARMOULA LAMB CHOPS ☺+

Serves 6

1 (3-inch) cinnamon stick
1 tablespoon coriander seeds
1 tablespoon cumin seeds
3 whole cloves
2 tablespoons paprika (not hot)
½ teaspoon cayenne
3 tablespoons olive oil
1 tablespoon finely chopped garlic
2 (8-rib) racks of lamb, frenched to the eye and
  cut into chops (about 2¾ lb frenched)
2 cups finely chopped fresh cilantro (2 large
  bunches)

Break cinnamon stick into 1-inch pieces and finely grind with coriander, cumin, and cloves in an electric coffee/spice grinder. Stir spices together with paprika and cayenne.

Stir together oil and garlic in a large bowl and add lamb, tossing to coat. Season with salt and toss with spice mixture and cilantro. Marinate lamb in a sealable plastic bag, chilled, at least 2 hours.

Prepare grill.

Season lamb with salt and grill on an oiled rack about 4 minutes on one side, then 2 minutes on the other for medium-rare. (Alternatively, broil lamb under a preheated broiler 2 to 3 inches from heat.) Serve lamb warm or at room temperature.

PHOTO ON PAGE 58

GRILLED LAMB CHOPS WITH SPICY
MANGO SAUCE ☺

Serves 2

1 mango
1 large shallot
¼ cup fresh lime juice
1 teaspoon sugar, or to taste
⅛ teaspoon cayenne
2 (½-inch-thick) center-cut shoulder lamb chops
  (about ¾ lb each)

Garnish: lime wedges and fresh cilantro sprigs

Prepare grill.

Peel, pit, and coarsely chop mango. Finely chop shallot. In a blender purée mango and shallot with lime juice, sugar, cayenne, and salt and pepper to taste until smooth. Transfer sauce to a bowl and if too thick whisk in some water, 1 tablespoon at a time.

Pat lamb dry and season with salt and pepper. Grill lamb on a lightly oiled rack set 5 to 6 inches over glowing coals about 4 minutes on each side for medium-rare.

Serve chops topped with sauce and garnished with lime wedges and cilantro.

GRILLED BUTTERFLIED LEG OF LAMB WITH LEMON,
HERBS, AND GARLIC ☺+

Serves 8

For herb rub
8 garlic cloves
3 tablespoons chopped fresh thyme
2 tablespoons chopped fresh rosemary
2 tablespoons chopped fresh flat-leaf parsley
½ teaspoon freshly ground black pepper
1 tablespoon kosher salt
3 tablespoons olive oil

1 (7- to 8-lb) leg of lamb, trimmed of all fat, boned,
  and butterflied by butcher (4 to 4¾ lb boneless)
1 lemon

Make herb rub:

Finely chop garlic and in a small bowl stir together with remaining herb-rub ingredients.

Put lamb in a large dish and with tip of a sharp small knife held at a 45-degree angle cut ½-inch-deep slits all over lamb, rubbing herb mixture into slits and all over lamb. Marinate lamb at room temperature 1 hour.

Prepare grill.

Lightly pat lamb dry. On a lightly oiled rack set 5 to 6 inches over glowing coals grill lamb about 10 minutes on each side, or until an instant-read thermometer horizontally inserted into thickest part of meat registers 125°F for medium-rare. (Alternatively, roast lamb in a roasting pan in middle of a 425°F oven about 25 minutes, or until an instant-read thermometer horizontally inserted into meat registers 125°F for medium-rare.) Transfer lamb to a cutting board. Halve and seed lemon.

Squeeze juice over lamb and let stand, loosely covered with foil, 15 minutes.

Cut lamb into slices and serve with any juices that have accumulated on cutting board.

Cooks' note:
- Butterflied leg of lamb can sometimes get a little unwieldy. To secure loose flaps of meat, run 2 long metal skewers lengthwise and 2 skewers crosswise through the lamb, bunching the meat together. This will also help it cook more evenly.

PHOTO ON PAGE 44

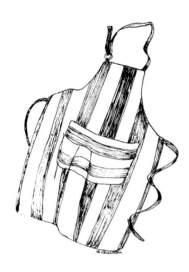

GREEN OLIVE, LEMON, AND GARLIC-ROASTED LEG
OF LAMB WITH POTATOES AND PAN GRAVY

Serves 6 with lamb left over

1 large lemon
⅓ cup brine-cured green olives (preferably Italian)
4 large garlic cloves
¼ cup packed fresh flat-leaf parsley
4 tablespoons olive oil
3 lb boiling potatoes (preferably Yukon Gold)
1 (7-lb) leg of lamb (ask butcher to remove pelvic bone and tie lamb for easier carving)
For pan gravy
½ tablespoon all-purpose flour
½ tablespoon unsalted butter
½ cup dry white wine
½ cup water

Garnish: lemon halves and olive branches
    (sources on page 252)

Preheat oven to 450°F.

With a vegetable peeler remove zest from lemon and reserve lemon. Pit olives. In a food processor finely chop zest, olives, garlic, and parsley with 2 tablespoons olive oil.

Peel potatoes and cut into 1½-inch pieces. In a large flameproof roasting pan toss potatoes with remaining 2 tablespoons oil to coat and season with salt and pepper. Arrange lamb on potatoes and with the tip of a sharp small knife cut small slits all over lamb. Rub olive mixture over lamb, pushing it into slits. Halve reserved lemon and squeeze juice over lamb. Season lamb with salt and pepper and roast with potatoes in middle of oven 20 minutes.

Reduce temperature to 350°F.

Roast lamb and potatoes, loosening potatoes from pan with a metal spatula and turning them occasionally, 1 hour more, or until a meat thermometer inserted into thickest part of meat registers 135°F. Transfer lamb to a cutting board and let stand while making gravy. Transfer potatoes to a large bowl and keep warm.

Make gravy:

In a cup with your fingers blend together flour and butter. Add wine and water to roasting pan and deglaze pan over moderately high heat, stirring and scraping up brown bits. Transfer mixture to a small saucepan and bring to a boil. Whisk in flour mixture, whisking until incorporated, and simmer gravy, stirring occasionally, 1 minute. With a slotted spoon remove any potato pieces from gravy.

Garnish lamb with lemon halves and olive branches and serve with gravy and potatoes.

PHOTO ON PAGE 35

POULTRY

MOROCCAN CHICKEN WITH PRESERVED MEYER LEMONS AND GREEN OLIVES

Serves 4

4 boneless skinless chicken breast halves
2 tablespoons olive oil
2 medium onions, sliced ¼ inch thick
2 garlic cloves, thinly sliced
½ teaspoon turmeric
½ teaspoon freshly ground black pepper
8 pieces preserved Meyer lemon (recipe follows)
½ cup chicken broth
¼ cup dry white wine
16 pitted green olives, halved
2 tablespoons coarsely chopped fresh cilantro

Pat chicken dry, then season with salt and pepper. Heat 1 tablespoon oil in a 12-inch nonstick skillet over moderately high heat until hot but not smoking, then sauté chicken until golden brown, about 3 minutes on each side. Transfer to a plate and keep warm, covered.

Add remaining tablespoon oil to skillet and reduce heat to moderate. Cook sliced onions and garlic, stirring frequently, until softened but not browned, 8 to 10 minutes. Add turmeric and pepper and cook, stirring, 1 minute.

Scrape pulp from preserved lemon, reserving for another use. Cut rind into thin strips and add to onions with broth, wine, and olives.

Return chicken, with any juices accumulated on plate, to skillet. Braise, covered, until chicken is cooked through, about 12 minutes. Serve chicken sprinkled with cilantro.

PRESERVED MEYER LEMONS

Makes 48 pieces

Preserving a Meyer lemon captures its glorious perfume. We've adapted cookbook author Paula Wolfert's quick method and made it even faster by blanching the lemons first. The rind of a preserved lemon is common in Moroccan dishes; we also use it in all kinds of soups, stews, and salads and as a low-fat alternative to olives.

2½ to 3 lb Meyer lemons (10 to 12)
⅔ cup kosher salt
¼ cup olive oil

Special equipment: 6-cup jar with tight-fitting lid

Blanch 6 lemons in boiling water 5 minutes. When cool enough to handle, cut lemons into 8 wedges each and discard seeds. Toss with salt in a bowl and pack into jar.

Squeeze enough juice from remaining lemons to measure 1 cup. Add enough juice to cover lemons and cover jar with lid. Let stand at room temperature, shaking gently once a day, 5 days. Add oil and chill.

Cooks' note:
• Preserved lemons keep, chilled, up to 1 year.

GOAT CHEESE AND OLIVE-STUFFED CHICKEN BREASTS ☻

Serves 2

6 Kalamata or other brine-cured black olives
1 oz soft mild goat cheese (about 2 tablespoons)
½ teaspoon chopped fresh thyme
2 boneless chicken breast halves with skin
1 teaspoon vegetable oil

Preheat oven to 300°F.
Pit and thinly slice olives. Stir together olives, goat

cheese, thyme, and salt and pepper to taste in a small bowl until combined well. Pat chicken dry and season with salt and pepper.

To form a pocket in chicken for filling: Put a chicken breast half on a cutting board and, beginning in middle of 1 side of breast half, horizontally insert a sharp thin knife three fourths of the way through center, moving knife in a fanning motion to create a pocket. Form pocket in remaining breast half in same manner. Divide filling between pockets and spread evenly with a finger.

Pat chicken dry and season with salt and pepper. In a small heavy ovenproof skillet heat oil over moderately high heat until hot but not smoking and brown chicken, skin sides down, about 2 minutes. Turn chicken over and brown about 2 minutes more. Transfer skillet to middle of oven and bake chicken until cooked through, about 15 minutes.

LEMON-PEPPER CHICKEN

Serves 4

2 lemons
1 (3-lb) chicken, quartered
1 teaspoon black peppercorns
1½ teaspoons coarse sea or kosher salt
¼ cup water

Preheat oven to 400°F.

With a vegetable peeler remove zest from lemon in strips and remove any white pith from strips. Coarsely chop enough zest to measure 1 tablespoon, reserving remainder for another use. Squeeze enough juice from lemons to measure ¼ cup. In a flameproof roasting pan combine juice and chicken, tossing to coat, and arrange chicken skin sides down. Marinate chicken 15 minutes.

In an electric coffee/spice grinder grind zest, peppercorns, and salt until finely chopped. Arrange chicken, skin sides up, and pat lemon-pepper onto it. Roast chicken in middle of oven, basting occasionally, until just cooked through, 45 to 50 minutes. Transfer chicken to a platter and keep warm.

Add water to juices in roasting pan and simmer, stirring and scraping up any browned bits, until liquid is slightly thickened, about 2 minutes. Pour sauce over roasted chicken.

ROASTED POUSSINS WITH CUMIN AND LEMON

Serves 2

½ stick unsalted butter, softened
3 tablespoons chopped fresh cilantro
½ teaspoon finely grated fresh lemon zest
¼ teaspoon ground cumin
¼ teaspoon salt
⅛ teaspoon freshly ground black pepper
2 *poussins* (young chickens; about 1 lb each)
   (sources on page 252)
⅓ cup dry white wine

Preheat oven to 425°F.

In a small bowl stir together 3 tablespoons butter, cilantro, zest, cumin, salt, and pepper until combined. Trim necks of *poussins* flush with bodies if necessary. Rinse birds inside and out and pat dry. Beginning at neck end of each bird, slide fingers between meat and skin to loosen skin (be careful not to tear skin). Divide seasoned butter into 4 portions. Using a teaspoon put 1 portion of butter under skin of each breast half. Spread seasoned butter evenly under skin by pressing outside of skin with fingers. If desired, tie legs of each bird together with kitchen string and secure wings to sides with wooden picks or skewers.

Arrange birds in a flameproof roasting pan just large enough to hold them. Melt remaining tablespoon butter. Brush butter onto birds and season them with salt. Roast birds in upper third of oven 45 minutes, or until an instant-read thermometer inserted in meatiest part of inner thigh registers 170°F.

Transfer birds to a platter and loosely cover with foil to keep warm. Add wine to roasting pan and deglaze over moderate heat, scraping up brown bits. Remove pan from heat and skim fat from sauce.

Serve *poussins* with sauce.

Cooks' note:
• Small Cornish hens (about 1¼ lb each) make a fine substitute for *poussins*.

PHOTO ON PAGE 23

TANDOORI-SPICED CHICKEN BREASTS

Serves 4

Tandoori chicken gets its name from the clay oven (heated by wood or coal) it is traditionally cooked in—a tandoor—which bakes meat, fish, poultry, and bread at temperatures upward of 500°F. In our version, the chicken is broiled and the signature yogurt and spice marinade contains only ingredients that are readily available on supermarket shelves.

For spice paste
1 large garlic clove
1½ teaspoons kosher salt
1 small fresh red or green chile such as
    serrano or cayenne
⅓ cup low-fat plain yogurt
1 tablespoon fresh lemon juice
2 teaspoons grated peeled fresh ginger
1½ teaspoons ground coriander seeds
¾ teaspoon turmeric
½ teaspoon ground cumin
½ teaspoon freshly ground black pepper
¼ teaspoon freshly grated nutmeg
⅛ teaspoon ground cloves

4 skinless boneless chicken breast halves
    (about 1¼ lb total)
1 small red onion
2 teaspoons vegetable oil
For yogurt sauce
½ cup low-fat plain yogurt
1 teaspoon fresh lemon juice
Pinch of cayenne

Make spice paste:
Mince garlic with salt and mash to a paste. Wearing protective gloves, mince chile (including seeds for a spicier paste) and in a bowl stir together with garlic paste and remaining spice paste ingredients.

Make 3 diagonal cuts about ¼ inch deep in each chicken breast and rub spice paste into cuts and all over chicken. Marinate chicken, covered, 30 minutes at cool room temperature.

Preheat broiler and line broiler pan with foil.

Halve onion through root end and reserve 1 half for sauce. Thinly slice remaining onion half, separating layers, and in a small bowl soak onion slices in ice water to cover while broiling chicken.

Arrange chicken without crowding on rack of broiler pan. Brush chicken with 1 teaspoon vegetable oil and broil about 3 inches from heat 8 minutes. Turn chicken over and brush with remaining teaspoon vegetable oil. Broil chicken until lightly browned and just cooked through, about 6 minutes more.

Make sauce while chicken is broiling:
Mince enough reserved onion to measure 1 tablespoon and in a small bowl stir together with all sauce ingredients.

Drain soaked onion and pat dry. Top chicken with onion slices and serve with yogurt sauce.

☞ each serving, including yogurt sauce, about 222 calories and 5 grams fat

PHOTO ON PAGE 81

BREAD-CRUMB-COATED CHICKEN

Serves 4

½ loaf country-style bread
½ cup freshly grated Parmesan (about 1½ oz)
1 tablespoon chopped fresh sage
½ stick unsalted butter
2 tablespoons Dijon mustard
2 whole skinless chicken legs (about ¾ lb total)
2 skinless boneless chicken breast halves
    (about ¾ lb total)

Preheat oven to 450°F and line a baking sheet with aluminum foil.

Tear bread into pieces and in a food processor pulse until finely ground. In a large bowl stir together 2 cups bread crumbs, Parmesan, sage, and salt and pepper to taste. Melt butter and stir in mustard and salt and pepper to taste.

With a sharp knife cut chicken thighs from legs. Pat chicken dry and brush all over with butter mixture. Roll chicken in bread-crumb mixture, pressing gently to adhere, and arrange chicken, without crowding, on baking sheet. Bake chicken in middle of oven until cooked through and golden, 25 to 30 minutes.

ROSEMARY-SCENTED CHICKEN AND POTATOES ☾

Serves 2

1 lb yellow-fleshed potatoes such as Yukon Gold
2 large garlic cloves
2 teaspoons chopped fresh rosemary
½ tablespoon olive oil
2 whole chicken legs (about 1½ lb total)

Preheat oven to 500°F.

Cut potatoes into ½-inch pieces and finely chop garlic. In a bowl stir together potatoes, half of garlic, half of rosemary, oil, and salt and pepper to taste. Pat chicken dry and season well with salt and pepper. Sprinkle chicken with remaining garlic and rosemary. In a roasting pan arrange chicken legs in one layer and scatter potatoes around chicken. Roast chicken and potatoes in middle of oven until chicken is cooked through and potatoes are crisp, about 35 minutes.

DEVILED CHICKEN WINGS

Serves 6 (hors d'oeuvre; 4 as a main course)

3 lb chicken wings (12 to 14)
6 slices firm white sandwich bread
2 teaspoons mustard seeds
½ cup Dijon mustard
2 tablespoons vegetable oil
2 teaspoons white-wine vinegar
1 teaspoon kosher salt
¼ teaspoon cayenne
3 oz freshly grated Parmesan (about ¾ cup)

Cut off wing tips, reserving for another use, and halve wings at joint. Discard crusts from bread and in a food processor finely grind bread. Measure out 1½ cups bread crumbs, reserving remainder for another use. With a mortar and pestle or in an electric coffee/spice grinder coarsely grind mustard seeds. Preheat oven to 450°F and oil rack of a broiler pan.

In a large bowl whisk together mustard seeds, mustard, oil, vinegar, salt, and cayenne. Add wings and stir to coat. In a shallow dish stir together bread crumbs and Parmesan. Press wings, thick-skin sides down, into bread-crumb mixture to coat and arrange, crumb sides up, on rack.

Roast wings in middle of oven until cooked through and golden, about 30 minutes. Serve chicken wings warm or at room temperature.

LIME, APRICOT, AND SOY-SAUCE CHICKEN WINGS ☾+

Serves 8 adults plus 10 children as part of a buffet

8 lb chicken wings
1 cup fresh lime juice (from 8 to 10 limes)
1 cup apricot preserves
1 cup soy sauce
⅔ cup sugar
4 large garlic cloves

Special equipment: 2 large roasting pans (about 16 by 12 inches)

Preheat oven to 425°F. Cut off wing tips, reserving for another use, and halve wings at joint. Divide wings between 2 roasting pans, arranging in single layers.

Purée remaining ingredients in a blender and pour mixture over wings, dividing evenly between pans. Bake wings in upper and lower thirds of oven 50 minutes. Turn wings over and switch position of pans in oven, then bake 45 minutes to 1 hour more, or until liquid is thick and sticky.

Serve wings warm or at room temperature.

PHOTO ON PAGE 70

GRILLED CHICKEN WINGS WITH TWO THAI SAUCES

Serves 6 (hors d'oeuvre; 4 as a main course)

Though it's not essential to make both sauces for these wings, we think the contrast between the rich peanut sauce and the light-yet-spicy gai yang—a classic Thai sauce for poultry—is a flavor combination that shouldn't be missed.

3 lb chicken wings (12 to 14)
¼ cup vegetable oil
3 tablespoons fresh lemon juice
For peanut sauce
3 shallots
2 garlic cloves
1 cup salted roasted peanuts
2 tablespoons vegetable oil
1 teaspoon Thai red curry paste (sources on
  page 252)
1 cup light coconut milk plus additional for thinning
1 tablespoon fresh lime juice
½ teaspoon brown sugar
For gai yang sauce
2 small fresh hot red chiles such as Thai
  or *serrano*
4 garlic cloves
¾ cup sugar
½ cup water
⅔ cup white-wine vinegar
¾ teaspoon salt

Accompaniment: cucumber salad (recipe follows)

Cut off wing tips, reserving for another use, and halve wings at joint. In a bowl whisk together oil, lemon juice, and salt to taste. Add wings and stir to coat. Marinate wings, covered and chilled, at least 1 hour and up to 8.

Make peanut sauce:
Mince shallots and garlic. In a food processor finely grind peanuts until they begin to get oily. In a small heavy saucepan heat oil over moderate heat until hot but not smoking and cook shallots, garlic, and curry paste, stirring, until fragrant, about 1 minute. Stir in ground peanuts and coconut milk and simmer, uncovered, stirring frequently, until mixture is slightly thickened, about 3 minutes. Stir in lime juice, brown sugar, and salt to taste. (If sauce is too thick, stir in additional coconut milk.)

Make gai yang sauce:
Wearing protective gloves, mince chiles. Mince garlic and in a small saucepan simmer with chiles and remaining ingredients, stirring occasionally, 10 minutes. Cool sauce to room temperature.

Prepare grill.

Drain wings in a colander and pat dry. Grill wings on an oiled rack set 5 to 6 inches over glowing coals until cooked through and golden brown, 8 to 10 minutes on each side.

Serve wings with sauces and cucumber salad.

Cooks' notes:
• Peanut sauce may be made 1 day ahead and chilled, covered. Bring sauce to room temperature before serving.
• *Gai yang* sauce may be made 1 day ahead and chilled, covered. Bring sauce to room temperature before serving.

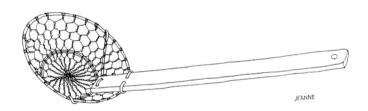

CUCUMBER SALAD ☽+

Makes about 4 cups

1 English cucumber
1 carrot
1 small red onion
⅔ cup distilled white vinegar
¼ cup sugar
⅛ teaspoon cayenne

Halve cucumber lengthwise and seed. Thinly slice cucumber and carrot crosswise. Thinly slice onion and transfer to a bowl with cucumber and carrot.

In a small saucepan heat vinegar, sugar, and cayenne over moderate heat, stirring until sugar is dissolved. Cool vinegar mixture and pour over vegetables. Marinate salad at least 2 hours and up to 3 days.

FRIED CHINESE FIVE-SPICE CHICKEN WINGS

Serves 6 (hors d'oeuvre; 4 as a main course)

3 lb chicken wings (12 to 14)
1 onion
a 1½-inch piece peeled fresh ginger
2 tablespoons soy sauce (preferably Kikkoman)
1½ tablespoons medium-dry Sherry
1 tablespoon Chinese five-spice powder (sources on
     page 252)
1 tablespoon sugar
2 tablespoons plus 1 teaspoon kosher salt
2 teaspoons freshly ground black pepper, or to taste
½ cup cornstarch
6 cups vegetable oil

Cut off wing tips, reserving for another use, and halve wings at joint. Coarsely chop onion and finely chop ginger. In a large sealable plastic bag combine onion, ginger, soy sauce, Sherry, five-spice powder, sugar, and 1 teaspoon salt. Add wings and seal bag, pressing out excess air. Turn bag until wings are completely coated. Marinate chicken wings in bag in a large bowl, chilled, turning bag once, 2 hours.

Preheat oven to 350°F.

Transfer wings and marinade to a roasting pan or large shallow baking pan and bake, covered with foil, in middle of oven 1 hour. Cool wings until they can be handled and drain in a colander, discarding marinade.

Reduce temperature to 250°F.

In a small serving bowl combine remaining 2 tablespoons salt and pepper. Put cornstarch in a small bowl and dredge each wing, knocking off excess cornstarch and transferring to a shallow pan. In a 5- to 6-quart heavy kettle heat oil until a deep-fat thermometer registers 370°F. Working in batches of 6 or 7, fry wings in oil until golden brown, about 3 minutes, and with a slotted spoon transfer to paper towels to drain. Keep wings warm on a baking sheet in oven. Fry remaining wings in same manner, returning oil to 370°F between batches.

Serve wings with salt and pepper mixture.

Cooks' note:
• Wings may be marinated and baked 1 day ahead and chilled, covered.

ROASTED CHICKEN WINGS WITH SMOKED-PAPRIKA MAYONNAISE

Serves 4

These chicken wings need to marinate for at least 8 hours—we recommend putting them in the refrigerator before you go to bed so they'll be ready for roasting the next day.

The deep, almost beeflike flavor of these wings comes from the red wine in the marinade; both the wings and the mayonnaise get a boost from the Spanish smoked paprika.

3 lb chicken wings (12 to 14)
3 garlic cloves
¾ cup dry red wine
¼ cup water
1 teaspoon sweet Spanish smoked paprika
     (sources on page 252)
1½ tablespoons Sherry vinegar
2 teaspoons sugar
2 teaspoons salt
For smoked-paprika mayonnaise
⅓ cup mayonnaise
1 teaspoon medium-dry Sherry
¼ teaspoon sweet Spanish smoked paprika

Cut off wing tips, reserving for another use, and halve wings at joint. Put wings in a large sealable plastic bag. Finely chop garlic and add to bag with wine, water, paprika, vinegar, sugar, and salt. Seal bag, pressing out excess air. Marinate wings in bag in a large bowl, chilled, turning bag once, at least 8 hours and up to 24.

Preheat oven to 400°F.

Arrange wings in a roasting pan or large shallow baking pan large enough to hold them in one layer and pour marinade over them. Roast wings in middle of oven 30 minutes. Turn wings over and roast until marinade is reduced to a glaze and wings are golden brown, 25 to 30 minutes more.

Make mayonnaise:
In a bowl whisk together all mayonnaise ingredients.
Serve wings with mayonnaise.

GRILLED INDIAN-STYLE CHICKEN WINGS WITH
CARROT-CUMIN YOGURT SAUCE

Serves 6 (hors d'oeuvre; 4 as a main course)

*Some advance preparation is required for these wings: The
yogurt needs to drain for 2 hours and the wings need to marinate for at least 2 hours.*

For yogurt sauce
2 cups plain yogurt
2 teaspoons cumin seeds
2 carrots
¼ cup finely chopped fresh mint

3 lb chicken wings (12 to 14)
1 cup kosher salt
2 cups water
1½ tablespoons *garam masala* (Indian spice mix)
   such as Frontier brand (sources on page 252)
1 tablespoon vegetable oil

Make sauce:
In a sieve set over a bowl drain yogurt, covered and
chilled, 2 hours. In a dry small heavy skillet toast cumin
seeds over moderate heat, shaking skillet frequently,
until a shade darker, 2 to 3 minutes. Cool and with a
mortar and pestle or in an electric coffee/spice grinder
coarsely grind. Finely grate carrots into a bowl and stir
in yogurt, cumin, mint, and salt and pepper to taste.

Cut off wing tips, reserving for another use, and
halve wings at joint. In a bowl dissolve salt in water.
Marinate wings in brine, covered and chilled, stirring
occasionally, at least 2 hours and up to 24.

Prepare grill.

In a colander drain wings and rinse well. Pat wings
dry and in a bowl rub *garam masala* and oil onto wings.
Grill wings on an oiled rack set 5 to 6 inches over glowing coals until cooked through and golden brown, 8 to
10 minutes on each side.

Serve wings with sauce.

Cooks' note:
• Yogurt sauce may be made 8 hours ahead and chilled.

ASSORTED FOWL

TURKEY CHEDDAR SANDWICHES WITH
HONEY MUSTARD ◐

Makes 2

1 tablespoon honey
1 tablespoon coarse-grained mustard
4 slices 7-grain or whole-grain bread
3 oz coarsely grated sharp Cheddar (about ¾ cup)
1 plum tomato, sliced lengthwise
¼ lb sliced turkey breast
4 small *radicchio* leaves

Preheat broiler.

In a small bowl stir together honey and mustard.
Arrange bread on a baking sheet and toast under broiler
until golden on one side. Turn bread over and spread
honey mustard on untoasted sides. Sprinkle Cheddar
over honey mustard and broil until cheese is melted.
Arrange tomato, turkey, and *radicchio* between melted
Cheddar toasts, seasoning with salt and pepper.

BOURSIN-STUFFED TURKEY BURGERS ◐

Serves 2

½ small red onion
¾ lb ground turkey
2 tablespoons Boursin cheese (preferably peppered)
4 slices challah or 2 English muffins
1½ tablespoons olive oil

Accompaniments: tomato slices and watercress sprigs

Prepare grill.

Finely chop onion. In a bowl gently combine onion
and turkey (do not overmix) and form into four ½-inch-
thick patties. Center 1 tablespoon Boursin on each of 2
patties and top with remaining 2 patties, pressing edges
together to seal. Season burgers with salt and pepper
and grill on a lightly oiled rack set 5 to 6 inches over
glowing coals 6 to 8 minutes on each side, or until just
cooked through.

While burgers are grilling, brush bread with oil and toast on grill. Serve burgers on bread with tomato and watercress.

CHILAQUILES WITH TURKEY AND ROASTED TOMATILLO SALSA

Serves 6

For tortilla strips
3 cups vegetable oil
2 (8-oz) packages corn tortillas, cut into
  ½-inch-wide strips

1 large onion, chopped
1 (14½-oz) can chicken broth
1¼ lb shredded cooked turkey meat (4 cups)
Roasted tomatillo salsa (recipe follows)
6 oz Monterey Jack, shredded (1½ cups)
¼ cup *crème fraîche* or sour cream
1½ tablespoons milk
½ cup fresh cilantro sprigs
3 oz *queso fresco* or feta, crumbled

Fry tortilla strips:
Heat oil in a 3½-quart flameproof nonreactive shallow casserole or deep skillet to 375°F. Fry tortillas in batches, turning occasionally, until golden, about 1 minute, and transfer to paper towels to drain (return oil to 375°F between batches). Carefully pour off all but 1 tablespoon hot oil into a large metal bowl to cool before discarding.
Make chilaquiles:
Preheat oven to 375°F. Cook onion in oil in casserole over moderately high heat, stirring, until softened. Add broth and turkey and simmer, uncovered, stirring, until liquid is reduced to about ½ cup, about 15 minutes. Add 2½ cups salsa and bring to a boil. Remove from heat and toss with Monterey Jack and tortilla strips. Bake *chilaquiles*, uncovered, in middle of oven until bubbling, about 15 minutes. Whisk together *crème fraîche* and milk. Serve *chilaquiles* topped with *crème fraîche*, cilantro, and cheese.

Cooks' note:
• We used a 12- by 2-inch round enameled cast-iron casserole to assemble and bake our chilaquiles. The wide shallow casserole gave us just enough room for frying and mixing. It also allowed for a nice balance of crisp tortillas on top and softer ones on the bottom.

ROASTED TOMATILLO SALSA ⊚

Makes about 3 cups

If you're pressed for time, you may want to try a jarred brand of tomatillo salsa instead of making it from scratch. We like Rick Bayless's, which has a fine, robust flavor. (Look for it in specialty foods stores and in some supermarkets.)

1½ lb fresh tomatillos or 3 (11-oz) cans tomatillos
5 fresh *serrano* chiles
3 garlic cloves, unpeeled
½ cup fresh cilantro
1 large onion, coarsely chopped
2 teaspoons kosher salt

Preheat broiler.
If using fresh tomatillos, remove husks and rinse under warm water to remove stickiness. If using canned tomatillos, drain and measure out 2 cups. Broil chiles, garlic, and fresh tomatillos (do not broil canned) on rack of a broiler pan 1 to 2 inches from heat, turning once, until tomatillos are softened and slightly charred, about 7 minutes.
Peel garlic and pull off tops of chiles. Purée all ingredients in a blender.

Cooks' note:
• Salsa can be made 1 day ahead and chilled, covered.

ROAST TURKEY WITH HERBED BREAD STUFFING AND GIBLET GRAVY

Serves 8

Kosher turkey, salted during the koshering process, is just as flavorful and succulent as a brined one, without all the fuss. You'll need to "groom" a kosher bird, removing remaining feathers and quills with tweezers or needlenose pliers. (This is a happy sign that the bird has been minimally processed.)

12- to 14-lb kosher turkey, feathers removed if
  necessary, neck and giblets (excluding liver)
  reserved for making stock
Herbed bread stuffing (page 139)
¾ stick unsalted butter
¼ cup chicken broth
¼ cup water
For gravy
Pan juices reserved from turkey
4 cups turkey giblet stock (recipe follows)
¼ cup all-purpose flour

Garnish: fresh sage, rosemary, and thyme sprigs

Make turkey giblet stock and herbed bread stuffing as directed in separate recipes.
Roast turkey:
Preheat oven to 425°F.

Rinse turkey inside and out and pat dry. Season with salt and pepper inside and out. Loosely fill neck cavity with some of stuffing. Fold neck skin under body and fasten with a small skewer. Loosely fill body cavity with some stuffing and tie drumsticks together with kitchen string. Transfer remaining stuffing to a buttered 3-quart shallow baking dish and chill, covered. Secure wings to body with small skewers if desired for a nicer appearance.

Put turkey on a rack set in a flameproof roasting pan. Roast turkey in middle of oven 30 minutes. Melt ½ stick butter. Reduce oven temperature to 325°F and pour melted butter over turkey. Roast turkey, basting every 20 minutes, for 3 to 3½ hours more, or until a thermometer inserted in center of stuffing in body cavity registers 165°F (thigh will be about 180°F). Transfer turkey to a heated platter and keep juices in pan. Remove skewers and discard string. Transfer stuffing from cavities to a serving dish and keep warm, covered. Let turkey stand at least 30 minutes and up to 45.

Increase temperature to 375°F. Stir together chicken broth and water and drizzle over uncooked stuffing in baking dish. Dot stuffing with remaining 2 tablespoons butter and bake in middle of oven 40 minutes while turkey stands; for moist stuffing, bake covered entire time; for less moist stuffing with a slightly crisp top, uncover after 10 minutes.
Make gravy:
Skim fat from pan juices and reserve ¼ cup fat. Add 1 cup giblet stock to roasting pan and deglaze over moderately high heat, scraping up brown bits. Add to remaining 3 cups stock and bring to a simmer. Whisk together reserved fat and flour in a large heavy saucepan and cook roux over moderately low heat, whisking, 3 minutes. Add hot stock to roux in a fast stream, whisking constantly to prevent lumps, and simmer, whisking occasionally, until thickened, about 10 minutes. Stir in additional juices from turkey platter and season gravy with salt and pepper.

Cooks' note:
• If you choose not to cook your stuffing inside the bird, your turkey will take less time to roast, only about 2 to 3 hours (thigh should register 170°F).

PHOTO ON PAGE 67

TURKEY GIBLET STOCK

Makes about 4 cups

Giblets are the edible internal organs of poultry—heart, liver, kidneys, and gizzard—often collected in a tidy plastic packet (along with the neck) and tucked inside the fowl. Minus the liver (which results in bitterness), they add depth and richness to stock or, minced, to gravy.

1 tablespoon vegetable oil
Neck and giblets (excluding liver) from a
  12- to 14-lb turkey
1 celery rib, coarsely chopped
1 carrot, coarsely chopped
1 onion, quartered
4 cups water
1¾ cups chicken broth
1 bay leaf
1 teaspoon whole black peppercorns
1 teaspoon dried thyme

Heat oil in a 2-quart saucepan over moderately high heat until hot but not smoking and brown neck and giblets. Add remaining ingredients and simmer until reduced to about 4 cups, 40 to 45 minutes. Pour stock through a fine sieve into a bowl. Skim off and discard any fat.

Cooks' note:
• Stock can be made 1 day ahead. Cool completely, uncovered, then chill, covered.

HERBED BREAD STUFFING

Makes about 12 cups

Any previously frozen turkey destined for stuffing should be completely thawed. (Check the body cavity for ice crystals; if you find any, submerge the turkey in cold water, changing the water every 30 minutes, until the turkey is thoroughly thawed.) Bring the stuffing to room temperature before spooning it into the bird. Don't pack it in too tightly; stuffing expands as it cooks. And be sure to stuff the turkey immediately before roasting to prevent food poisoning.

10 cups (1-inch) cubes crusty country-style
    bread (1 lb)

3 medium onions, chopped
3 celery ribs, thinly sliced crosswise
1 teaspoon dried thyme
½ teaspoon dried sage
½ teaspoon dried rosemary
1 stick unsalted butter
1½ cups chicken broth
½ cup water

Preheat oven to 325°F.

Toast bread in a large shallow baking pan in middle of oven until just dry, 25 to 30 minutes. Cook onions, celery, and herbs in butter in a large heavy skillet over moderately low heat, stirring occasionally, until celery is softened, about 10 minutes. Stir together bread, vegetables, broth, water, and salt and pepper to taste, then cool completely, uncovered.

Cooks' notes:
• To change this stuffing try a hearty multigrain or nut loaf. Precooked sausage, bacon, or oysters will add richness and more complex flavors. Lightly sautéed celery or diced apple and/or lightly toasted nuts add some crunch.
• You can make stuffing 1 day ahead and keep it covered and chilled.

BREAKFAST, BRUNCH, & CHEESE DISHES

BAKED ASPARAGUS AND YELLOW PEPPER FRITTATA

Serves 12 (as part of a buffet)

2 lb thin asparagus
2 large yellow bell peppers
3 shallots
1 medium zucchini
3 scallions
1 tablespoon unsalted butter
10 large eggs
½ cup heavy cream
3 tablespoons chopped fresh flat-leaf parsley
1½ teaspoons salt
¼ teaspoon freshly ground black pepper

Preheat oven to 350°F and butter a 13- by 9- by 2-inch glass baking dish (3-quart).

Trim asparagus and diagonally cut into ¼-inch-wide slices. Cut bell peppers into ¼-inch-wide strips and mince shallots. Halve zucchini lengthwise and diagonally cut both zucchini and scallions into thin slices.

Have ready a bowl of ice and cold water. In a large saucepan of boiling salted water blanch asparagus 1 minute and drain in a colander. Immediately transfer asparagus to ice water to stop cooking. Drain asparagus well in colander and pat dry.

In a large skillet cook bell peppers and shallots in butter over moderately low heat, stirring occasionally, until peppers are softened, about 10 minutes. In a large bowl whisk together eggs, cream, parsley, salt, and pepper. Stir in asparagus, bell pepper mixture, zucchini, and scallions. Pour custard into baking dish and bake in middle of oven until golden and set, about 35 minutes. Cool frittata on a rack. If desired, loosen frittata from edges of pan and slide onto a platter.

Cooks' note:
· Frittata may be made 1 day ahead and chilled, covered. Bring to room temperature before serving.

PHOTO ON PAGE 30

SCRAMBLED EGGS WITH AVOCADO, ONION, AND CHEDDAR ☾

Serves 2

1 small onion
½ firm-ripe California avocado
4 large eggs
⅔ cup grated extra-sharp Cheddar (about 2½ oz)
2 teaspoons unsalted butter

Garnish: chopped fresh cilantro

Chop onion. Halve, pit, and peel avocado and cut into ¼-inch pieces. In a bowl whisk together eggs and Cheddar and season with salt and pepper. In a nonstick skillet heat butter over moderately high heat until foam subsides and sauté onion, stirring, until just beginning to soften, about 2 minutes. Add egg mixture and cook, stirring constantly, until eggs are just set, about 1 minute. Remove skillet from heat and stir in avocado.

Serve eggs garnished with cilantro.

BAKED EGGS ON CREAMED SPINACH ☾

Serves 2

1 bunch spinach (about ¾ lb)
2 tablespoons minced onion
1 tablespoon unsalted butter
3 tablespoons heavy cream
Freshly grated nutmeg to taste
2 large eggs

Preheat oven to 400°F and butter two ⅓- to ½-cup ramekins.

Discard coarse stems from spinach. In a 2- to 3-quart saucepan of boiling salted water cook spinach 2 minutes and drain in a sieve, pressing with back of a spoon to remove as much water as possible. Finely chop spinach.

In a small nonstick skillet cook onion in butter over

moderately low heat, stirring, until softened. Stir in spinach, cream, nutmeg, and salt and pepper to taste and cook, stirring, until hot.

Divide creamed spinach between ramekins and break an egg into each. On a baking sheet bake eggs in upper third of oven until whites are cooked through, or until desired doneness, about 12 minutes. (The yolks will not be fully cooked, which may be of concern if there is a problem with salmonella in your area.)

Season baked eggs with salt and pepper and serve immediately.

ALMOND COCONUT GRANOLA

Makes about 6 cups

This granola is delicious topped with fresh fruit (we suggest kiwifruit and pineapple) or on its own, served with milk or yogurt.

3 cups old-fashioned rolled oats
⅔ cup sliced almonds
½ cup unsweetened desiccated coconut
    (sources on page 252)
⅓ cup hulled green pumpkin seeds (sources
    on page 252) or sunflower seeds
½ teaspoon salt
½ stick unsalted butter
6 tablespoons honey
1 cup mixed dried fruits such as raisins,
    cherries, and apricots

Preheat oven to 325°F.

In a large bowl stir together oats, almonds, coconut, pumpkin or sunflower seeds, and salt. In a small saucepan melt butter with honey over low heat, stirring. Pour butter mixture over oat mixture and stir until combined well.

In a large jelly-roll pan spread granola evenly and bake in middle of oven, stirring halfway through baking, until golden brown, about 15 minutes. Cool granola in pan on a rack and stir in dried fruits.

Cooks' note:
• Granola keeps in an airtight container at cool room temperature 2 weeks.

PHOTO ON PAGE 18

BUTTERMILK WAFFLES WITH CRISP PROSCIUTTO

Serves 2

Vegetable-oil cooking spray
1 cup all-purpose flour
1 teaspoon baking powder
¼ teaspoon baking soda
½ teaspoon salt
¾ stick unsalted butter
1 cup well-shaken buttermilk
1 large egg
4 thin slices prosciutto

Accompaniments: sour cream and pure maple syrup

Preheat oven to 250°F. Spray an unheated nonstick or well-seasoned Belgian waffle iron with cooking spray and preheat iron.

Into a large bowl sift together flour, baking powder, baking soda, and salt. Melt 5 tablespoons butter and in a small bowl whisk together with buttermilk and egg until combined. Stir butter mixture into flour mixture until smooth (batter will be thick).

Spoon batter into waffle iron, using 1 cup batter for two 4-inch-square Belgian waffles (see note, below) and spreading evenly, and cook according to manufacturer's instructions. Transfer waffles to a baking sheet and keep warm, uncovered, in middle of oven. Make more waffles in same manner (do not respray iron).

In a large heavy skillet heat remaining tablespoon butter over moderate heat until foam subsides and cook prosciutto slices until crisp and golden, about 1 minute on each side.

Serve warm waffles with prosciutto, sour cream, and maple syrup.

Cooks' note:
• We used a Belgian waffle iron, but a standard waffle iron will also work. The batter yields four 4-inch-square Belgian waffles or eight 4-inch-square standard waffles.

PHOTO ON PAGE 19

Preheat oven to 350°F.

In a shallow baking pan spread pecans evenly and toast in middle of oven until fragrant, about 8 minutes. Toss pecans in pan with 1 teaspoon butter and salt.

Increase temperature to 400°F.

Sprinkle pecans and blueberries evenly over bread mixture. Cut ½ stick butter into pieces and in a small saucepan heat with remaining ¼ cup brown sugar, stirring, until butter is melted. Drizzle butter mixture over bread and bake mixture 20 minutes, or until any liquid from blueberries is bubbling.

Make syrup while French toast is baking:

In a small saucepan cook blueberries and maple syrup over moderate heat until berries have burst, about 3 minutes. Pour syrup through a sieve into a heatproof pitcher, pressing on solids, and stir in lemon juice.

Serve French toast with syrup.

Cooks' note:
· Syrup may be made 1 day ahead and chilled, covered. Reheat before serving.

PHOTO ON PAGE 36

BAKED BLUEBERRY-PECAN FRENCH TOAST WITH BLUEBERRY SYRUP

Serves 6

You don't have to be in the kitchen at the crack of dawn to prepare this dish. The French toast is soaked overnight like bread pudding— in the morning all you need to do is add the topping and pop it in the oven. Serve it with coffee, juice, and fresh fruit for a well-rounded breakfast.

1 (24-inch) baguette
6 large eggs
3 cups whole milk
½ teaspoon freshly grated nutmeg
1 teaspoon vanilla
1 cup packed brown sugar
1 cup pecans (about 3 oz)
½ stick plus 1 teaspoon unsalted butter
¼ teaspoon salt
2 cups blueberries (about 12 oz)
For syrup
1 cup blueberries (about 6 oz)
½ cup pure maple syrup
1 tablespoon fresh lemon juice

Butter a 13- by 9-inch baking dish. Cut 20 (1-inch) slices from baguette and arrange in one layer in baking dish. In a large bowl whisk together eggs, milk, nutmeg, vanilla, and ¾ cup brown sugar and pour evenly over bread. Chill egg mixture, covered, until all liquid is absorbed by bread, at least 8 hours, and up to 1 day.

BACON, LETTUCE, AND CANTALOUPE SANDWICHES

Makes 4

12 bacon slices (about ¾ lb)
6 tablespoons mayonnaise
2 tablespoons Dijon mustard
2 teaspoons fresh lemon juice
2 teaspoons honey
½ cantaloupe
8 soft lettuce leaves such as Boston
    or Bibb
8 slices crusty bread

Preheat oven to 425°F.

In a shallow baking pan cook bacon in one layer in middle of oven, turning occasionally, until golden and crisp, 16 to 18 minutes, and transfer to paper towels.

In a small bowl whisk together mayonnaise, mustard, lemon juice, and honey until smooth.

Seed cantaloupe. Cut melon into 12 slices and discard rind. Cut out and discard lettuce ribs.

Spread mayonnaise mixture on all 8 slices of bread.

Stack lettuce, cantaloupe, and bacon on 4 of the slices and top with remaining 4 slices, gently pressing them together.

OPEN-FACED BACON AND CUCUMBER-SALAD SANDWICHES ◯

Serves 2

½ cup plain yogurt
2 large slices country-style bread
½ English cucumber
½ teaspoon minced garlic
6 bacon slices
2 teaspoons packed brown sugar

In a fine sieve set over a bowl drain yogurt 20 minutes. Lightly toast bread. Finely chop cucumber and in a bowl stir together with yogurt, garlic, and salt and pepper to taste.

In a large heavy skillet cook bacon over moderate heat, turning it, until it begins to brown and is almost crisp. Sprinkle sugar evenly over bacon and turn it. Cook bacon until golden and crisp and transfer to paper towels to drain. Divide cucumber salad between toasts and top with bacon.

TOMATO GRUYÈRE MELTS ◯

Serves 2

2 English muffins, split
1 large beefsteak tomato, cut into 4
  (¾-inch-thick) slices and seeded
1 cup coarsely grated Gruyère (4 oz)
¼ cup chopped fresh basil
2 tablespoons dry bread crumbs
2 small garlic cloves,
  minced

Preheat oven to 375°F.

Toast muffins until golden. Put 1 slice tomato on top of each muffin half and season with salt and pepper. Bake on a baking sheet in middle of oven until tomatoes are softened, 17 to 20 minutes.

Stir together cheese, basil, bread crumbs, and garlic and season with salt and pepper. Mound mixture on top of tomatoes and bake until melted, about 5 minutes.

PASTA AND GRAINS

PASTA

MINTED APRICOT COUSCOUS ○

Serves 6 (side dish)

1⅓ cups water
3 tablespoons olive oil
2 teaspoons honey
1 teaspoon ground cumin
1 cup couscous
½ English cucumber
4 fresh apricots
3 tablespoons chopped fresh mint
1 tablespoon fresh lemon juice

In a 3-quart saucepan bring water, oil, honey, and cumin to a boil and stir in couscous. Immediately remove pan from heat and let couscous stand, covered, 5 minutes. Seed cucumber and cut into ¼-inch dice. Pit apricots and cut into ¼-inch dice. Fluff couscous with a fork and stir in cucumber, apricots, mint, lemon juice, and salt and pepper to taste. Serve warm or chilled.

ISRAELI COUSCOUS WITH ROASTED BUTTERNUT SQUASH AND PRESERVED LEMON

Serves 50

When cooking in large quantities, shortcuts come in handy. Here, a U-shaped peeler with a horizontal blade (available at most supermarkets) makes peeling the squash easier. And, it's okay to pulse the parsley in a food processor rather than chop it by hand, but pat it dry with paper towels first. A "scaled back" version of this recipe (serving 6) follows.

4 to 5 preserved lemons (sources on page 252)
5 lb butternut squash, peeled and seeded
¾ to 1 cup olive oil
3 cups chopped onion
7 cups Israeli couscous or *acini di pepe* (tiny peppercorn-shaped pasta; about 3 lb) (sources on page 252)
4 (3-inch) cinnamon sticks
3 cups chopped fresh flat-leaf parsley
2 cups pine nuts, toasted
2 cups golden raisins
1 teaspoon ground cinnamon

Preheat oven to 475°F.

Halve lemons and scoop out flesh, keeping both flesh and peel. Cut enough peel into ¼-inch dice to measure 1 cup. Put lemon flesh in a sieve set over a bowl and press with back of a spoon to extract juice.

Cut enough squash into ¼-inch dice to measure about 12 cups and toss with ⅓ cup oil and salt to taste. Roast squash in single layers in batches in your largest shallow baking pan in upper third of oven 15 minutes, or until just tender.

Cook ½ of onion in 3 tablespoons oil in a 12-inch heavy skillet over moderately high heat, stirring occasionally, until just beginning to turn golden. Add to squash. Repeat with remaining onion and more oil.

Cook couscous with cinnamon sticks in an 8-quart pot of boiling salted water 10 minutes, or until just tender, and drain in a colander (do not rinse). Toss couscous with 3 tablespoons oil in a large bowl. Add squash, onion, lemon peel and juice, and remaining ingredients. Season with salt (you'll need a lot) and toss to mix well.

Cooks' note:
• Preserved lemons may be prepared and squash, onion, and couscous cooked (toss couscous with a little oil) 1 day ahead and chilled *separately* in sealable plastic bags. Bring to room temperature before combining.

PHOTO ON PAGE 56

ISRAELI COUSCOUS WITH ROASTED BUTTERNUT SQUASH AND PRESERVED LEMON

Serves 6

1 preserved lemon (sources on page 252)
1½ lb butternut squash, peeled, seeded, and cut
    into ¼-inch dice
3 tablespoons olive oil
1 large onion, chopped
1¾ cups Israeli couscous or *acini di pepe* (tiny
    peppercorn-shaped pasta; about 1 lb)
    (sources on page 252)
1 (3-inch) cinnamon stick
1 cup chopped fresh flat-leaf parsley
½ cup pine nuts, toasted
½ cup golden raisins
¼ teaspoon ground cinnamon

Preheat oven to 475°F.

Halve lemon and scoop out flesh, keeping both flesh and peel. Cut enough peel into ¼-inch dice to measure ¼ cup. Put lemon flesh in a sieve set over a bowl and press with back of a spoon to extract juice.

Toss squash with 1 tablespoon oil and salt to taste in a large shallow baking pan and spread in 1 layer. Roast in upper third of oven 15 minutes, or until squash is just tender, and transfer to a large bowl.

Cook onion in 1 tablespoon oil in a 10-inch heavy skillet over moderately high heat, stirring occasionally, until just beginning to turn golden. Add to squash.

Cook couscous with cinnamon stick in a large pot of boiling salted water 10 minutes, or until just tender, and drain in a colander (do not rinse). Add couscous to vegetables and toss with 1 tablespoon oil to coat.

Add lemon peel and juice, parsley, nuts, raisins, ground cinnamon, and salt to taste. Toss to mix well.

PHOTO ON PAGE 58

FETTUCCINE WITH SUMMER SQUASH AND ROSEMARY BUTTER ☺

Serves 4

1 lb dried *tagliatelle* or fettuccine
1 lb small zucchini (about 5)
1 lb small yellow squash (about 4)

5 tablespoons unsalted butter
1 tablespoon finely chopped fresh rosemary

Accompaniment: grated Parmigiano-Reggiano

Fill a 6-quart pasta pot three fourths full with salted water and bring to a boil for pasta.

Trim vegetables and cut into 1½- by ¼-inch sticks. In a deep 12-inch heavy skillet melt butter over moderate heat and cook vegetables with salt and pepper to taste, stirring gently, 2 minutes. Add rosemary and cook, stirring gently, until vegetables are just tender, about 2 minutes more. Remove skillet from heat.

Cook pasta in boiling water, stirring occasionally, until al dente and ladle out and reserve 1 cup pasta water. Drain pasta in a colander and add to sauce with ¼ cup reserved pasta water and salt and pepper to taste. Heat mixture over low heat, gently tossing (and adding more pasta water as needed if mixture becomes dry), until just heated through.

Serve pasta with Parmigiano-Reggiano.

WILTED MUSTARD-GREEN PASTA

Serves 4 (main course; 6 as a first course)

½ lb short pasta such as *gemelli*
1 to 2 bunches mustard greens (about 1 lb)
3 garlic cloves
2 lemons
2 tablespoons olive oil

Bring a 6-quart kettle three fourths full with salted water to a boil for pasta.

Remove and discard ribs from mustard greens. Coarsely chop greens and finely chop garlic. Finely grate zest from lemons.

Cook pasta in boiling water until al dente. While pasta is cooking, in a 12-inch nonstick skillet cook zest and garlic in oil over moderate heat, stirring, until garlic is golden and remove skillet from heat. Add greens to garlic mixture with salt and pepper to taste, tossing with tongs until greens are wilted. Reserve ½ cup pasta cooking water and drain pasta in a colander. Add hot pasta and ¼ cup reserved cooking water to greens and cook over moderately low heat, tossing until combined well. If mixture is too dry, stir in more cooking water.

GEMELLI WITH GARLIC, HERBS, AND BOCCONCINI MOZZARELLA

Serves 4

Here we call for bocconcini bite size pieces of mozzarella—but regular fresh mozzarella cut into ½-inch cubes would work just as well.

1 lb dried *gemelli* or *fusilli*
2 large garlic cloves
2 cups packed fresh basil
1 cup packed fresh flat-leaf parsley
½ lb lightly salted *bocconcini* mozzarella
   (sources on page 252)
½ teaspoon dried hot red pepper flakes
¼ cup extra-virgin olive oil
2 tablespoons red-wine vinegar, or to taste
1 cup packed small arugula leaves

Fill a 6-quart pasta pot three fourths full with salted water and bring to a boil for pasta.

Mince garlic and chop herbs. Quarter large *bocconcini* and halve smaller ones. In a bowl toss cheese with garlic, herbs, red pepper flakes, oil, and salt to taste.

Cook pasta in boiling water, stirring occasionally, until al dente and ladle out and reserve ½ cup pasta water. Drain pasta in a colander. Stir vinegar and arugula into cheese mixture and add hot pasta and ¼ cup reserved pasta water, gently tossing (and adding more pasta water as needed if mixture becomes dry) until combined well.

Cooks' note:
• When incorporating raw garlic into a dish such as this, buy the freshest garlic you can find. The cloves should be dry and tightly packed together, and they should feel firm. Old garlic may impart a bitter, strong flavor—overwhelming the other components.

WILD MUSHROOM LASAGNE

Serves 6

For mushroom filling
3 cups water
2 oz dried *porcini* mushrooms (about 1 cup)
2 lb fresh white mushrooms
2 large zucchini (about 1 lb)
1 large onion
3 garlic cloves
5 tablespoons unsalted butter
6 tablespoons Sherry
2 teaspoons chopped fresh thyme
2½ teaspoons salt
¼ teaspoon freshly ground black pepper
For sauce
1 stick unsalted butter
½ cup all-purpose flour
5 cups whole milk
4½ oz freshly grated Parmesan (about 1½ cups)
2 teaspoons Dijon mustard
1½ teaspoons salt

18 (7- by 3½-inch) sheets dry no-boil lasagne
   (about 1 lb)
½ lb freshly grated mozzarella (about 2 cups)
1½ oz freshly grated Parmesan (about ½ cup)

Make filling:

In a small saucepan bring water to a boil and remove pan from heat. Stir in *porcini* and soak 20 minutes. Lift out *porcini*, squeezing out excess liquid, and reserve soaking liquid. In a sieve rinse *porcini* to remove any grit and pat dry. Chop *porcini* and transfer to a large bowl. Simmer reserved soaking liquid until reduced to about ¼ cup. Pour liquid through a sieve lined with a dampened paper towel into bowl with *porcini*.

Quarter white mushrooms and in a food processor pulse in 3 batches until finely chopped. Cut zucchini into ¼-inch dice. Chop onion and mince garlic. In a 12-inch heavy skillet heat 1 tablespoon butter over moderate heat until foam subsides and cook one third white mushrooms with 2 tablespoons Sherry, stirring, until liquid mushrooms give off is evaporated and they begin to brown. Add mushroom mixture to *porcini*. Cook remaining mushrooms in 2 batches in butter with remaining Sherry in same manner and add to *porcini* mixture. In skillet cook zucchini in 1 tablespoon butter until tender and stir into *porcini* mixture. In skillet cook onion in remaining tablespoon butter, stirring, until softened. Stir in garlic, thyme, salt, and pepper and cook, stirring, until fragrant, about 30 seconds. Stir onion into mushroom mixture until combined.

Make sauce:

In a 3-quart heavy saucepan melt butter over moderately low heat and whisk in flour. Cook *roux*, whisking, 3 minutes and whisk in milk. Bring sauce to a boil, whisking constantly, and simmer, whisking occasionally, 3 minutes. Stir in Parmesan, mustard, and salt. Remove pan from heat and cover surface of sauce with wax paper.

Preheat oven to 375°F and butter a 13- by 9-inch (3-quart) baking dish.

Assemble lasagne:

Spread 1¼ cups sauce in baking dish and cover with 3 pasta sheets, making sure they don't touch each other. Spread one third filling over pasta sheets in dish and top with 3 more pasta sheets, gently pressing down layers to remove air pockets. Top pasta sheets with one third mozzarella. Continue layering in same manner with sauce, pasta sheets, filling, and mozzarella, ending with mozzarella (dish will be filled to rim). Spread remaining sauce over top and sprinkle with Parmesan.

On a foil-lined large baking sheet bake lasagne in middle of oven until bubbling and golden, about 45 minutes. Let lasagne stand 20 minutes.

Cooks' notes:
• Filling may be made 1 day ahead and chilled, covered.
• Sauce may be made 1 day ahead and chilled, covered. Bring sauce to room temperature before proceeding.
• Lasagne may be made 1 day ahead and chilled, covered. Bring to room temperature and reheat before serving.

PHOTO ON PAGE 28

LINGUINE WITH PARSLEY-PECAN PESTO SAUCE ◐

Serves 4 to 6

A cup or so of the linguine cooking water is the secret to a properly made pasta with pesto.

½ cup pecans
2 cups packed fresh flat-leaf parsley
¾ cup freshly grated Parmesan (about 1½ oz)
2 tablespoons fresh lemon juice
1 cup extra-virgin olive oil
1 lb linguine

Preheat oven to 350°F.

On a baking sheet toast pecans in one layer in middle of oven until fragrant and one shade darker, about 7 minutes. Cool pecans and in a blender purée with parsley, Parmesan, lemon juice, and oil.

In a 6-quart kettle bring 5 quarts salted water to a boil for linguine. Cook pasta in boiling water until al dente and ladle out and reserve 1½ cups pasta cooking water. Drain pasta in a colander and in kettle toss with pesto, 1 cup reserved pasta cooking water, and salt and pepper to taste, adding as much of remaining ½ cup pasta cooking water for desired consistency.

Cooks' note:
• Parsley-pecan pesto may be made 1 day ahead and chilled, covered.

CREAMY MACARONI WITH SAGE ◐

Serves 2

½ lb elbow macaroni
½ tablespoon unsalted butter
2 tablespoons fine dry bread crumbs
1½ teaspoons finely chopped fresh sage
½ cup *mascarpone* cheese
½ cup freshly grated Parmesan (about 1½ oz)

Fill a 4-quart kettle three fourths full with salted water and bring to a boil for macaroni. Cook macaroni in boiling water until al dente and drain in a colander.

While macaroni is cooking, in a non-stick skillet heat butter over moderate heat until foam subsides and add bread crumbs, sage, and salt and pepper to taste. Cook bread crumb mixture, stirring, until golden brown, about 3 minutes. In a large bowl stir together *mascarpone* and Parmesan. Add macaroni and salt and pepper to taste, tossing to combine.

Divide macaroni between 2 bowls and sprinkle with seasoned bread crumbs.

Macaroni and Cheese with Garlic Bread Crumbs—Plain and Chipotle 🌣+

Serves 8 adults plus 10 children as part of a buffet

We make half of this mac 'n' cheese plain, for kids, and into the other half we stir some chipotle chiles for a grown-up kick.

For bread crumbs
2 tablespoons unsalted butter
2 tablespoons olive oil
2 large garlic cloves, finely chopped
2 cups coarse fresh bread crumbs

2½ to 3 tablespoons chopped *chipotle* chiles
   in *adobo* (sources on page 252)
½ stick unsalted butter
½ cup all-purpose flour
3 cups whole milk
2 cups heavy cream
1 tablespoon dry mustard
1 lb macaroni
2 lb extra-sharp Cheddar (preferably white), grated

Make bread crumbs:

Heat butter and oil in a 10-inch heavy skillet over moderate heat until foam subsides, then cook garlic and bread crumbs, stirring, until crumbs are golden. Transfer to paper towels to drain and season with salt.

Make macaroni:

Preheat oven to 350°F. Chop *chipotles*.

Melt butter in a 3- to 4-quart saucepan over moderate heat, then add flour and cook, whisking, 1 minute. Gradually whisk in milk, cream, and mustard and simmer, whisking occasionally, 3 minutes.

Cook macaroni in a 6- to 7-quart pot of boiling salted water until just tender. Drain in a colander and transfer to a large bowl. Stir in sauce, cheese, and salt to taste.

Fill a 1½-quart shallow casserole with half of macaroni mixture. Stir *chipotles* into remaining macaroni. Spoon into another 1½-quart shallow casserole and sprinkle both with bread crumbs. Bake casseroles in middle of oven 30 minutes, or until bubbly.

Cooks' note:
• Macaroni and cheese may be made 2 days ahead, put into casseroles, cooled completely, and chilled, covered. Do not add bread crumbs until ready to bake.

PHOTO ON PAGE 70

Bean-Thread Noodles with Beef and Asian Pear 🌣

Serves 4

¼ lb bean-thread noodles (also known as
   cellophane noodles)
4 garlic cloves, minced
⅓ cup soy sauce
2 tablespoons sugar
1 tablespoon Asian sesame oil
1 teaspoon dried hot red pepper flakes
½ cup plus 1 teaspoon rice vinegar
   (not seasoned)
1 lb filet mignon, cut into ¼-inch-thick
   julienne strips
2 (14½-oz) cans beef broth
¼ cup water
1 Asian pear, cut into julienne strips
2 scallions (green parts only), thinly sliced

Soak noodles in a bowl of cold water until pliable, about 15 minutes, and drain. Cut into 2-inch lengths.

While noodles are soaking, stir together garlic, soy sauce, sugar, oil, pepper flakes, and ½ cup vinegar. Add beef and marinate at room temperature, stirring occasionally, 15 minutes. Bring broth and water to a boil. Add beef and marinade and cook 2 minutes. Stir in noodles and cook until just tender, about 2 minutes.

Toss pear and scallions with remaining teaspoon vinegar. Spoon noodles and broth into bowls and top with pear and scallions.

ORZO WITH FETA AND CHERRY TOMATOES ◑

Serves 2

½ lb *orzo* (rice-shaped pasta; about 1 cup)
1½ tablespoons olive oil
⅓ cup pine nuts
1 small garlic clove
½ cup packed fresh flat-leaf parsley
6 oz cherry tomatoes (about ½ pint)
¼ lb feta
1½ tablespoons red-wine vinegar

Fill a 4-quart pasta pot three fourths full with salted water and bring to a boil for *orzo*.

In a small heavy skillet heat ½ tablespoon oil over moderate heat until hot but not smoking and sauté pine nuts with salt to taste, stirring frequently, until golden, about 2 minutes. Transfer nuts to paper towels to drain and cool.

Mince garlic and chop parsley. Quarter tomatoes and coarsely crumble feta. In a large bowl whisk together garlic, parsley, vinegar, remaining tablespoon oil, and salt and pepper to taste. Add tomatoes and feta and gently toss to combine.

Cook *orzo* in boiling water, stirring occasionally, until al dente. In a large sieve drain *orzo* and rinse slightly until just warm. Drain *orzo* well and add to tomato mixture, tossing until just combined.

Serve *orzo* topped with nuts.

PAPPARDELLE IN LEMON CREAM SAUCE WITH ASPARAGUS AND SMOKED SALMON ◑

Serves 4

We found this pasta just as delicious without the salmon.

1 lb asparagus
2 large shallots
2 lemons
¼ lb sliced smoked salmon (optional)
1 lb dried *pappardelle* or fettuccine
3 tablespoons unsalted butter
¾ cup heavy cream

Trim asparagus and diagonally cut into ¼-inch-thick slices. Finely chop shallots. Finely grate enough lemon zest to measure 1½ teaspoons and squeeze enough juice to measure 3 tablespoons. Cut smoked salmon into 2- by ½-inch strips.

Fill a 6-quart pasta pot three fourths full with salted water and bring to a boil for asparagus and pasta. Have ready a bowl of ice and cold water.

Cook asparagus in boiling water until crisp-tender, about 3 minutes, and with a slotted spoon transfer to ice water to stop cooking. Reserve water in pot over low heat, covered. Drain asparagus and set aside some asparagus tips for garnish.

In a deep 12-inch heavy skillet cook shallots in butter with salt and pepper to taste over moderately low heat, stirring, until softened, about 5 minutes. Stir in cream and zest and simmer, stirring occasionally, until slightly thickened, about 10 minutes. Stir in 2 tablespoons lemon juice and remove skillet from heat. Return water in pot to a boil. Cook pasta in boiling water, stirring occasionally, until al dente and ladle out and reserve 1 cup pasta water. Drain pasta in a colander and add to sauce with asparagus, ½ cup pasta water, three fourths salmon, remaining tablespoon lemon juice, and salt and pepper to taste. Heat mixture over low heat, gently tossing (and adding more remaining pasta water as needed if mixture becomes dry), until just heated through.

Serve pasta garnished with reserved asparagus tips and remaining salmon.

PHOTO ON PAGE 84

PENNE WITH TUNA, BASIL, AND LEMON ◑

Serves 2

½ lb *penne*
1 garlic clove
1 lemon
¼ cup packed fresh basil
1 (6-oz) can tuna in olive oil (not drained)

Bring a 4-quart pasta pot three fourths full with salted water to a boil for *penne*. Mince garlic. Finely grate enough lemon zest to measure 1 tablespoon and squeeze 1 teaspoon juice. Cut basil into thin strips. In a large bowl toss together garlic, zest, juice, basil, and tuna with oil from can.

Boil *penne* until al dente and drain. Add *penne* to bowl and toss with salt and pepper to taste.

RATATOUILLE WITH PENNE

Serves 6

2 eggplants (1½ lb), cut into ½-inch cubes
4 onions, chopped
½ cup olive oil
Kosher salt to taste
4 yellow squash (1½ lb), cut into ½-inch cubes
2 large red bell peppers, cut into ½-inch cubes
8 plum tomatoes, peeled (see note, below),
   seeded, and chopped
7 garlic cloves, minced
1 teaspoon chopped fresh thyme
1½ lb *penne rigate* (with ridges)
½ cup finely chopped fresh flat-leaf parsley
¼ cup finely chopped fresh basil

Accompaniment: grated Parmigiano-Reggiano

Preheat oven to 450°F.

Stir together eggplants, onions, ¼ cup oil, and kosher salt in a large roasting pan, then roast mixture in middle of oven, stirring occasionally, 15 minutes. Stir in squash, bell peppers, 2 tablespoons oil, and more kosher salt and roast mixture, stirring occasionally, until bell peppers are tender, 25 to 30 minutes.

While vegetables are roasting, simmer tomatoes, garlic, thyme, remaining 2 tablespoons oil, and kosher salt in a heavy saucepan, stirring occasionally, until thickened, 12 to 15 minutes. Stir tomatoes into roasted vegetables and season *ratatouille*.

Cook *penne rigate* in a 6-quart pot of boiling salted water until al dente and drain. While pasta is cooking, stir parsley and basil into *ratatouille* and season.

Toss *penne rigate* with ⅓ of *ratatouille* and serve topped with remainder.

Cooks' notes:
• To peel a tomato, first cut an X in the end opposite the stem and immerse in boiling water (10 seconds). Transfer it to ice water and then peel.
• *Ratatouille* may be made 2 days ahead and chilled, covered. Reheat before using in recipe.

PHOTO ON PAGE 61

ROTINI WITH FRESH TOMATO AND THYME ◯

Serves 2

½ lb dried *rotini* or other spiral pasta
3 small tomatoes
2 garlic cloves
1½ tablespoons finely chopped fresh thyme
1 to 2 tablespoons balsamic vinegar
3 tablespoons extra-virgin olive oil
½ cup crumbled *ricotta salata* or feta

Fill a 4-quart pasta pot three fourths full with salted water and bring to a boil for *rotini*. Coarsely chop tomatoes and mince garlic. In a large bowl toss together tomatoes, garlic, thyme, vinegar, oil, and salt and pepper to taste. Marinate tomatoes 20 minutes.

Cook *rotini* in boiling water until al dente and drain well in a colander. Add pasta to tomatoes and toss. Serve pasta sprinkled with *ricotta salata*.

GRAINS

PECAN BULGUR SALAD ◯

Serves 2

⅓ cup medium or coarse bulgur
   (sources on page 252)
1½ teaspoons salt
2 cups boiling-hot water
½ cup pecans
1 small tomato
¼ English cucumber
2 tablespoons fresh lemon juice
1 teaspoon honey
½ teaspoon cinnamon
½ teaspoon ground cumin
½ teaspoon cayenne, or to taste
¼ teaspoon freshly ground black pepper
3 tablespoons olive oil
2 tablespoons chopped fresh dill
1 cup loosely packed salad greens
   such as *frisée*

In a bowl combine bulgur, 1 teaspoon salt, and water. Let bulgur soak, uncovered, until softened, 20 to 25 minutes.

While bulgur is soaking, in a dry small heavy skillet toast pecans over moderately low heat, shaking skillet frequently, until pecans are a shade darker, 4 to 5 minutes. Cool pecans and chop. Seed tomato and chop. Chop cucumber.

In a large bowl whisk together lemon juice, honey, spices, pepper, remaining ½ teaspoon salt, and oil until emulsified. Drain bulgur in a sieve and press out any excess water. Add bulgur, tomato, cucumber, pecans, and dill to dressing and toss well. Divide salad greens between 2 plates and top with bulgur.

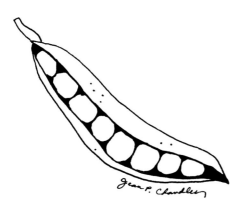

Jean P. Chandler

FOOLPROOF LONG-GRAIN RICE ◒

Makes about 4½ cups

3 cups water
1½ cups long-grain rice (not converted)
1¼ teaspoons salt

In a 2½- to 3-quart heavy saucepan combine all ingredients and boil, uncovered, until steam holes appear in rice and grains on surface appear dry, about 8 minutes. Cover pan and cook rice over very low heat 15 minutes more. Remove pan from heat and let rice stand, covered, 5 minutes.

Fluff rice with a fork before serving.

BASMATI RICE AND MUSTARD-SEED PILAF ◒

Serves 4

2 shallots
1 teaspoon vegetable oil
2 teaspoons mustard seeds
⅔ cup white *basmati* rice
1 cup water
½ teaspoon salt

Thinly slice shallots and in a 2-quart heavy saucepan cook in oil over moderate heat, stirring occasionally, until golden. Stir in mustard seeds and cook until they begin to pop. Add rice and cook, stirring, 1 minute. Add water and salt and bring to a boil. Cook pilaf, covered, over low heat until rice is tender and water is absorbed, about 25 minutes. Fluff rice with a fork.

🍃 each serving about 125 calories
and 2 grams fat

PHOTO ON PAGE 81

FRIED RICE WITH CILANTRO AND PEAS ◒

Serves 4 to 6

This recipe is a super way to use up leftover white rice from Chinese takeout—or substitute long-grain rice cooked as directed (recipe opposite).

1 cup fresh cilantro
4 scallions
2 teaspoons cumin seeds
1 tablespoon vegetable oil
4 cups chilled cooked white rice
1 tablespoon seasoned rice vinegar
1 tablespoon soy sauce (preferably Kikkoman)
1 cup frozen peas

Chop cilantro and thinly slice scallions. In a large nonstick skillet cook cumin seeds in oil over moderately high heat, stirring, until fragrant, about 1 minute. Add rice and fry, stirring occasionally, until heated through, about 3 minutes. Add vinegar and soy sauce, stirring to coat rice, and stir-fry until liquid is evaporated. Stir in cilantro, scallions, and peas and stir-fry until heated through, about 2 minutes, seasoning with salt if desired.

SAGE, ONION, AND WILD-RICE RISOTTO CAKES

Serves 8 to 10 (main course)
(makes about 32 cakes)

For wild-rice risotto
4 cups water
½ teaspoon salt
½ cup wild rice
5 to 6 cups light vegetable stock
    (page 96) or broth
1 tablespoon unsalted butter
2 tablespoons olive oil
¼ cup thinly sliced fresh sage
3 yellow onions, finely chopped (3 cups)
3 large celery ribs, finely chopped
    (1 cup)
2½ cups Arborio rice (1 lb)
½ cup dry Marsala wine
1 tablespoon chopped fresh thyme
Freshly ground black pepper
¾ cup finely grated fresh Parmesan
½ cup chopped fresh parsley

3 large eggs, separated
About ½ cup olive oil

Make wild-rice risotto:
Bring water with salt to a boil in a heavy saucepan, then simmer wild rice, covered, until tender, about 45 minutes. Remove from heat and let rice stand in cooking liquid, uncovered, 30 minutes. Drain rice in a sieve set over a saucepan and reserve rice. Add vegetable stock to cooking liquid and bring to a simmer. Keep liquid hot, covered, over low heat.

Heat butter and oil in a 6- to 8-quart heavy pot over moderately high heat until hot but not smoking, then sauté sage, stirring, 1 minute. Add onions and sauté, stirring, until softened. Stir in celery with salt to taste and sauté, stirring, until onions begin to turn golden brown, about 7 minutes.

Stir in Arborio rice and cook over moderate heat, stirring constantly, 2 minutes. Add wine, thyme, and pepper to taste and cook, stirring constantly, until wine is absorbed. Stir in 1 cup hot broth and simmer, stirring frequently, until broth is absorbed. Continue adding broth, 1 cup at a time, and simmering, stirring frequently and letting each addition be absorbed before adding

the next, until rice is tender but still al dente and creamy-looking and liquid is absorbed, 20 to 22 minutes. Toward end of cooking, stir in wild rice.

Remove pot from heat and stir in Parmesan, parsley, and salt and pepper to taste. Cool risotto and chill, covered, at least 4 hours and up to 12. Bring risotto to room temperature before proceeding with recipe.

Make risotto cakes:
Lightly beat yolks and stir into risotto. Beat whites and a pinch of salt with an electric mixer until they just hold stiff peaks. Stir half of whites into risotto to lighten slightly and fold in remaining whites. Let batter stand at room temperature 15 minutes before proceeding.

Heat 1 tablespoon oil in a 12-inch nonstick skillet over moderate heat until hot but not smoking. Scoop 4 (rounded ¼-cup) mounds of batter into skillet, flattening with back of a spoon to form cakes 3 inches across by ½ inch thick. Cook cakes until golden brown on underside (this is critical to prevent cakes from breaking when turning), adjusting heat if browning too quickly, 5 minutes. Carefully turn cakes over with a metal spatula and cook until golden brown on underside, 3 to 4 minutes. Transfer as browned to a large shallow baking pan and arrange in one layer. Make more cakes in same manner, wiping skillet clean with paper towels between batches and adding more oil as necessary.

Preheat oven to 450°F.

Just before serving, bake risotto cakes until sizzling, about 6 minutes. Serve immediately.

PHOTO ON PAGE 64

PERSIAN RICE WITH GOLDEN CRUST

Serves 4 to 6 (side dish)
Tah-dig is the Persian word for the crunchy layer of rice that forms on the bottom of the pan. We think it tastes fantastic.

2 quarts water
2 tablespoons salt
1½ cups long-grain rice (not converted; preferably
    basmati or *jasmine*)
3 tablespoons unsalted butter

In a large saucepan bring water with salt to a boil. Add rice and boil 10 minutes. In a colander drain rice and rinse under warm water.

In a 2- to 3-quart nonstick saucepan melt butter.

Spoon rice over butter and cover pan with a kitchen towel and a heavy lid. Fold edges of towel up over lid and cook rice over moderately low heat until tender and a crust forms on bottom, 30 to 35 minutes.

Spoon loose rice onto a platter and dip bottom of pan in a large bowl of cold water 30 seconds to loosen *tah-dig*. Remove *tah-dig* and serve over rice.

PINE NUT AND BASIL RICE ☉

Serves 2

¼ cup pine nuts
2 teaspoons olive oil
⅓ cup long-grain white rice
⅔ cup water
¼ cup packed fresh basil

In a 1½-quart heavy saucepan cook nuts in oil over moderate heat, stirring occasionally, until golden, about 2 minutes. With a slotted spoon transfer nuts to a bowl. Add rice to oil in pan and cook over moderately low heat, stirring, 1 minute. Add water and bring to a boil. Cover rice and cook over very low heat until water is absorbed and rice is tender, about 18 minutes. Remove pan from heat and let rice stand, undisturbed, 5 minutes.

Finely chop basil. Fluff rice with a fork and stir in basil, pine nuts, and salt and pepper to taste.

SQUID RISOTTO

Serves 4

1 lb cleaned squid
1 tablespoon olive oil
2 teaspoons chopped fresh oregano, or to taste
½ teaspoon chopped fresh rosemary
Pinch of dried hot red pepper flakes
4 garlic cloves, minced

5½ cups fish stock, or 2 (8-oz) bottles
    clam juice mixed with 3½ cups water
1¼ cups Arborio rice (8 oz)
1 cup dry white wine
¾ cup fresh flat-leaf parsley
1 teaspoon fresh lemon juice, or to taste

Accompaniment: lemon wedges

Pat squid dry, then cut bodies lengthwise into ¼-inch-wide strips and quarter tentacles lengthwise. Season with salt and pepper.

Heat 1 teaspoon oil in a 12-inch nonstick skillet over high heat until hot but not smoking, then cook oregano, rosemary, red pepper flakes, and 1 teaspoon garlic, stirring, until fragrant, about 30 seconds. Add squid strips and tentacles and sauté, stirring constantly, until opaque and curled, about 1 minute. (Do not overcook, or squid will toughen.) Transfer to a sieve set over a bowl to catch juices squid releases.

Combine squid juices from bowl with fish stock in a saucepan and bring to a simmer. Season with salt and keep at a bare simmer.

Heat remaining 2 teaspoons oil in a large heavy saucepan over moderate heat until hot but not smoking, then cook remaining garlic, stirring frequently, until pale golden, 2 to 3 minutes. Stir in rice and cook, stirring constantly, until rice is translucent, 4 to 5 minutes. Add wine and cook, stirring constantly, until absorbed. Stir in 1 cup simmering broth mixture and cook at a strong simmer, stirring frequently, until broth is absorbed. Continue cooking at a strong simmer and adding broth, ½ cup at a time, stirring frequently and letting each addition be absorbed before adding the next, until rice is tender but still al dente and creamy looking, 18 to 20 minutes total. (There may be broth left over.)

Stir in squid and parsley and cook just until heated through, about 1 minute. Add lemon juice and salt and pepper to taste.

☞ each serving about 386 calories and 4 grams fat

VEGETABLES AND BEANS

BRAISED BABY ARTICHOKES AND SHALLOTS

Serves 6

½ lb shallots
3 lb baby artichokes (20 to 30)
2 tablespoons olive oil
1 tablespoon unsalted butter
½ cup chicken broth
½ cup dry white wine
1 tablespoon chopped fresh flat-leaf parsley

Halve shallots lengthwise. Pull off tough outer leaves (about 5 layers) from artichokes to resemble tight rose-buds. Cut off top third of each artichoke and discard. Trim stem ends and halve artichokes through stems.

In a large heavy skillet heat oil and butter over moderately high heat until hot but not smoking and sauté artichokes and shallots, stirring occasionally, until golden. Add broth and simmer, covered, 15 minutes, or until artichokes are almost tender. Add wine and boil, uncovered, until liquid is evaporated.

Toss braised vegetables with parsley and season with salt and pepper.

PHOTO ON PAGE 35

GREEN BEANS WITH CRUSHED ALMONDS ☺

Serves 2

½ lb green beans, trimmed
1½ tablespoons unsalted butter
1 garlic clove, minced
¼ cup blanched whole almonds, finely ground

Cook beans in a 3-quart saucepan of boiling salted water until crisp-tender, about 4 minutes, and drain.

Melt butter in a large nonstick skillet over moderate heat, then cook garlic, stirring, until it just begins to turn golden, about 1 minute. Add almonds and cook, stirring, until they begin to color slightly, about 2 minutes. Add beans and cook, stirring, until tender and heated through, about 2 minutes. Season with salt and pepper.

GREEN BEANS IN SALTED WATER ☺

Serves 4

Salt is a magnificent flavor enhancer. This simple recipe demonstrates how salt—and little else—can bring out the best in beans.

1 lb green beans
8 cups water
3½ tablespoons salt
1 teaspoon unsalted butter

Trim beans and cut into 1-inch pieces. In a 3-quart saucepan bring water with salt to a boil and simmer beans until just tender, about 5 minutes. Drain beans in a colander and return to pan. Toss beans with butter and pepper to taste.

GREEN BEANS, TOASTED PECANS, AND BLUE CHEESE ☺

Serves 2 (side dish)

¼ teaspoon Dijon mustard
1 teaspoon cider vinegar
2 teaspoons finely chopped shallot
1 tablespoon olive oil
½ cup pecans
¾ lb green beans
1½ oz blue cheese such as Maytag

In a large bowl whisk together mustard, vinegar, shallot, and ½ tablespoon oil to make dressing.

In a small heavy skillet heat remaining ½ tablespoon

oil over moderately high heat until hot but not smoking and sauté pecans with salt to taste, stirring frequently, until a shade darker, about 1 minute. Transfer nuts to paper towels to drain and cool. Coarsely chop nuts.

Have ready a bowl of ice and cold water. In a large saucepan of boiling salted water blanch beans until just tender, about 3 minutes, and drain in a colander. Transfer beans to ice water, stirring until just cool. Drain beans well and add to dressing. Crumble blue cheese over beans and gently toss with half of nuts and salt and pepper to taste. Serve beans at room temperature topped with nuts.

SWEET-GARLIC FRENCHED GREEN BEANS ○+

Serves 6

1 large head garlic
1½ lb green beans, trimmed
3 tablespoons olive oil
3 tablespoons water

Preheat oven to 400°F.

Tightly wrap garlic in foil and bake until very tender, about 1 hour. Cool garlic and halve head horizontally. Squeeze enough garlic from cloves to measure 2 tablespoons. Halve beans lengthwise with a thin sharp knife. Cook in boiling salted water until crisp-tender, 6 to 8 minutes, and drain in a colander.

Heat oil in a large heavy skillet over moderately high heat and cook garlic with water, stirring, until a smooth paste. Add beans and cook, stirring to coat, 1 minute. Season with salt and pepper.

PHOTO ON PAGE 74

ROASTED BEETS WITH GARLIC-BEET PURÉE

Serves 4

6 large garlic cloves, unpeeled
4 medium beets (about 1 lb)
½ lb boiling potatoes
1½ tablespoons balsamic vinegar
1 tablespoon whole milk
¼ teaspoon fresh lemon juice
4 to 6 tablespoons water

Preheat oven to 450°F.

Wrap garlic cloves together tightly in foil. Trim beet stems to 1 inch if necessary and scrub beets. Wrap beets together tightly in foil. Roast garlic and beets in middle of oven until garlic is soft, about 30 minutes. Remove garlic from oven and continue to roast beets until very tender, about 45 minutes more. In a saucepan cover potatoes with cold salted water and simmer until tender, about 30 minutes. Drain and keep warm, covered.

Unwrap garlic and peel skin from cloves, transferring garlic to a food processor. Unwrap beets carefully and, when cool enough to handle, slip off skins and stems and discard. Reserve 1 beet. Quarter remaining beets and add to processor. Peel and halve potatoes. Add potatoes to processor with vinegar and milk and pulse until mixture is just smooth (do not over-process or potatoes will become gluey).

Transfer purée to cleaned saucepan and stir in lemon juice, 2 tablespoons water, and salt and pepper to taste. Heat purée over low heat, stirring, until hot. Stir in 2 tablespoons water and add enough remaining water to reach desired consistency. Cut reserved beet into 8 wedges and serve with purée.

☞ each serving about 98 calories and
less than 1 gram fat

PHOTO ON PAGE 79

STIR-FRIED BOK CHOY ○

Serves 2

1 head bok choy
2 tablespoons water
1½ teaspoons soy sauce (preferably Kikkoman)
1½ teaspoons oyster sauce
1 tablespoon vegetable oil
½ teaspoon salt
1 tablespoon unsalted butter

Trim bok choy and cut crosswise into ¼-inch-thick slices. In a bowl stir together water and soy and oyster sauces. In a 10- to 12-inch heavy skillet heat oil over moderately high heat until hot but not smoking and stir-fry bok choy with salt 2 minutes. Add soy mixture and butter and stir-fry until bok choy is crisp-tender, 1 to 2 minutes.

STEAMED BROCCOLI WITH OLIVE OIL, GARLIC, AND LEMON ☉

Serves 2

1 small bunch broccoli (about ¾ lb)
1 garlic clove
1½ tablespoons olive oil
1½ teaspoons fresh lemon juice

Discard tough lower third of broccoli stem. Peel remaining stem and cut crosswise into ½-inch-thick slices. Cut broccoli into 2-inch florets. In a steamer set over boiling water steam broccoli, covered, until crisp-tender, 4 to 5 minutes.

While broccoli is steaming, finely chop garlic and in a small skillet combine with oil, lemon juice, and salt and pepper to taste. Heat garlic mixture over moderate heat until garlic is fragrant. In a bowl toss broccoli with garlic mixture.

STEAMED BROCCOLI ☉

Serves 2

½ lb broccoli

Cut broccoli into very small florets. In a steamer steam broccoli over boiling water, covered, until crisp-tender, about 1½ minutes. Season with salt and pepper.

BUTTERED BRUSSELS SPROUTS ☉

Serves 8

2 lb Brussels sprouts, trimmed
3 tablespoons unsalted butter, softened

Cook Brussels sprouts in a large pot of boiling salted water until just tender, 8 to 10 minutes. Drain in a colander and toss with butter and salt and pepper to taste.

Cooks' note:
• To vary this recipe you can add vacuum-packed chestnuts sautéed in butter, toasted pine nuts, or finely chopped red onion.

PHOTO ON PAGE 68

HONEY MUSTARD CARROTS ☉

Serves 2

4 medium carrots
1 tablespoon Dijon mustard
1 teaspoon honey
½ teaspoon fresh lemon juice

Cut carrots into ¼-inch-thick matchsticks and in a steamer steam over boiling water, covered, until tender, 4 to 5 minutes. Stir together remaining ingredients and salt and pepper to taste and toss with hot carrots.

COLLARD GREENS AND TURNIPS WITH HAM HOCK AND PEPPER VINEGAR

Serves 8 to 10

An added bonus to cooking up a mess o' greens is the resultant pot liquor—the delicious, nutritious broth left in the bottom of the cooking pot or serving dish. It is usually served as an accompaniment to that last piece of corn bread.

6 cups water
1 large ham hock (about 1¼ lb)
3 lb collard greens
1½ lb turnips

Accompaniment: pepper vinegar (recipe follows)

In a 6-quart kettle bring water with ham hock to a boil (water will not cover hock) and simmer, covered, turning hock over halfway through cooking, 1 hour.

While hock is simmering, remove and discard stems and center ribs of collard greens and cut leaves into 1-inch pieces. Stir collards into hock mixture and simmer, partially covered, until almost tender, about 45 minutes. Cut turnips into ½-inch cubes. Stir turnips into collards and simmer, partially covered, until turnips are tender, 12 to 15 minutes. Season collard and turnip mixture with salt and pepper.

Serve collards and turnips with pepper vinegar.

Cooks' note:
• Collards and turnips may be cooked 8 hours ahead and cooled completely before being chilled, covered. Reheat before serving.

PHOTO ON PAGE 16

PEPPER VINEGAR ⊙+

Makes about 1½ cups

Pepper vinegar—the aromatic, piquant liquid from chiles that have been pickled for at least 3 weeks—is a household staple in many parts of the South. It is used in the kitchen and on the table to liven up stews and vegetable dishes. Store-bought pepper vinegar is available in southern supermarkets and West Indian markets and by mail order from The Lee Bros. Boiled Peanuts Catalogue, tel. (843) 720-8890.

6 oz fresh red or green hot chiles such as cayenne, *serrano*, or Thai
1½ cups distilled white vinegar
¼ teaspoon salt
Pinch of ground cayenne

In a sterilized 1-pint Mason-type jar (sterilizing procedure follows) pack hot chiles. In a small bowl stir together remaining ingredients until salt is dissolved and pour over chiles. Seal jar with lid. Let pepper vinegar stand at cool room temperature at least 3 weeks.

Cooks' note:
• Pepper vinegar keeps up to 6 months at cool room temperature.

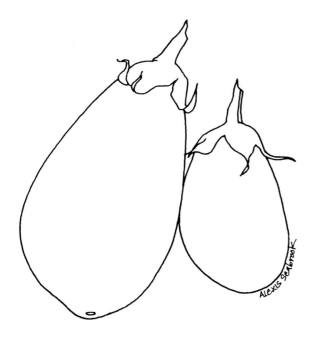

TO STERILIZE JARS FOR PICKLING ⊙

Wash jars in hot suds and rinse in scalding water. Put jars and lids in a kettle and cover completely with hot water. Bring water to a boil, covered, and boil jars 15 minutes from the time that steam emerges from kettle. Turn off heat and let jars stand in hot water. Just before they are to be filled, invert jars onto a kitchen towel to dry. (Jars should be filled while still hot.)

BROILED EGGPLANT WITH CILANTRO VINAIGRETTE

Serves 50

This recipe serves a crowd. It is followed by an adjusted recipe (on page 158) for a more intimate gathering.

25 small (4-oz) eggplants
1¾ cups olive oil
2 teaspoons cumin seeds, toasted
1 cup fresh cilantro
1 cup fresh flat-leaf parsley
4 garlic cloves
1 teaspoon salt
½ teaspoon cayenne
¾ cup fresh lemon juice

Preheat broiler.
Halve eggplants lengthwise. Brush cut sides with ¼ cup oil and season with salt. Arrange as many eggplants, cut sides up, as will fit in 1 layer on rack of a broiler pan and broil 2 to 3 inches from heat until browned, about 5 minutes. Turn oven setting to 450°F and move pan to middle of oven. Roast until tender when pierced with a fork, about 12 minutes. Repeat with remaining eggplants.
Blend remaining 1½ cups oil and remaining ingredients in a blender until emulsified.
Serve eggplants at room temperature, drizzled with vinaigrette.

Cooks' notes:
• Eggplants may be cooked 1 day ahead and chilled, covered.
• You can make the vinaigrette without lemon juice 8 hours ahead (with lemon juice, only 1 hour ahead) and chill it, covered.

PHOTO ON PAGE 56

BROILED EGGPLANT WITH CILANTRO VINAIGRETTE ◔

Serves 6

6 small eggplants (4 oz each)
8 tablespoons olive oil
½ teaspoon cumin seeds, toasted
¼ cup fresh cilantro
¼ cup fresh flat-leaf parsley
1 garlic clove
¼ teaspoon salt
⅛ teaspoon cayenne
3 tablespoons fresh lemon juice

Preheat broiler.

Halve eggplants lengthwise. Brush cut sides with 2 tablespoons oil and season with salt. Broil, cut sides up, on rack of a broiler pan 2 to 3 inches from heat until browned, about 5 minutes. Turn oven setting to 450°F and move pan to middle of oven. Roast until tender when pierced with a fork, about 12 minutes.

Blend remaining 6 tablespoons oil and remaining ingredients in a blender until emulsified. Serve eggplants at room temperature with vinaigrette.

PHOTO ON PAGE 58

CARROTS VICHY ◔

Serves 4

In France many swear by cooking these carrots in the pure water of Vichy, said to best bring out the vegetable's delicate flavor, but in truth the dish is delicious made with good water of any origin.

1 lb carrots
2 tablespoons unsalted butter
¼ cup water
1 teaspoon sugar

Diagonally cut carrots into ⅛-inch-thick slices. In a heavy saucepan combine butter, carrots, water, and sugar and cook, covered, over low heat, stirring occasionally, until tender, about 15 minutes.

SAUTÉED ESCAROLE WITH CURRANTS AND CAPERS ◔

Serves 4

1 tablespoon pine nuts
2 heads escarole (about 2 lb total)
4 garlic cloves
2 tablespoons olive oil
2 tablespoons dried currants
1 tablespoon chopped drained capers

Preheat oven to 350°F.

In a shallow baking pan toast nuts in middle of oven until golden, about 5 minutes. Cut escarole into 1-inch pieces and chop garlic.

In a 12-inch nonstick skillet sauté garlic in oil over moderately high heat, stirring, until fragrant, about 1 minute. Add escarole in 3 batches, tossing each batch with tongs until wilted before adding next. Stir in currants, capers, and salt and pepper to taste and cook, covered, over moderately low heat until escarole is tender, about 3 minutes. Remove lid and cook over moderately high heat until most liquid is evaporated, about 2 minutes more. Stir in nuts.

PARMESAN-STUFFED PORTABELLA MUSHROOMS ◔

Serves 2 (side dish)

¼ cup coarse fresh bread crumbs
¾ oz freshly grated Parmesan (about ¼ cup)
1 tablespoon chopped fresh flat-leaf parsley
2 portabella mushrooms (each about 4 inches in
    diameter)
1 tablespoon extra-virgin olive oil

Preheat broiler.

Stir together bread crumbs, Parmesan, parsley, and salt and pepper to taste. Cut off and discard mushroom stems. Put mushrooms, gill sides down, on a baking sheet and brush tops with ½ tablespoon oil. Broil mushrooms 2 to 3 inches from heat until golden, about 3 minutes. Turn mushrooms over and season with salt and pepper. Broil 3 minutes more. Mound bread-crumb mixture onto mushroom centers and drizzle with remaining ½ tablespoon oil. Broil stuffed mushrooms until stuffing is golden brown, 1 to 2 minutes.

STUFFED PORTABELLA MUSHROOMS

Serves 2 (serves 4 as a side dish)

3 tablespoons olive oil
1 cup coarse fresh bread crumbs
1 medium onion, finely chopped
1 tablespoon minced garlic
4 medium portabella mushrooms (¾ lb),
   stems finely chopped
3 canned plum tomatoes, chopped
½ teaspoon chopped fresh sage
½ cup dry white wine

Heat 1 tablespoon oil in a large nonstick skillet over moderate heat until hot but not smoking and lightly brown bread crumbs, stirring occasionally. Transfer to a large bowl.

Heat 1 tablespoon oil in skillet over moderately high heat until hot but not smoking and sauté onion, stirring, until tender. Add garlic and sauté, stirring, 1 minute. Add chopped mushroom stems and salt and pepper to taste and sauté, stirring, until tender, about 3 minutes. Add tomatoes, sage, and ¼ cup wine and cook, stirring, until almost all of liquid is evaporated. Set aside half of bread crumbs and stir mushroom mixture into remaining bread crumbs.

Heat remaining tablespoon oil over moderately low heat until hot but not smoking and cook mushroom caps, gill sides down, covered, 5 minutes. Turn mushroom caps over and add remaining ¼ cup wine and salt and pepper to taste. Cook, covered, until just tender but still juicy and mound filling in caps. Heat mushrooms until hot, about 3 minutes.

Serve sprinkled with remaining bread crumbs.

SAUTÉED MUSHROOMS

Serves 2

1 tablespoon fresh lemon juice
½ tablespoon soy sauce
1 teaspoon sugar
2 tablespoons olive oil
10 oz mushrooms, quartered
1 tablespoon unsalted butter
1 garlic clove, chopped

Stir together lemon juice, soy sauce, and sugar. Heat a 12-inch heavy skillet over moderately high heat until very hot. Add oil, then sauté mushrooms, stirring, until golden brown, about 5 minutes. Add butter and garlic and sauté, stirring, until butter is absorbed. Add lemon mixture to mushrooms, stirring until sauce is absorbed.

SMOKED PORTABELLA MUSHROOMS AND TOMATOES

Makes 6 smoked portabellas and ¾ pound tomatoes

These mushrooms and tomatoes make great side dishes and add zing to sandwiches, salads, and risottos. But we think they're best tossed with pasta and a little extra-virgin olive oil and chopped flat-leaf parsley or basil.

6 medium portabella mushrooms (about 1½ lb total)
1 lb plum tomatoes

Special equipment and kitchen supplies: stove-top
   smoker/cooker (sources on page 252) and 3
   tablespoons fine wood chips such as hickory
   or oak (sources on page 252)

Cut out and discard mushroom stems and halve tomatoes lengthwise. Arrange mushrooms, gill sides down, and tomatoes, cut sides up, on rack of smoker.

Line drip tray of smoker with foil and spread wood chips evenly over center of smoker pan. Put tray on top of chips and put rack in tray. Put smoker on stove, using 2 burners, and heat, uncovered, over moderate heat until chips begin to smolder. Smoke mushrooms and tomatoes, covered, over moderate heat 30 minutes. Remove smoker from heat. Let mushrooms and tomatoes stand, covered, 30 minutes.

ROASTED WILD MUSHROOMS IN RED-WINE REDUCTION

Serves 8 to 10 (main course)

If you can't find fresh porcini mushrooms, buy whole frozen ones, defrost them in the fridge, and drain them on paper towels. Then roast them, uncovered, until tender and golden brown (and for about half the time as the fresh ones). As a last resort, other exotic fresh mushrooms mixed with reconstituted dried porcini would provide the body and flavor the dish needs. (Avoid dried porcini that are broken up.)

3 lb fresh *porcini* (also known as *cèpes*) or 3 lb other
    exotic mushrooms (sources on page 252) and 2 oz
    large dried *porcini* slices
2 medium onions, cut into ½-inch-thick wedges
6 garlic cloves, minced
3 tablespoons chopped fresh thyme
¼ cup dry Marsala wine
4 tablespoons extra-virgin olive oil
1 teaspoon salt
1½ lb assorted pearl onions, blanched and peeled
2 cups red-wine reduction (recipe follows)

If using dried *porcini*, soak in boiling-hot water to cover until soft, about 45 minutes. Lift out *porcini*, squeezing out excess liquid, and discard soaking liquid. Rinse in a sieve to remove any grit and pat dry. Halve larger slices.

Preheat oven to 375°F.

If using fresh *porcini*, halve or quarter larger ones, keeping smaller ones whole, and transfer all to a baking pan. Toss all mushrooms with onion wedges, garlic, thyme, wine, 3 tablespoons oil, salt, and pepper to taste. Toss pearl onions with remaining tablespoon oil and salt and pepper to taste in a shallow baking pan.

Roast mushroom mixture, covered with foil, in upper third of oven and pearl onions, uncovered, in lower third, stirring occasionally and switching position of pans halfway through roasting, until pearl onions are tender and golden brown, about 45 minutes total. Remove pearl onions from oven.

Uncover mushroom mixture and stir in ½ cup red-wine reduction. Continue roasting mixture in middle of oven, uncovered, stirring occasionally, until vegetables are tender and liquid is reduced by half, about 30 minutes. Stir in pearl onions and roast until hot, about 10 minutes more. Heat remaining red-wine reduction.

Season mushrooms and onions with salt and pepper. Drizzle with some red-wine reduction and serve the rest on the side.

Cooks' note:
• Mushrooms and onions may be roasted 1 day ahead, cooled completely, and chilled, covered. Reheat before serving.

PHOTO ON PAGE 64

RED-WINE REDUCTION ◐+

Makes 2 cups

1 large onion, chopped
2 small celery ribs, chopped
2 carrots, chopped
3 garlic cloves, chopped
1½ tablespoons olive oil
1½ (750-ml) bottles dry red wine (4½ cups)
1 (750-ml) bottle Ruby Port wine (3 cups)

Sauté onion, celery, carrots, and garlic in olive oil in a 6-quart heavy pot over moderately high heat, stirring, until golden, about 10 minutes. Add wines and simmer, stirring occasionally, until mixture is reduced to 1 quart, about 1 hour.

Pour through a sieve into a saucepan and simmer until reduced to 2 cups. Reheat reduction and season with salt and pepper before using.

Cooks' note:
• Reduction may be made 2 days ahead, cooled completely, and chilled, covered. Reheat before using.

SAUTÉED PEAS AND SMALL POTATOES ◐

Serves 6

2 lb small boiling potatoes (preferably red)
¾ lb fresh peas in pods or 1 cup frozen baby peas
½ lb sugar snap peas
1½ tablespoons olive oil

In a 4-quart saucepan cover potatoes with salted cold water by 1 inch and simmer 10 minutes, or until potatoes are tender when pierced with a sharp knife. Drain potatoes in a colander.

Shell peas if using fresh and trim sugar snap peas. In a large skillet heat oil over moderately high heat until hot but not smoking and sauté all vegetables, stirring frequently, until sugar snaps are crisp-tender and potatoes are heated through, about 4 minutes. Season vegetables with salt and pepper.

Cooks' note:
• Potatoes may be cooked 1 day ahead and cooled before being chilled in a sealable plastic bag. Bring to room temperature before proceeding.

PHOTO ON PAGE 42

CREAMED ONIONS

Serves 4

1⅓ lb small (1½-inch) onions
1 tablespoon unsalted butter
1 tablespoon all-purpose flour
1 cup heavy cream
⅛ teaspoon ground cloves
2 tablespoons chopped fresh flat-leaf parsley

Cut off tip and root ends of onions. Peel, quarter, then separate onion layers. Cook onions in boiling salted water to cover in a 2-quart saucepan until tender, 15 to 20 minutes, and drain in a colander.

Melt butter in saucepan over moderate heat. Add flour and cook, whisking, 1 minute. Add cream in a slow stream, whisking, and simmer, whisking, until thickened, about 2 minutes. Add onions, cloves, and salt and pepper to taste and gently simmer 5 minutes. Stir in chopped parsley.

Cooks' note:
• Save the onion-cooking liquid to use as a stock.

ROASTED PEPPERS STUFFED WITH CHERRY TOMATOES, ONION, AND BASIL

Serves 8

4 red bell peppers
2 tablespoons olive oil plus additional
1 pint cherry tomatoes

1 medium onion
1 cup packed fresh basil
3 garlic cloves

Preheat oven to 425°F and lightly oil a large shallow baking pan.

Halve bell peppers lengthwise and discard seeds and ribs. Arrange peppers, cut sides up, in baking pan and lightly oil cut edges and stems. Halve tomatoes and chop onion and basil. Finely chop garlic and in a bowl toss with tomatoes, onion, basil, 2 tablespoons oil, and salt and pepper to taste. Divide mixture among peppers and roast in upper third of oven until peppers are tender, about 20 minutes.

PHOTO ON PAGE 47

PARSLEYED STEAMED POTATOES

Serves 8

2 lb small potatoes (about 2 inches in diameter)
2 tablespoons unsalted butter, softened
⅓ cup finely chopped fresh flat-leaf parsley

Steam potatoes on a steamer rack set over boiling water, covered, until tender, 10 to 15 minutes. Toss with butter, parsley, and salt and pepper to taste.

PHOTO ON PAGE 66

ROASTED POTATO WEDGES

Serves 2

2 medium boiling potatoes (about ¾ lb)
1 tablespoon vegetable oil
½ teaspoon kosher salt

Preheat oven to 425°F.
Peel potatoes and cut into ½-inch-thick wedges. In a small roasting pan toss potatoes with oil and salt and roast in oven until golden and crisp, about 45 minutes.

PHOTO ON PAGE 23

THE GOLD FAMILY LATKES

Serves 6

This recipe makes two large latkes (which are cut into small wedges for serving), as opposed to the more common individual latkes.

2 lb large boiling potatoes
3 tablespoons coarsely grated onion
1 teaspoon kosher salt
Freshly ground white pepper
¼ cup olive oil

Accompaniment: apple-cranberry sauce
   (recipe follows)

Cook potatoes in salted water to cover until barely tender, about 15 to 20 minutes. Rinse under cold water. Cool potatoes and peel with a sharp knife. Coarsely shred potatoes lengthwise (long strands help hold the latkes together) into a bowl using large holes of a grater and stir in onion, salt, and white pepper to taste.

Heat 1 tablespoon oil in a 10-inch nonstick skillet over moderate heat until hot but not smoking, then add half of potatoes, spreading with a spatula to form an even cake. Cook until underside is golden brown, 10 to 12 minutes. Invert a large plate over skillet and invert latke onto plate. Add 1 tablespoon oil to skillet and slide latke back in. Cook until underside is golden brown, 10 to 12 minutes.

Slide latke onto serving plate and keep warm. Make another in same manner.

Cut latkes into wedges and serve with apple-cranberry sauce.

PHOTO ON PAGE 74

APPLE-CRANBERRY SAUCE

Makes about 3 cups

3 large Granny Smith apples, peeled and cut
   into ½-inch pieces
1 cup cranberries (fresh or unthawed frozen)
1 cup water
7 tablespoons sugar

Bring all ingredients to a boil in a 3-quart saucepan. Cook, covered, over moderate heat, stirring occasionally, 20 minutes. Serve at room temperature.

Cooks' note:
• Sauce keeps, covered and chilled, 1 week.

GOLDEN POTATO WEDGES

Serves 8

5 lb boiling potatoes (preferably Yukon Gold;
   6 to 8 medium)
2 tablespoons olive oil

Preheat oven to 425°F and oil a large shallow baking pan large enough to hold potatoes in one layer.

Peel potatoes and cut each lengthwise into 6 wedges. Toss potatoes with oil and salt and pepper to taste and roast in lower third of oven until undersides are golden, about 40 minutes. Turn potatoes over and continue roasting until undersides are golden and potatoes are tender, about 20 minutes more.

PHOTO ON PAGE 47

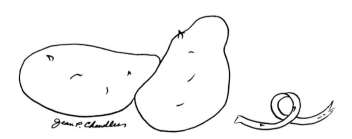

CREAMY MASHED POTATOES ◌

Serves 8

3 lb baking (russet) potatoes
¾ stick unsalted butter, cut into bits and softened
1 to 1½ cups heavy cream or half-and-half, heated
 until hot

Special equipment: potato ricer or food mill

Bring a large pot of water to a boil (enough to cover potatoes by 1 inch) and add salt to taste. Peel potatoes and quarter. Add potatoes to water, then return to a boil. Gently boil potatoes until tender, 15 to 20 minutes, and drain in a colander. Force potatoes, while still warm, through ricer into a large bowl. Add butter and stir with a wooden spoon, letting butter melt completely. Add 1 cup heavy cream and incorporate by gently stirring with wooden spoon, adding more cream to thin to desired consistency.

Cooks' note:
• To vary this recipe simmer garlic with the potatoes. Add Spanish smoked paprika (sources on page 252) or sautéed leeks to the potatoes after mashing.

PHOTO ON PAGE 66

CANDIED SWEET-POTATO PURÉE

Serves 8 to 10

4 lb sweet potatoes (about 5 medium)
1 large navel orange
¾ stick unsalted butter, softened
½ cup sugar
1½ tablespoons bourbon
½ teaspoon freshly grated nutmeg
¼ teaspoon salt

Preheat oven to 400°F and line a baking sheet with aluminum foil.
Prick sweet potatoes in several places with a fork and bake on baking sheet in middle of oven until very tender, 1 to 1¼ hours.
Finely grate enough zest from orange to measure 1 teaspoon and squeeze enough juice from orange to measure ½ cup. In a small saucepan melt 4 tablespoons butter over moderate heat and stir in zest, orange juice, sugar, bourbon, nutmeg, and salt, stirring until sugar is dissolved.

When potatoes are just cool enough to handle, peel and put flesh in a food processor. Add butter mixture and purée just until smooth.
Transfer purée to a serving dish and dot with remaining 2 tablespoons butter, letting it melt to form pools.

Cooks' note:
• Purée may be made 2 days ahead (before dotting with remaining butter) and chilled in a 1½ quart shallow baking dish, covered. Reheat, covered, in middle of 350°F oven before proceeding.

PHOTO ON PAGE 16

CANDIED SWEET POTATOES

Serves 8

3 lb large sweet potatoes, peeled and
 halved crosswise
1 cup packed light brown sugar
½ stick unsalted butter
¼ cup water
¼ teaspoon salt
¼ to ⅓ cup bourbon

Preheat oven to 375°F.
Cut each sweet potato half lengthwise into fourths. Steam potatoes on a steamer rack set over boiling water, covered, until just tender, 10 to 15 minutes, then cool, uncovered. Transfer to a buttered 3-quart shallow baking dish.
Simmer brown sugar, butter, water, and salt, stirring occasionally, until sugar is dissolved and syrup is thickened, about 5 minutes. Stir in bourbon to taste. Drizzle syrup over potatoes and bake in middle of oven, basting occasionally, until syrup is thickened, about 1¼ hours.

Cooks' notes:
• To vary this recipe add some toasted pecans. In place of bourbon, substitute dark rum or medium-dry Sherry.
• Sweet potatoes may be made 1 day ahead and chilled, covered. Reheat before serving.

PHOTO ON PAGE 68

ZUCCHINI GREMOLATA ⊙

Serves 2

4 small zucchini (about 1 lb)
2 garlic cloves
2 bottled or canned flat anchovies
1 tablespoon olive oil
1 teaspoon lemon zest
1 tablespoon finely chopped fresh
   flat-leaf parsley

Halve zucchini lengthwise and diagonally cut into ½-inch-thick slices. Finely chop garlic. Pat anchovies dry and coarsely chop.

In a large nonstick skillet heat oil and anchovies over moderate heat, stirring, until anchovies are dissolved, 1 to 2 minutes. Add zucchini and salt and pepper to taste and cook, stirring frequently, until zucchini is crisp-tender, 5 to 7 minutes. Add garlic, zest, and parsley and cook, stirring, 1 minute.

VEGETABLE GREEN CURRY ⊙

Serves 4

The sweet potato and coconut milk balance the spiciness of this dish. Serve it over white rice, and dinner is ready.

2 red bell peppers, cut into ¼-inch-thick strips
1 medium onion, thinly sliced
1 tablespoon vegetable oil
1 tablespoon minced garlic
1 to 1½ tablespoons Thai green curry paste
   (sources on page 252)
2 medium sweet potatoes (1 lb), peeled, halved
   lengthwise, and cut crosswise into ¼-inch-thick
   half-moons
1 (14-oz) can unsweetened coconut milk
½ cup water
½ lb snow peas
1 tablespoon chopped fresh cilantro

Sauté bell peppers and onion in oil with salt and pepper to taste in a 12-inch nonstick skillet over moderately high heat until edges of vegetables are golden, about 5 minutes. Stir in garlic and curry paste and cook, stirring, 1 minute. Add sweet potatoes, coconut milk, and water and simmer, covered, stirring occasionally, until potatoes are almost tender, about 3 minutes. Add snow peas and simmer, uncovered, until sauce is slightly thickened. Stir in cilantro.

BUTTER-BRAISED ROOT VEGETABLES AND GREEN BEANS ⊙

Serves 2

1 (1-lb) celery root (sometimes called celeriac)
2 large carrots
4 large shallots
1½ tablespoons unsalted butter
¾ teaspoon salt
¼ lb green beans

With a sharp knife peel celery root and cut into 1-inch pieces. Diagonally cut carrots into 1-inch-thick pieces. Quarter shallots lengthwise. In a 2-quart heavy saucepan melt butter over moderately low heat. Add celery root, carrots, shallots, salt, and pepper to taste, stirring to coat vegetables with butter, and cook, covered, stirring occasionally, 20 minutes.

While root vegetables are cooking, trim beans. Stir beans into root vegetables and cook, covered, stirring once or twice, until all vegetables are tender, about 10 minutes.

BEANS

BLACK BEANS WITH GARLIC, CUMIN, AND CILANTRO ⊙

Serves 2

1 (16- to 19-oz) can black beans
2 garlic cloves
1 teaspoon ground cumin
2 tablespoons olive oil
⅓ cup tomato juice or water
¾ teaspoon salt
2 tablespoons chopped fresh cilantro

Rinse black beans and drain. Chop garlic. Cook garlic and cumin in oil in a nonstick skillet over moderate heat, stirring, until fragrant. Add black beans, juice or water, and salt and cook, stirring, until beans are heated through. Stir in cilantro.

CHICK-PEAS AND SWISS CHARD ◔

Serves 2

Pairing chick-peas and Swiss chard is not new—Armenians have been doing it for generations. Add a great tomato and lemon, and you have a quick vegetable stew.

1 small onion, thinly sliced
1 garlic clove, thinly sliced
1½ tablespoons olive oil
1 small tomato, cut into ¼-inch dice
1 cup canned chick-peas, rinsed
½ lb Swiss chard, stems discarded and leaves
   coarsely chopped
½ tablespoon fresh lemon juice

Cook onion and garlic in oil in a large nonstick skillet over moderately low heat, stirring, until softened. Add tomato and chick-peas and cook, stirring, 5 minutes. Add Swiss chard and cook, covered, until wilted, about 2 minutes. Add lemon juice and season with salt and pepper.

PICKLED BLACK-EYED PEAS

Serves 8 to 10

1 lb dried black-eyed peas
1 bay leaf
2 teaspoons salt
2 red bell peppers
1 small onion
2 large garlic cloves
6 tablespoons red-wine vinegar
⅔ cup vegetable oil
¼ cup finely chopped fresh
   flat-leaf parsley

Pick over black-eyed peas and rinse. In a 5-quart kettle simmer peas with bay leaf in water to cover by 2 inches until tender, 25 to 30 minutes, and remove kettle from heat. Stir in salt and let peas stand 5 minutes. Drain peas in a colander and discard bay leaf.

While peas are simmering, finely chop bell peppers and onion and mince garlic. In a large bowl whisk together vinegar and oil until combined well and stir in hot peas, bell pepper, onion, garlic, and salt and pepper to taste. Just before serving, stir parsley into peas.

Cooks' note:
• Peas may be made 1 day ahead and chilled, covered. Bring
  to room temperature before serving.

PHOTO ON PAGE 16

VEGETABLE AND BEAN CHILI ◔

Serves 4

2 large onions (1 lb), coarsely chopped
1 green bell pepper, cut into ½-inch
   pieces
3 large garlic cloves, finely chopped
½ fresh jalapeño chile, finely chopped
   (including seeds)
2 tablespoons olive oil
1 tablespoon chili powder
1 teaspoon ground cumin
2 teaspoons salt
28-oz can whole tomatoes, coarsely chopped,
   with juice
2 zucchini, cut into ½-inch cubes
2 (15-oz) cans kidney beans, rinsed
1 tablespoon chopped semisweet chocolate
3 tablespoons chopped fresh cilantro

Sauté onions, bell pepper, garlic, and jalapeño in oil in a 4-quart heavy pot over moderately high heat, stirring, until softened, about 5 minutes. Add chili powder, cumin, and salt and cook, stirring, 1 minute. Add tomatoes with juice and zucchini and simmer, partially covered, stirring occasionally, 15 minutes. Stir in beans and chocolate and simmer, stirring occasionally, 5 minutes. Stir in cilantro.

Red Lentil and Tofu Curry ◔

Serves 2

Contrary to what their name suggests, the color of "red" lentils is actually closer to orange. You can also use brown lentils, but the results will be different. Red lentils fall apart as they cook, creating a creamier base, whereas brown ones hold their shape (and take a little longer to cook).

1 small onion
1 garlic clove
1 (½-inch) piece fresh ginger
½ cup red lentils (sources on page 252)
2 tablespoons vegetable oil
3½ cups water
½ lb firm tofu
½ teaspoon cumin seeds
½ teaspoon *garam masala* (sources on
   page 252) or curry powder
½ teaspoon salt
Generous pinch of cayenne
3 tablespoons chopped fresh cilantro

Accompaniment: cooked rice

Thinly slice onion and mince garlic. Peel ginger and mince. In a sieve rinse lentils and drain. In a 2-quart heavy saucepan cook onion and garlic in 1 tablespoon oil over moderate heat, stirring, until golden. Add ginger and cook, stirring, 1 minute. Add lentils and water and gently boil, uncovered, until lentils fall apart, about 20 minutes.

While lentils are boiling, rinse tofu and trim ends. Cut tofu into ½-inch cubes and gently press between paper towels to remove excess moisture.

In a small heavy skillet heat remaining tablespoon oil over moderate heat until hot but not smoking and cook cumin seeds, stirring, until a shade darker, about 1 minute. Add *garam masala*, salt, and cayenne and cook, stirring, until fragrant, 15 to 30 seconds. Stir hot spice oil into lentils and gently stir in tofu cubes. Let curry stand, covered, 5 minutes to allow flavors to develop. Stir in cilantro and salt to taste.

Serve curry over rice.

Lentils with Butternut Squash and Walnuts

Serves 2

1 small butternut squash (about 1 lb)
1 large shallot
2 tablespoons olive oil
1½ teaspoons curry powder
½ cup walnuts
⅓ cup lentils
2 tablespoons chopped fresh cilantro
Fresh lime juice to taste (optional)

Preheat oven to 425°F.

Halve, peel, and seed squash and cut into ½-inch pieces. Finely chop shallot and in a shallow baking pan toss with squash, oil, curry powder, and salt and pepper to taste until combined well. Bake squash mixture in middle of oven until almost tender, about 15 minutes.

Chop walnuts and sprinkle over squash. Bake squash mixture 10 minutes more, or until walnuts are lightly toasted and squash is tender.

While squash is baking, in a saucepan of boiling water cook lentils until just tender but not falling apart, about 20 minutes. Drain lentils in a sieve and transfer to a bowl.

To lentils add squash mixture, cilantro, lime juice, and salt and pepper to taste and toss until combined.

SALADS

MAIN COURSE SALADS

CRUNCHY TUNA SALAD

Serves 2

½ small *jícama*
1 large celery rib
¼ cup packed fresh cilantro
1 (6-oz) can tuna in olive oil
2½ tablespoons mayonnaise
1½ teaspoons Dijon mustard
Fresh lime juice to taste (optional)

Accompaniment: sliced bread or crackers

Peel *jícama*. Cut enough *jícama* and celery into ¼-inch dice to measure ⅓ cup each. Chop cilantro. Drain tuna and in a bowl with a fork break up flakes to desired consistency. Stir in *jícama*, celery, cilantro, mayonnaise, mustard, and lime juice to taste.
Serve salad with bread or crackers.

> *The following chicken, asparagus, roasted pepper, and white bean recipes, when served together, make a lovely composed salad that will serve 6 for lunch.*

SAUTÉED CHICKEN BREASTS WITH CAPERS

Serves 6

6 small boneless chicken breast halves, with
    or without skin (about 2¼ lb total)
1 tablespoon olive oil
2 tablespoons drained capers
¼ cup lemon vinaigrette (recipe follows)

Pat chicken dry and season with salt and pepper. In a 12-inch nonstick skillet heat oil over moderately high heat until hot but not smoking and sauté chicken, skin or skinned sides down, 3 minutes, or until golden. Turn chicken over and sauté 1 minute more. Reduce heat to moderately low and cook chicken, covered, until just cooked through, about 10 minutes. Coarsely chop capers and in a large bowl toss chicken with any juices from skillet, capers, and vinaigrette. Serve chicken warm or at room temperature.

PHOTO ON PAGE 39

LEMON VINAIGRETTE

Makes about 1 cup

Lemon adds a subtle acidity and a fresh tang to a wide range of dishes without overpowering other flavors. Our simple lemon vinaigrette is used in several components of the composed salad (making preparation that much easier) and it brings out something different in each.

3 lemons
⅔ cup extra-virgin olive oil

Squeeze enough juice from lemons to measure ⅓ cup. In a bowl combine lemon juice with salt and pepper to taste. Whisk in oil in a slow stream.

Cooks' note:
• Vinaigrette may be made 3 hours ahead and chilled, covered. Bring to room temperature before proceeding.

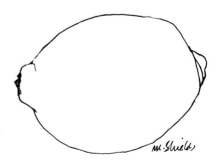

Asparagus with Lemon Vinaigrette ◐

Serves 6

2 lb thin asparagus
¼ cup lemon vinaigrette (recipe precedes)

Trim asparagus and have ready a large bowl of ice and cold water. In a large saucepan of boiling salted water cook asparagus until just tender, 3 to 4 minutes, and with tongs transfer to ice water to stop cooking. Drain asparagus well in a colander and pat dry.

Gently toss asparagus with vinaigrette and salt and pepper to taste.

PHOTO ON PAGE 39

Roasted Peppers with Garlic ◐+

Serves 6

These peppers get even better when made ahead because the flavors develop more fully over time.

2 red bell peppers
2 yellow bell peppers
1 large garlic clove
2 tablespoons extra-virgin olive oil

Preheat broiler.

Quarter bell peppers lengthwise and discard stems, seeds, and ribs. Arrange peppers, skin sides up, on rack of a broiler pan and broil about 2 inches from heat until skins are blistered, 8 to 12 minutes. (Alternatively, lay whole peppers on their sides on racks of burners of a gas stove and turn flames on high. Char peppers, turning them with tongs, until skins are blackened, 5 to 8 minutes.)

Transfer roasted peppers to a bowl and let stand, covered, until cool enough to handle. Peel peppers and cut each quarter lengthwise into 2 or 3 strips. Thinly slice garlic and in a bowl toss with peppers, oil, and salt to taste. Marinate, covered and chilled, at least 3 hours.

Cooks' note:
• Peppers can marinate up to 3 days, covered and chilled.

PHOTO ON PAGE 39

White Bean Salad

Serves 6

1⅔ cups dried white beans such as Great Northern
⅓ cup lemon vinaigrette (page 167)
4 celery ribs
4 scallions
½ cup packed fresh flat-leaf parsley
3 large garlic cloves
¼ cup chopped fresh chives
1 tablespoon chopped fresh tarragon
Fresh lemon juice to taste

In a large bowl soak beans in cold water to cover by 2 inches at least 6 hours and up to 1 day. Drain beans. In a 3- to 4-quart saucepan cover beans with cold water by 2 inches and simmer until tender, 1 to 1¼ hours. After about 45 minutes, season beans with salt. Drain beans in a colander and transfer to a bowl. Gently stir vinaigrette into warm beans.

Thinly slice celery and scallions. Chop parsley and mince garlic. Add celery, scallions, parsley, garlic, chives, and tarragon to beans and stir in lemon juice and salt and pepper to taste. Serve beans warm or at room temperature.

Cooks' notes:
• We find that beans cook more evenly and hold their shape better with a long soak—which is why the ones in this recipe are soaked for 6 hours. But, you can use the following quick-soak method if you prefer: In a saucepan cover beans with cold water by 2 inches. Bring water to a boil and boil beans 2 minutes. Remove pan from heat and soak beans 1 hour.
• Beans in vinaigrette may be prepared 1 day ahead and cooled, uncovered, before being chilled, covered. Bring to room temperature before proceeding.

PHOTO ON PAGE 39

Shrimp, Avocado, and Noodle Salad ◐

Serves 2

1 tablespoon honey
1 tablespoon fresh lemon juice
1½ teaspoons minced peeled fresh ginger
2 tablespoons vegetable oil

3 scallions
1 large carrot
¾ lb large shrimp (about 12)
4 oz Asian rice-stick noodles
    (sources on page 252)
1 firm-ripe California avocado

In a small bowl whisk together honey, lemon juice, and ginger until combined. Add oil in a slow stream, whisking until emulsified, and season with salt and pepper. Thinly slice scallions diagonally and cut carrot into 1-inch-long thin julienne strips.

In a 4-quart kettle bring 3 quarts salted water to a boil. Shell and devein shrimp. Simmer shrimp until just cooked through, about 1½ minutes. With a slotted spoon transfer shrimp to a plate. Return water to a boil and add noodles. Cook noodles until just tender, about 3 minutes. In a colander rinse noodles under cold water to stop cooking and drain well. With scissors cut noodles into 4-inch lengths.

Pit and peel avocado and cut into ¼-inch dice. In a large bowl gently toss together shrimp, noodles, vegetables, dressing, and salt and pepper to taste.

SALADS WITH GREENS

BIBB LETTUCE WITH BUTTER DRESSING ☉

Serves 4

½ lb Bibb lettuce (about 4 heads) or Boston lettuce
    (about 1 head)
1 garlic clove
½ stick unsalted butter
4 teaspoons fresh lemon juice

Separate lettuce leaves and put in a large bowl. Halve garlic and in a small heavy skillet heat with butter over moderate heat, stirring occasionally, until garlic is golden and butter has a slight nutty aroma, about 3 minutes. Remove skillet from heat and discard garlic. Add lemon juice and salt and pepper to taste, swirling skillet to incorporate (butter will foam).

Pour warm dressing over lettuce and toss to coat. Serve salad immediately.

ARUGULA, FENNEL, AND PARMESAN SALAD ☉

Serves 4

1 medium fennel bulb (sometimes called anise)
2 tablespoons chicken broth
1 tablespoon fresh lemon juice
1 tablespoon extra-virgin olive oil
¼ teaspoon sugar
½ lb arugula, stems removed
1 small red onion, coarsely chopped
1 (2-oz) piece fresh Parmesan

Remove fronds, stalks, and tough outer layer from fennel. Halve bulb lengthwise and cut into paper-thin slices with a *mandoline* or other manual slicer.

Whisk together chicken broth, lemon juice, olive oil, sugar, and salt and pepper to taste in a large bowl. Add sliced fennel, arugula, and onion, then toss together. Thinly shave enough Parmesan with a vegetable peeler to measure ¼ cup.

Serve salad sprinkled with Parmesan.

☞ each serving about 79 calories and 4 grams fat

ENDIVE AND PEAR SALAD ☉

Serves 2

3 tablespoons extra-virgin olive oil
1 tablespoon white-wine vinegar
1 firm-ripe pear (about ½ lb)
2 Belgian endives (about 1 lb)
1 small head chicory (curly endive; about ½ lb)

In a small bowl whisk together oil, vinegar, and salt and pepper to taste. Halve and core pear and thinly slice lengthwise. Cut endives crosswise into ½-inch-wide slices and tear chicory into bite-size pieces. In a bowl toss greens with pear and vinaigrette.

MUSHROOM, RADISH, AND BIBB LETTUCE SALAD
WITH AVOCADO DRESSING ☺

Serves 6

For avocado dressing
1 ripe California avocado
2 tablespoons fresh lemon juice
½ teaspoon Dijon mustard
½ teaspoon sugar
¾ teaspoon salt
2 tablespoons heavy cream
¼ cup packed fresh flat-leaf parsley
¼ cup olive oil

4 heads Bibb lettuce
6 oz mushrooms
1 cup radishes
¼ cup packed fresh flat-leaf parsley

Make dressing:
Pit and peel avocado and mash enough to measure ¼ cup. In a blender purée mashed avocado with remaining dressing ingredients until smooth.

Discard any discolored lettuce leaves. Separately cut mushrooms and radishes into thin slices.

In a small bowl combine mushrooms and 2 tablespoons dressing and toss to coat. Divide lettuce among 6 salad bowls and top with mushrooms, radishes, and parsley. Drizzle salads with some remaining dressing.

PHOTO ON PAGE 34

BABY GREENS WITH OLIVE OIL ☺

Serves 8

Tossed with your best-quality olive oil, this simple salad needs no vinegar or lemon juice to taste unbelievably good. For extra crunch, mix in tender shoots from the farmers market.

1 lb mixed baby greens such as *frisée,* baby spinach
    or arugula, and Lolla Rosa
3 tablespoons extra-virgin olive oil
1 teaspoon kosher salt

In a large bowl toss greens with oil and salt. Serve salad immediately.

PHOTO ON PAGE 47

RED-LEAF LETTUCE WITH SHALLOT VINAIGRETTE ☺

Serves 6

1 large shallot, minced
2 teaspoons white-wine vinegar
2 teaspoons Dijon mustard
3½ tablespoons olive oil
Kosher salt to taste
1 large head red-leaf lettuce

Stir together shallot and vinegar and let stand 10 minutes. Whisk in mustard, oil, kosher salt, and pepper to taste until blended. Tear lettuce into bite-size pieces and toss with shallot vinaigrette.

Cooks' note:
• You can wash lettuce a day ahead—wrap it in paper towels, then chill it in plastic bags.

ROMAINE SALAD WITH PARMESAN DRESSING ☺

Serves 2

1 heart of romaine
2 teaspoons white-wine vinegar
2 tablespoons extra-virgin olive oil
2 oz freshly grated Parmesan (about ⅔ cup)

Separate romaine leaves. In a large bowl whisk together vinegar, oil, half of Parmesan, and salt and pepper to taste.

Toss romaine with dressing and serve sprinkled with remaining Parmesan.

FARMERS MARKET GREEN SALAD WITH
FRIED SHALLOTS ☺

Serves 6

½ lb shallots
1½ cups vegetable oil for frying
6 oz *mizuna* and *tatsoi* (mixed; about 6 cups loosely
    packed) (sources on page 252)
⅓ cup radish sprouts
1 tablespoon white-wine vinegar
Sea salt to taste

Cut shallots into ⅛-inch-thick slices. In a heavy 10-inch skillet fry shallots in oil over moderate heat, stirring occasionally, until golden, 15 to 20 minutes. With a slotted spoon transfer shallots to paper towels to drain and season with salt. Reserve 3 tablespoons oil for dressing salad and cool shallots to room temperature.

Just before serving, in a large bowl toss together greens, radish sprouts, reserved oil, vinegar, and sea salt. Sprinkle shallots over salad.

Cooks' note:
• Shallots may be fried 2 days ahead and kept in an airtight container at room temperature.

PHOTO ON PAGE 41

SPINACH AND ROASTED RED PEPPER SALAD ◐

Serves 6

4 red bell peppers
1 teaspoon honey
1 teaspoon Dijon mustard
1 tablespoon balsamic vinegar
2½ tablespoons extra-virgin olive oil
½ lb fresh baby spinach (about 8 cups packed)

Quick-roast and peel peppers (procedure page 87). Cut roasted peppers into ½-inch-wide strips. In a small bowl whisk together honey, mustard, and vinegar. Add oil in a slow stream, whisking until emulsified, and season with salt and black pepper.

In a large bowl toss roasted peppers and spinach with vinaigrette and salt and black pepper to taste.

Cooks' note:
• Roasted peppers and vinaigrette may be prepared 2 days ahead and chilled separately, covered.

PHOTO ON PAGE 20

CREAMY SPINACH AND BACON SALAD ◐

Serves 4 (first course)

Cold steak from last weekend's cookout would taste great sliced and laid over this salad.

4 bacon slices
1 small garlic clove
2 tablespoons extra-virgin olive oil
2 tablespoons sour cream
2 tablespoons fresh lemon juice
1 teaspoon brown or white sugar
½ lb baby spinach
¼ cup coarsely grated Parmesan (1 oz)

Cook bacon until crisp and drain on paper towels.

While bacon is cooking, mince garlic and mash to a paste with a pinch of salt. Whisk together oil, sour cream, lemon juice, sugar, and garlic paste in a large bowl and season with salt and pepper. Add spinach and crumble bacon over it. Toss with cheese and dressing.

VEGETABLE SALADS AND SLAWS

APPLE AND CELERY SALAD ◐

Serves 2 (side dish)

2 tablespoons mayonnaise
1 tablespoon chopped fresh cilantro
1 tablespoon fresh lemon juice
1½ celery ribs
1 crisp red apple

In a small bowl whisk together mayonnaise, cilantro, lemon juice, and salt and pepper to taste until combined. Cut celery and apple into 1½-inch-long thin julienne strips. Toss together celery, apple, dressing, and salt and pepper to taste.

Apple and Celery Salad with Peanuts ◔

Serves 8 adults plus 10 children as part of a buffet

2 tablespoons fresh lemon juice
½ teaspoon Dijon mustard
¼ cup olive oil
3 crisp red apples such as Fuji or Rome, cut into
    ¼-inch-thick julienne
2 tart green apples such as Granny Smith, cut into
    ¼-inch-thick julienne
4 large celery ribs, cut into ¼-inch-thick julienne
¼ cup chopped fresh parsley
⅓ cup dry-roasted peanuts, coarsely chopped

Whisk together lemon juice and mustard in a large bowl. Add oil in a stream, whisking until emulsified. Add apples, celery, and parsley, tossing to coat. Just before serving, sprinkle with peanuts.

Cooks' note:
• Salad may be made 3 hours ahead and chilled, covered.

PHOTO ON PAGE 70

Cabbage Salad with Mustard Vinaigrette ◔

Serves 6

1 (1½-lb) piece white or green cabbage
1 (½-lb) piece red cabbage
½ cup packed fresh flat-leaf parsley
1½ teaspoons Dijon mustard
2½ tablespoons red-wine vinegar
¾ teaspoon salt
5 tablespoons extra-virgin olive oil

Cut cabbage into thin shreds and chop parsley. In a small bowl whisk together mustard, vinegar, and salt until combined. Whisk in oil in a slow stream, whisking until emulsified.

In a large bowl toss together cabbage, parsley, vinaigrette, and salt and pepper to taste until combined. Chill salad, covered, at least 30 minutes and up to 2 hours.

PHOTO ON PAGE 28

Beet and Jícama on Endive with Garlic Yogurt Dressing

Serves 50

For dressing
32 oz whole-milk plain yogurt
    (sources on page 252)
2 to 3 teaspoons minced garlic
⅓ cup chopped fresh mint
For salad
2 lb trimmed beets
2½ lb *jícamas* (about 1½)
3 tablespoons sugar
½ teaspoon finely grated fresh orange zest
¼ cup fresh orange juice
2 tablespoons red-wine vinegar
2 tablespoons extra-virgin olive oil
2 teaspoons crushed fennel seeds
2 tablespoons fresh lemon juice
8 Belgian endives

Make dressing:
Drain yogurt in a large sieve lined with double thickness of cheesecloth, chilled, at least 8 hours, then stir drained yogurt with garlic, mint, and salt to taste.
Make salad:
Preheat oven to 425°F.
Wrap beets in foil and roast in middle of oven 1¼ hours, or until tender when pierced with a knife. Cool beets. Peel beets and *jícamas* and cut into ¼-inch dice. Toss with sugar, zest, orange juice, vinegar, oil, fennel, and salt to taste.
Stir lemon juice into a large bowl of cold water. Cut ends from endives and separate into leaves. Soak in lemon water 10 minutes to keep endive from discoloring. Drain and spin dry.
Spread some dressing on each leaf and spoon beet salad over it.

Cooks' notes:
• You can make dressing 2 days ahead and chill it, covered.
• Beets may be roasted, and beets and *jícama* diced, 1 day
  ahead. Keep separate, chilled, in sealable plastic bags.

PHOTO ON PAGE 56

Carrot Salad with Lime and Cilantro ☺

Serves 4

4 medium carrots
1 tablespoon fresh lime juice
⅛ teaspoon finely grated fresh lime zest
2 tablespoons finely chopped fresh cilantro
1 teaspoon vegetable oil

Garnish: fresh cilantro sprigs

Finely shred carrots and in a bowl toss together with remaining ingredients and salt and pepper to taste.
Serve salad garnished with cilantro.

☞ each serving about 42 calories and 1 gram fat

PHOTO ON PAGE 81

Avocado and Sweet Onion Salad ☺

Serves 8

For dressing
3 limes
2 fresh jalapeño chiles
⅓ cup extra-virgin olive oil
1½ teaspoons sugar

1 large sweet onion such as Vidalia
4 California avocados
1 cup packed fresh cilantro sprigs

Make dressing:
Squeeze enough juice from limes to measure ¼ cup. Wearing protective gloves, coarsely chop chiles. In a blender purée chiles with lime juice, oil, sugar, and salt and pepper to taste.
Cut onion in half through stem end and thinly slice crosswise. Quarter avocados lengthwise. Peel avocados and cut lengthwise into ¼-inch-thick slices.
Arrange avocado, onion, and cilantro sprigs on a platter and season with salt and pepper. Drizzle dressing over salad.

Cooks' note:
• Dressing may be made 2 days ahead and chilled in an airtight container.

PHOTO ON PAGE 52

Jícama, Cucumber, and Chile Slaw ☺

Serves 2 (side dish)

½ English cucumber
1 (¼-lb) piece *jícama*
2 medium carrots
2½ tablespoons seasoned rice vinegar
3 tablespoons chopped fresh cilantro
1 tablespoon vegetable oil
¼ teaspoon Asian chili paste, or to taste
   (sources on page 252)

Seed cucumber and peel *jícama*. Cut cucumber, *jícama*, and carrots into 1½-inch-long thin strips. Toss vegetables together with remaining ingredients and season with salt and pepper.

Zesty Bell Pepper Slaw ☺

Serves 2

¼ medium head cabbage
½ small red bell pepper
½ small yellow bell pepper
2 scallions
3 tablespoons mayonnaise
1 tablespoon plain yogurt
1 tablespoon cider vinegar
Pinch of cayenne, or to taste
2 tablespoons shredded fresh basil

Coarsely chop cabbage, bell peppers, and scallions. In a bowl whisk together mayonnaise, yogurt, vinegar, and cayenne. Add vegetables, basil, and salt and pepper to taste and toss well. Chill slaw, covered, 20 minutes.

SAUCES

APRICOT MOJO SAUCE ◐

Makes about 1¼ cups

Inspired by Florida chef Norman Van Aken's mango habanero mojo, this sauce is a wonderful accompaniment to grilled pork or chicken. Wear protective gloves while mincing the chile.

4 fresh apricots
5 tablespoons fresh orange juice
1½ teaspoons sugar
1 teaspoon fresh lemon juice
½ teaspoon minced fresh hot chile, or to taste
4 fresh cilantro sprigs

Pit apricots and in a blender purée with remaining ingredients until smooth. Season sauce well with salt.

BEURRE MEUNIÈRE ◐

BROWN BUTTER SAUCE WITH LEMON

Makes about 5 tablespoons

This simple sauce enhances the natural sweetness in foods—try it on steamed cauliflower or asparagus or with sautéed fish.

½ stick unsalted butter
1½ teaspoons fresh lemon juice
¼ teaspoon salt
1 tablespoon chopped fresh flat-leaf parsley

Cut butter into pieces and in a small heavy skillet melt over moderately low heat. Simmer butter until golden brown with a nutty aroma, about 5 minutes. Remove skillet from heat and immediately add lemon juice, salt, parsley, and pepper to taste, swirling skillet to incorporate (butter will foam).
Serve sauce immediately.

BEURRE NANTAIS ◐

WHITE BUTTER SAUCE WITH CREAM

Makes about ¾ cup

This sauce is traditionally served with fish, but we like it over steak and vegetables as well.

1 stick unsalted butter
2 tablespoons dry white wine
2 tablespoons white-wine vinegar
1 tablespoon chopped shallot
3 tablespoons heavy cream
A few drops fresh lemon juice

Cut butter into small pieces and chill. In a small heavy saucepan simmer wine, vinegar, and shallot over moderate heat until liquid is reduced to about 1 tablespoon, about 5 minutes. Add cream and simmer mixture until slightly thickened, about 2 minutes. Gradually add butter a few pieces at a time, whisking and adding more before previous pieces are fully incorporated (mixture will be creamy and pale). Remove pan from heat and pour sauce through a fine sieve into a sauceboat, pressing on solids. Season sauce with lemon juice and salt and pepper.
Serve sauce immediately.

FENNEL TSATSIKI ◐

Makes about 3 cups

This sauce makes a terrific accompaniment to grilled fish or lamb.

1 medium fennel bulb with fronds
  (sometimes called anise; about ¾ lb)
1 teaspoon fennel seeds
2 garlic cloves
1 lemon
2 cups plain yogurt (16 oz)
1½ teaspoons salt

Trim fennel stalks flush with bulb, reserving fronds and discarding stalks, and trim any discolored outer layers. Halve bulb lengthwise and discard core. Finely chop fronds and bulb. In a dry small skillet toast fennel seeds over moderate heat, shaking skillet, until fragrant and a shade darker. In an electric coffee/spice grinder grind seeds. Mince garlic cloves and squeeze juice from lemon.

In a bowl stir together chopped fennel, ground fennel seeds, garlic, yogurt, salt, and lemon juice to taste.

Cooks' note:
• *Tsatsiki may be made 3 days ahead and chilled, covered.*

TONNATO SAUCE ◑

Makes about 2 cups

This is traditionally served with sliced cold veal, but we also like it with turkey or as a dip for vegetables.

1 cup mayonnaise
½ cup extra-virgin olive oil
1 (6-oz) can tuna in olive oil (not drained)
3 anchovy fillets
2 tablespoons fresh lemon juice
3 tablespoons drained capers

In a blender purée all ingredients, including oil from tuna can, until smooth and season with salt and pepper.

Vicky

CRANBERRY SAUCE ◑

Makes about 2½ cups

1 cup water
1 cup sugar
12-oz bag fresh or frozen cranberries (3 cups)
½ teaspoon freshly grated orange zest

Bring water and sugar to a boil, stirring until sugar is dissolved. Add cranberries and simmer, stirring occasionally, until berries just pop, 10 to 12 minutes. Stir in zest, then cool.

Cooks' notes:
• Possible variations to this sauce include sliced kumquats or orange sections, chopped pecans, citrus zest, minced shallot, or minced *serrano* chile.
• Cranberry sauce may be made 3 days ahead and chilled, covered.

PHOTO ON PAGE 69

CRANBERRY GINGER SAUCE ◑+

Makes about 4½ cups

Be sure to use firm, dense apples such as Granny Smith, Fuji, or Pippin, which will hold their shape when cooked.

1½ lb fresh or frozen cranberries
1½ cups sugar
2 medium Granny Smith apples, peeled and cut into ¼-inch dice
2¼ tablespoons minced peeled fresh ginger
1½ cups water
3 tablespoons cider vinegar
1 tablespoon finely grated fresh orange zest

Stir together all ingredients in a nonreactive 4- to 5-quart deep heavy pot and bring to a boil, stirring until sugar is dissolved. Boil sauce (adjust heat if sauce spits too much), stirring frequently, 10 minutes, or until slightly thickened. Cool about 30 minutes and chill at least 1½ hours.

Cooks' note:
• Sauce may be made 1 week ahead and chilled, covered.

PHOTO ON PAGE 64

CHIMICHURRI SAUCE ◐

Makes about 2 cups

This Argentinian sauce is served with both grilled meats and fish. Its spice and herbal flavors go well with the smokiness imparted by the grill.

3 large bunches fresh flat-leaf parsley
5 large garlic cloves
¾ cup extra-virgin olive oil
½ cup distilled white vinegar
½ teaspoon dried hot red pepper flakes

Remove enough leaves from parsley to measure 4 packed cups and in a food processor purée with remaining ingredients.

Cooks' note:
• Sauce may be made 1 day ahead and chilled, covered.

PHOTO ON PAGE 52

JÍCAMA AND CILANTRO RELISH

Makes about 6 cups

1 cup tender fresh cilantro sprigs
1 tablespoon chopped fresh mint
1 large fresh jalapeño, seeded and finely chopped
1 teaspoon sugar
3 tablespoons fresh lime juice, or to taste
2 lb *jícama*, peeled and cut into 1-inch cubes
¼ teaspoon salt

Pulse cilantro, mint, jalapeño, sugar, and 3 tablespoons lime juice in a food processor until cilantro is finely chopped. Add half of *jícama* and pulse until *jícama* is very coarsely chopped (you want a chunky, crunchy slaw, not a purée). Transfer relish to a bowl.

Pulse remaining *jícama* in food processor in same manner and add to relish with salt and lime juice to taste. Chill relish well, about 2 hours.

Cooks' note:
• Taste jalapeño before adding it, to control amount of heat.

PHOTO ON PAGE 64

MEYER LEMON "JAM"

Makes about ½ cup

Inspired by the lemon-oregano jam Mario Batali serves at Babbo, in New York City, this "jam" is delicious with poached or grilled fish or chicken or steamed asparagus or artichokes.

2 Meyer lemons (½ lb)
1 tablespoon sugar
1 tablespoon water
2 tablespoons olive oil

Remove zest from lemons with a vegetable peeler. Remove any white pith from zest and lemon with a sharp knife. Blanch zest only in boiling water 5 minutes. Cut peeled lemons into quarters and discard seeds.

Purée zest, lemons, sugar, and water in a blender until smooth. With motor running, add oil in a slow stream, blending until "jam" is thick, and season with salt. Transfer to a bowl and chill, covered, 8 hours to allow flavors to mellow.

Cooks' note:
• "Jam" keeps, covered and chilled, 5 days.

DESSERTS

POPPY-SEED ANGEL FOOD CAKES WITH LEMON SYRUP

Serves 4

Vegetable-oil cooking spray
4 large egg whites
¼ teaspoon cream of tartar
½ cup superfine sugar
⅓ cup cake flour (not self-rising)
¼ teaspoon salt
1 teaspoon freshly grated lemon zest
¼ teaspoon vanilla
1 teaspoon poppy seeds

Special equipment: 4 (3- by 1½-inch) stainless-steel
   entremet (pastry) rings

Garnish: 1½ teaspoons confectioners sugar
Accompaniment: lemon syrup (recipe follows)

Preheat oven to 350°F. Set rings on a baking sheet and lightly spray insides with cooking spray.

In a large bowl with an electric mixer beat whites until frothy. Add cream of tartar and beat until whites just hold soft peaks. Beat in superfine sugar, a little at a time, and beat until whites just hold stiff peaks. Sift flour with salt over whites and gently fold in with remaining ingredients.

Spoon batter into rings, mounding batter, and bake in middle of oven until golden brown, about 20 minutes (cakes will fall slightly). Transfer rings on sheet to a rack to cool. Run a thin knife around edges of rings and gently remove cakes, transferring them to plates.

Dust cakes with confectioners sugar and spoon syrup around them.

Cooks' note:
• You can use ½-cup muffin cups instead of the pastry rings. The batter will fill 6 muffin cups, making smaller cakes.

☞ each serving, including syrup, about 233 calories and
less than 1 gram fat

LEMON SYRUP ◐+

Makes about 1 cup

½ vanilla bean
1 large lemon
6 tablespoons superfine sugar
½ cup water
1½ teaspoons fresh lemon juice

Halve vanilla bean lengthwise and scrape seeds into a small saucepan. Finely grate enough zest from lemon to measure ½ teaspoon. Cut remaining peel from lemon, removing all white pith. Cut enough sections free from membranes to measure ¼ cup and cut into ¼-inch pieces. Add lemon pieces to pan with sugar, water, and grated zest. Simmer mixture, stirring, until sugar is dissolved and stir in lemon juice. Cool syrup to room temperature and serve with cakes.

☞ each ¼-cup serving about 78 calories and less than 1 gram fat

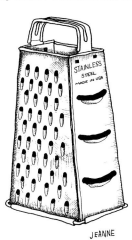

JEANNE

177

MARBLED PUMPKIN CHEESECAKE

Serves 8 to 10

1 crumb-crust (recipe follows)
3 (8-oz) packages cream cheese,
   softened
1¾ cups sugar
3 tablespoons all-purpose flour
5 large eggs
½ teaspoon vanilla
2 large egg yolks
¾ teaspoon ground cinnamon
⅛ teaspoon ground ginger
⅛ teaspoon ground allspice
⅛ teaspoon freshly grated nutmeg
15-oz can solid-pack pumpkin

Make crumb crust. Preheat oven to 550°F.

Beat together cream cheese, sugar, and flour with an electric mixer until smooth and add whole eggs, 1 at a time, then vanilla, beating on low speed until each ingredient is incorporated and scraping down bowl between additions. Transfer 2½ cups filling to another bowl and beat yolks, spices, and pumpkin into remaining filling until smooth.

Put springform pan with crust in a shallow baking pan. Pour half of pumpkin filling into crust, then half of plain. Repeat procedure with remaining fillings (springform pan will be completely full), drizzling the plain so that some of pumpkin filling is still visible. Gently swirl a small spoon once through batters in a figure-eight pattern without touching crust. Bake in baking pan (to catch drips) in middle of oven 12 minutes, or until puffed. Reduce temperature to 200°F and bake 30 minutes (do not open oven). Dome a piece of lightly oiled foil over cake and continue baking until mostly firm (center will still be slightly wobbly when pan is gently shaken), about 1 hour more.

Run a knife around top edge of cake to loosen and cool completely in springform pan on a rack. Chill, loosely covered, at least 6 hours. Remove side of pan and transfer cake to a plate. Bring to room temperature before serving.

Cooks' note:
• Cheesecake keeps, covered and chilled, 1 week.

CRUMB CRUST ☺

Makes enough for a 24-centimeter cheesecake

1½ cups (5 oz) finely ground gingersnaps
5 tablespoons unsalted butter, melted
⅓ cup sugar
⅛ teaspoon salt

Stir together crust ingredients and press onto bottom and 1 inch up side of a buttered 24-centimeter springform pan. Fill right away or chill up to 2 hours.

Cooks' note:
• When buying the springform pan make sure it is marked "24 centimeters." (Depending on the manufacturer, the pans are variously sized as 9 or 9½ inches across, but disregard this.)

BLOSSOM-TOPPED CUPCAKES

Makes 16

When choosing edible flowers to garnish these cupcakes, make sure that they are unsprayed and organically grown.

For cupcakes
2 cups cake flour (not self-rising)
1 teaspoon baking powder
½ teaspoon salt
2 sticks unsalted butter, softened
1½ cups granulated sugar
4 large eggs
¼ cup whole milk
1 teaspoon vanilla
For frosting
2 (8-oz) packages cream cheese, softened
1 cup confectioners sugar
1 teaspoon fresh lemon juice
¼ teaspoon rosewater (sources on page 252)
   (optional)

Special equipment: 16 (2½-inch) paper muffin-cup
   liners

Garnish: nontoxic and organic (pesticide-free) small
   roses, pansies, and scented geranium leaves
   (sources on page 252) and blackberries dusted
   with confectioners sugar

Make cupcakes:

Preheat oven to 350°F and line 16 (⅓-cup) muffin cups with paper muffin-cup liners.

Sift together flour, baking powder, and salt. Beat together butter and sugar in a large bowl with an electric mixer until light and fluffy. Add eggs 1 at a time, beating well after each addition, and with mixer on low speed beat in milk and vanilla until just combined (batter will separate). Add flour mixture in 3 batches, beating until just combined after each addition.

Divide batter among muffin cups and bake in middle of oven until a tester comes out clean, about 20 minutes. Cool cupcakes in pan on a rack 5 minutes and remove from pan.

Make frosting:

Beat cream cheese with an electric mixer until smooth. Add confectioners sugar and beat on low speed until incorporated. Add lemon juice and rosewater and beat until smooth.

Frost cupcakes and garnish.

Cooks' notes:
• You can make cupcakes 1 day ahead (leave them unfrosted) and keep them in an airtight container at room temperature.
• Frosting may be made 2 days ahead and chilled, covered (beat until smooth before using).

PHOTO ON PAGE 59

CHOCOLATE CARAMEL DIAMONDS

Makes about 42

For cake
4 oz fine-quality bittersweet chocolate
    (not unsweetened)
1 stick unsalted butter
¾ cup sugar
3 large eggs
¼ cup all-purpose flour
¼ cup unsweetened cocoa powder
For ganache
5 oz fine-quality bittersweet chocolate
    (not unsweetened)
⅓ cup sugar
⅓ cup heavy cream
For caramel topping
¼ cup sugar

Make cake:

Preheat oven to 375°F. Butter a 9-inch square baking pan and line bottom with wax paper.

Chop chocolate into small pieces. In a double boiler or a metal bowl set over a saucepan of barely simmering water melt chocolate and butter, stirring until smooth. Remove top of double boiler or bowl from heat and whisk sugar into chocolate mixture. Whisk in eggs 1 at a time until combined well. Sift flour and cocoa powder over chocolate mixture and whisk until just combined. Pour batter into baking pan and bake in middle of oven until a tester comes out clean, about 20 minutes. Cool cake completely in pan on a rack and invert onto a baking sheet lined with wax paper.

Make ganache:

Chop chocolate. In a dry heavy saucepan cook sugar over moderate heat, without stirring, until it begins to melt. Continue to cook sugar, stirring with a fork, until a deep-golden caramel. Remove pan from heat and add cream (mixture will bubble up and steam). Simmer mixture, stirring, until caramel is dissolved. Remove pan from heat and add chocolate, stirring until mixture is smooth. Pour *ganache* over top of cake and smooth with a spatula. Chill, uncovered, at least 30 minutes.

Make topping:

Lightly grease a baking sheet.

In a dry small heavy saucepan cook sugar over moderately low heat, stirring slowly with a fork (to help sugar melt evenly), until a pale-golden caramel. Continue to cook caramel, without stirring, gently swirling pan, until golden. Remove pan from heat and pour caramel onto baking sheet. Cool completely.

Pry caramel from baking sheet with your fingers and in a food processor pulse caramel until coarsely ground. Sprinkle the ground caramel evenly over top of cake and with a sharp knife cut cake into 1¼-inch diamonds.

Cooks' note:
• Cake topped with *ganache* can be chilled up to 3 days, covered.

PHOTO ON PAGE 25

CHOCOLATE MOUSSE SPONGE ◐+

Serves 6

Vegetable-oil cooking spray
8 oz fine-quality semisweet chocolate (preferably
    Callebaut or Valrhona), finely chopped
8 large eggs, separated
¼ teaspoon salt
¼ cup confectioners sugar, plus more for dusting

Preheat oven to 350°F. Lightly spray side of an 8½-inch springform pan with cooking spray and line bottom with wax paper.

Melt chocolate in a metal bowl set over a saucepan of simmering water, stirring until smooth. Whisk yolks until thick and pale, about 2 minutes with a standing mixer or 4 minutes with a hand-held. (Do not beat to ribbon stage.) Fold chocolate into yolks.

Beat whites with salt and sugar, using cleaned beaters, until they just hold soft peaks. Fold one fourth of whites into chocolate mixture to lighten, then fold in remaining whites gently but thoroughly.

Pour batter into pan and bake in middle of oven, 25 to 30 minutes, just until cake is almost set but still trembles slightly in center when shaken gently. Do not cook it beyond this stage, or you won't get a mousselike center. Cool cake on a rack (it will settle as it cools) and chill (still in pan), covered, at least 6 hours.

Let cake stand at room temperature 30 minutes before serving, then dust with confectioners sugar.

Cooks' notes:
• Do not overbeat yolks and whites.
• Cake may be chilled up to 5 days.

PHOTO ON PAGE 75

MINI BROWNIE CUPCAKES ◐+

Makes about 72 mini-cupcakes

We used waxed candy/muffin liners for these cupcakes, which kept them from sticking and helped them develop attractive domed tops. (Spraying your muffin tins will keep them from sticking but tends to result in flat-topped cupcakes.)

Vegetable-oil cooking spray
4 sticks unsalted butter, cut into pieces
8 oz unsweetened chocolate, chopped
1¾ cups all-purpose flour
½ cup unsweetened cocoa powder (preferably
    Dutch-process)
½ teaspoon salt
3¾ cups granulated sugar
8 large eggs
Confectioners sugar (optional)

Special equipment: mini–muffin tins and about 72
    (1- by 1-inch) waxed paper liners (sources on
    page 252)

Preheat oven to 350°F and line mini–muffin tins with waxed paper liners. Spray liners with cooking spray.

Melt butter and chocolate in a 4-quart heavy pot over moderately low heat, stirring until smooth. Whisk together flour, cocoa, and salt. Remove pan from heat and whisk in granulated sugar. Add eggs, 1 at a time, whisking after each addition until incorporated, and stir in flour mixture just until blended.

Spoon batter into muffin liners, filling cups to top, and bake in middle of oven 25 to 30 minutes, or until a tester comes out with crumbs adhering. Cool 5 minutes in tins and turn out onto racks. Repeat with remaining batter.

Dust with confectioners sugar if desired.

Cooks' note:
• Cupcakes may be made 2 days ahead and kept in an airtight container at room temperature.

WARM CHOCOLATE RASPBERRY PUDDING CAKE

Serves 6 to 8

The frosting for this cake is baked in the same pan with the batter. When the cake is inverted, it is bathed with frosting.

For frosting
3 oz fine-quality bittersweet chocolate
    (not unsweetened)
½ cup seedless raspberry jam (about 5 oz)
½ cup heavy cream
For cake batter
½ cup boiling-hot water
⅓ cup plus 2 teaspoons unsweetened cocoa
    powder (not Dutch process)
¼ cup whole milk
½ teaspoon vanilla
⅓ cup seedless raspberry jam (about 3½ oz)
1 stick unsalted butter, softened
⅓ cup packed light brown sugar
⅓ cup granulated sugar
2 large eggs
1 cup all-purpose flour
¾ teaspoon baking soda
¼ teaspoon salt

Garnish: raspberries

Preheat oven to 350°F and generously butter a 9- by 2-inch round cake pan.
    Make frosting:
Chop chocolate. In a small heavy saucepan bring jam, cream, and chocolate to a simmer, stirring occasionally, until smooth. Pour frosting into cake pan.
    Make cake batter:
In a bowl whisk together boiling-hot water and cocoa powder until smooth and whisk in milk, vanilla, and jam. In a large bowl with an electric mixer beat together butter and sugars until light and fluffy and add eggs 1 at a time, beating well after each addition. Into another bowl sift together flour, baking soda, and salt and add to egg mixture in batches alternately with cocoa mixture, beginning and ending with flour mixture and beating well after each addition.
    Pour batter evenly over frosting mixture and bake in middle of oven 30 to 35 minutes, or until a tester comes out clean (frosting on bottom will still be liquid). Cool cake slightly in pan on a rack, 10 to 20 minutes.

Run a thin knife around edge of pan and twist pan gently back and forth on a flat surface to loosen cake. Invert a cake plate with a slight lip over pan and, holding pan and plate together with both hands, invert cake onto plate. Frosting will cover cake and run onto plate.
    Serve cake warm or at room temperature garnished with raspberries.

Cooks' note:
- Cake may be made 1 day ahead, cooled completely in pan and left in pan, covered, at room temperature. Reheat, uncovered, at 350°F 10 to 15 minutes.

PHOTO ON PAGE 15

STAR ANISE AND CORIANDER SPICE CAKE

Serves 10 to 12

1¼ cups all-purpose flour
1 teaspoon baking powder
¾ teaspoon salt
3 tablespoons coriander seeds
5 points of star anise (sources on page 252)
1 stick unsalted butter, softened
1 cup sugar
½ cup uncooked farina such as Cream of Wheat
1 large egg
2 large yolks
⅔ cup whole milk

Garnish: strawberries

Preheat oven to 350°F and butter and flour an 8- by 2-inch round cake pan.
    Into a bowl sift together flour, baking powder, and salt. In an electric coffee/spice grinder finely grind coriander seeds and star anise. In a large bowl with an electric mixer beat together butter and sugar until light and fluffy. Add flour mixture, ground spices, and remaining ingredients and beat on low speed until combined. Increase speed to high and beat batter 3 minutes. Pour batter into pan and bake in middle of oven until cake pulls away from side of pan, about 50 minutes.
    Cool cake in pan on a rack 10 minutes. Invert cake onto rack and remove pan. Invert another rack onto cake and turn cake right side up. Cool cake completely.

PHOTO ON PAGE 43

WEDDING CAKE WITH BLACKBERRIES AND ROSES

Serves 50

We wanted to make a cake that would look wonderful, taste great, but still be manageable. The layers are a basic pound cake, and the frosting is a simple cream-cheese variation. Sandwiched between the layers is store-bought jam.

You'll need some sort of base for the assembled cake. This can be anything from a very large platter to a piece of wood covered with tulle. For more tips on preparing this cake, see box, page 184.

Important: Two separate batches of the following batter are required in this recipe. You'll need twice the quantity of the batter ingredients below, but do not double when mixing the ingredients.

For each batch of batter
12 large eggs
¾ cup milk
2 tablespoons vanilla
1½ teaspoons salt
6 cups cake flour (not self-rising)
6 sticks unsalted butter, softened
3 cups sugar
For assembly
4 cups lemon syrup (recipe follows)
2⅓ cups rose hip, rose fruit, or seedless blackberry jam (about 3 jars, 12 oz each)
Cream-cheese frosting (page 183)
8 (½-pint) containers blackberries (about 8 cups)

Special equipment:
1 (12- by 2-inch) cake pan
1 (9- by 2-inch) cake pan
1 (6- by 2-inch) cake pan
2 packages Magi-Cake or homemade foil strips (sources and tips in box, page 184)
1 (12-inch) serrated knife
4 (11-inch) cardboard rounds
4 (8-inch) cardboard rounds
4 (6-inch) cardboard rounds, trimmed to 5-inch rounds
1 medium-size piping bag with 3⁄16-inch plain tip
Cake base or large platter
5 (8-inch) plastic straws
Cake-decorating turntable (optional but very helpful)

Garnish: petals from 3 large organic and nontoxic roses (sources on page 252) and blackberries (optional)

Bake cake layers:

Preheat oven to 350°F. Grease cake pans and line bottom of each with a round of wax paper. Grease paper and dust pans with flour, knocking out excess. Wet Magi-Cake strips and fasten around each pan.

Whisk together eggs, milk, and vanilla. Whisk salt into flour in another bowl. Beat butter (it should be room temperature) with sugar in a 5-quart standing electric mixer on medium speed until light and fluffy, about 5 minutes. Add flour and egg mixture alternately in 3 batches, ending with egg mixture and beating on low speed just until incorporated.

Divide batter among pans so each is filled to 1 inch from top. (If you have a wall oven or other small oven, see notes, below.) Bake in upper and lower thirds of oven, with 12-inch pan on upper rack, 20 minutes. Gently turn pans in place so that part of cake that was toward back of oven now faces front and bake cakes until a tester comes out of each with a few crumbs adhering, 10 to 20 minutes more, depending on cake size. Transfer each cake as done to a rack to cool. Cool cakes slightly (9-inch and 6-inch cakes for 10 minutes; 12-inch cake for 20 minutes) and invert onto racks, peeling off paper. Turn cakes right side up and cool completely.

Clean pans. Make second batch of batter; bake and cool cakes in same manner.

Assemble cake:

Work with 12-inch cakes first. Trim top of each with long serrated knife to make level, then cut cakes horizontally in half. Put each 12-inch layer, cut side up, on an 11-inch cardboard round. Brush cut sides generously with syrup. Stir jam until smooth and spread about ⅔ cup on a 12-inch layer. Invert another 12-inch layer (with cardboard), cut side down, onto jam. Discard top cardboard round and spread about 2½ cups frosting on top. Sprinkle with 1 layer of blackberries to cover frosting. (If berries are 1 inch or larger, halve them lengthwise.) Slide the third 12-inch layer, syrup side up, onto berries, discarding cardboard, and press gently. Spread about ⅔ cup jam on layer and invert the last 12-inch layer (with cardboard), cut side down, onto jam, then discard cardboard.

Spoon 2 cups frosting onto 12-inch tier and cover cake with a thin coating. (This is called crumb-coating. It tamps down any loose crumbs to keep them out of the top layer of frosting and fills in any crevices.) Chill 12-inch tier while working on remaining tiers.

Trim and halve 9-inch cakes similarly and put on 8-inch rounds. Brush cut sides generously with syrup. Assemble and crumb-coat 9-inch tier in same manner (use about ⅓ cup jam and 1¼ cups frosting between layers; crumb-coat with about 1½ cups frosting). Chill 9-inch tier.

Repeat procedure to make 6-inch tier (use about 2½ tablespoons jam and about ¾ cup frosting between layers; crumb-coat with about ¾ cup frosting) and chill until firm.

Reserve 2 cups frosting for piping. Place 12-inch tier on cake base (preferably on a cake turntable) and frost. Then frost remaining tiers. Chill frosted tiers (do not stack) at least 4 hours.

Cut 3 straws in half and insert 1 straw piece in center of 12-inch tier all the way to bottom. Insert remaining 5 straw pieces in a circle about 1½ inches from center straw and trim straws level with top of tier. (Straws support tiers.) Carefully put 9-inch tier (still on cardboard) in center of bottom tier. Cut remaining 2 straws in half and insert into middle tier in similar manner, with 1 straw piece in center and remaining 3 straw pieces in a circle around it. Carefully put 6-inch tier (still on cardboard) on top, in center of middle tier.

Fill in any gaps between tiers and any imperfections with frosting and transfer the remainder to pastry bag fitted with ³⁄₁₆-inch tip. Pipe a decorative border around the bottom edge of each tier. Save remaining frosting for touch-ups—just in case.

Cake should come to room temperature before serving (it may stand at cool room temperature about 6 hours). Garnish cake with roses and serve slices with blackberries.

Cooks' notes:
• Cake layers may be baked and frozen, wrapped well in foil and sealed in plastic bags, up to a month ahead. (Don't refrigerate them.) Thaw wrapped layers at room temperature a day before assembling the cake.
• If you can't fit the entire assembled cake on its base into your refrigerator, a good place to stop is after assembling and crumb-coating the 3 tiers but before stacking them together. Go to that point 1 day ahead and keep the tiers chilled. Cover each loosely with plastic wrap once the frosting is set. (No smelly things in the fridge, please!) After frosting the tiers, chill them overnight.
• Some of our ovens are wall ovens, which tend to be small (ours are about 19 inches wide, 15 inches high, and 17½ inches deep). We found that the cakes cooked more evenly when we cooked the 12-inch cake alone on the middle rack, then the 6-inch and 9-inch together on the middle rack. If you do this, fill all the pans at the same time but leave the 2 smaller cakes at room temperature while baking the 12-inch.

PHOTO ON PAGE 57

LEMON SYRUP ◐

Makes about 4 cups

2 cups fresh lemon juice
2 cups sugar
1 cup water
1 teaspoon rosewater (optional)
   (sources on page 252)

Stir together all ingredients until sugar is dissolved.

Cooks' note:
• You can make syrup up to 1 week ahead and chill it in an airtight container.

CREAM-CHEESE FROSTING ◐

Makes about 16 cups

12 (8-oz) packages cream cheese, softened
6 sticks unsalted butter, softened
2 (1-lb) boxes confectioners sugar (7½ cups)

Make frosting in 2 batches: For first batch, beat 6 packages cream cheese in a standing electric mixer until smooth and add 3 sticks butter and 1 box confectioners sugar. Beat on low speed until sugar is incorporated, then beat on medium speed 1 minute. Repeat with remaining ingredients and combine batches.

Cooks' note:
• Frosting may be made 3 days ahead and chilled, covered. You can ice cake with chilled frosting.

TIPS FOR MAKING A WEDDING CAKE

• **Magi-Cake Strips** ensure that the cake bakes to a level-topped finish. Without the strips, the layers form a dome shape as they bake. The aluminum-coated fabric strips, dampened and wrapped around a pan, keep the pan cooler so that the edges of the cake rise at the same rate as the center. See sources below, or make the strips yourself: You will need foil, paper towels, scissors, and large paper clips. Tear off three different lengths of foil, equivalent to the circumference of each of the three pans. (We did the math: The 6-inch pan will require a 19-inch sheet of foil; the 9-inch pan, a 29-inch sheet; the 12-inch pan, a 38-inch sheet.) Measure equal lengths of paper towels. Working with one paper towel at a time, moisten it (it should not be dripping) and fold into a strip measuring 1½ to 2 inches in width. Align one long side of the paper-towel strip with one long side of the sheet of foil that is the same length and fold the foil over twice, trimming excess width of foil sheet. Wrap it snugly around the side of the appropriate pan and fasten it with a paper clip.

• **A cake-decorating turntable** (sources below) will give you easy access to the entire cake. Frost each tier separately on the turntable. Use a spatula to help transfer the tiers, still on their cardboard rounds, to the turntable. Put a generous amount of frosting on top and spread it until it begins to slump over the side. Then go vertical: After spreading a small patch of frosting down the side with a 6- to 8-inch narrow offset metal spatula, keep that hand still and with the other slowly spin the turntable, spreading the frosting. To assemble the "official" wedding cake, transfer the largest tier to a cakestand and put that on the turntable. During this phase, it's fine to leave a few fingerprints—it's easy to smooth out the frosting to a satiny finish.

Note: Magi-Cake strips, turntable, and other baking supplies needed for making a wedding cake are available at bake shops and New York Cake and Baking Distributors, 800-942-2539.

CITRUS CHIFFON CAKE

Serves 6

It's unusual to butter and flour the pan when making a chiffon cake, but we liked the delicate crust that resulted. Because we did it this way, the cake must be cooled, inverted, on a rack, not on a bottle (the usual procedure for chiffons), or it will fall right out of the pan!

1 cup cake flour (not self-rising)
¾ cup granulated sugar
1 teaspoon baking powder
½ teaspoon salt
3 large eggs
5 tablespoons canola oil
⅓ cup fresh orange juice
2 teaspoons finely grated fresh orange zest
2 teaspoons finely grated fresh lemon zest
1 teaspoon vanilla
½ teaspoon cream of tartar
Confectioners sugar for sprinkling

Special equipment: a 1½-quart (about 8-inch) *Kugelhupf* or bundt pan

Accompaniment: citrus syrup (recipe follows)

Preheat oven to 350°F. Butter and flour pan, knocking out excess flour.

Into a large bowl sift together flour, ½ cup granulated sugar, baking powder, and salt. Separate eggs. In a small bowl whisk together yolks, oil, orange juice, zests, and vanilla and whisk mixture into flour mixture until batter is smooth.

In another large bowl with an electric mixer beat whites with cream of tartar until they just hold soft peaks. With mixer on low speed gradually add remaining ¼ cup granulated sugar and beat until whites hold stiff, glossy peaks. Stir about one third whites into batter to lighten and fold in remaining whites gently but thoroughly. Spoon batter into pan (batter will reach top of pan).

Bake cake in middle of oven until golden and a tester comes out clean, about 40 minutes. Immediately invert pan onto a rack and cool cake completely in pan upside down on rack. Run a thin knife around outer edge of pan and turn cake out of pan onto a serving plate.

Sprinkle cake with confectioners sugar and serve, sliced, with syrup.

Cooks' note:
• Cake may be made 2 days ahead and kept in an airtight container at cool room temperature.

PHOTO ON PAGE 21

CITRUS SYRUP ☉

Makes about 1¼ cups

¾ cup sugar
½ cup fresh orange juice
½ cup fresh lemon juice

In a 1½-quart saucepan stir together sugar and citrus juices and simmer, stirring occasionally, 5 minutes, or until sugar is dissolved and syrup is slightly thickened. Cool syrup.

Cooks' note:
• Syrup may be made 3 days ahead and chilled, covered.

COOKIES, BARS, AND CONFECTIONS

BLUEBERRY CHEESECAKE BARS

Makes 24

These treats are built upon a buttery shortbread foundation. Be sure to prepare your topping while the shortbread is baking— the cookie layer must be piping hot for the topping to spread properly.

For shortbread base
1½ sticks unsalted butter
2 cups all-purpose flour
½ cup packed light brown sugar
½ teaspoon salt
For topping
16 oz cream cheese, softened
2 large eggs
¾ cup sugar
1 teaspoon vanilla
¾ cup blueberry or other fruit preserves

Make base:
Preheat oven to 350°F.
Cut butter into ½-inch pieces. In a food processor process all base ingredients until mixture begins to form small lumps. Sprinkle mixture into a 13- by 9- by 2-inch baking pan and with a metal spatula press evenly onto bottom. Bake shortbread in middle of oven until golden, about 20 minutes.

While shortbread is baking, prepare topping:
In a bowl whisk cream cheese until smooth and whisk in eggs, sugar, and vanilla. Evenly spread preserves over hot shortbread and pour cream-cheese mixture over it. Bake in middle of oven until slightly puffed, about 30 minutes. Cool completely in pan and cut into 24 bars.

Cooks' note:
• Bar cookies keep, covered and chilled, 3 days.

BUTTER COOKIES

Makes about 100

2 cups all-purpose flour
½ teaspoon salt
¼ teaspoon baking powder
2 sticks unsalted butter, softened
1 cup sugar
1 large egg
1 teaspoon vanilla

Into a bowl sift together flour, salt, and baking powder. In a large bowl with an electric mixer beat butter until creamy. Gradually add sugar, beating until mixture is light and fluffy. Add egg and vanilla and beat until combined well. Gradually add flour mixture, beating until mixture just forms a dough.

Divide dough between 2 large sheets of wax paper and form each half into a 10- by 1½-inch log, wrapping it in wax paper. Chill logs until firm, at least 4 hours, and up to 5 days.

Preheat oven to 375°F. Lightly butter a baking sheet.

Cut dough into ⅛-inch-thick slices and arrange slices about ½ inch apart on baking sheet. Bake cookies in batches in middle of oven until golden around edges, 10 to 12 minutes, and transfer with a metal spatula to a rack to cool.

Cooks' notes:
• Dough logs may be frozen, wrapped in foil, 2 months. Let dough soften slightly before cutting.
• Cookies may be kept in an airtight container at room temperature 5 days.

OATMEAL COOKIES ◐

Makes 24

1¾ cups old-fashioned rolled oats
¾ cup all-purpose flour
¾ teaspoon cinnamon
½ teaspoon baking soda
½ teaspoon salt
1¼ sticks unsalted butter, softened
⅓ cup packed light brown sugar
⅓ cup granulated sugar
1 large egg
½ teaspoon vanilla

Preheat oven to 375°F. Grease baking sheets.

Stir together oats, flour, cinnamon, baking soda, and salt. Beat together butter, brown sugar, and granulated sugar in a large bowl with an electric mixer until light and fluffy. Add egg and vanilla and beat until combined well. Add oat mixture and beat until just combined.

Drop dough by heaping tablespoons 2 inches apart onto baking sheets and flatten mounds slightly with moistened fingers. Bake cookies in upper and lower thirds of oven, switching position of sheets halfway through baking, until golden, about 12 minutes total. Transfer to racks to cool.

CASHEW ORANGE BISCOTTI

Makes about 60

1½ cups roasted cashews (about 7 oz)
2 cups unbleached all-purpose flour
1 cup sugar
1 teaspoon baking soda
¼ teaspoon salt
4 large eggs
1 tablespoon freshly grated orange zest
1 teaspoon vanilla
1 teaspoon water

Preheat oven to 300°F. Butter a large baking sheet.

Coarsely chop cashews. Into a bowl sift together flour, sugar, baking soda, and salt. In another bowl with an electric mixer beat together 3 eggs, zest, and vanilla until just combined. Stir in flour mixture and beat until a stiff dough is formed. Stir in cashews.

In a small bowl beat together water and remaining egg to make an egg wash. On baking sheet with floured hands form dough into two 12-inch-long logs and flatten slightly. Brush logs with some egg wash and bake in middle of oven until golden, about 50 minutes. Cool logs on baking sheet on a rack 10 minutes.

On a cutting board with a serrated knife diagonally cut logs into roughly ⅓-inch-thick slices. Arrange *biscotti*, a cut side down, on baking sheet and bake in middle of oven until crisp, about 15 minutes. Cool *biscotti* on rack.

Cooks' note:
• *Biscotti* keep in an airtight container at cool room temperature 2 weeks.

PHOTO ON PAGE 29

CHOCOLATE MACAROON BARS

Makes 24

For shortbread base
1½ sticks unsalted butter
2 cups all-purpose flour
½ cup packed light brown sugar
½ teaspoon salt
For topping
4 large egg whites
1 cup sugar
1 teaspoon vanilla
½ cup all-purpose flour
1 (7-oz) bag sweetened flaked coconut
   (about 2⅔ cups)
1½ cups semisweet chocolate chips

Make base:
Preheat oven to 350°F.

Cut butter into ½-inch pieces. In a food processor process all base ingredients until mixture begins to form small lumps. Sprinkle mixture into a 13- by 9- by 2-inch baking pan and with a metal spatula press evenly onto bottom. Bake shortbread in middle of oven until golden, about 20 minutes.

While shortbread is baking, prepare topping:
In a bowl whisk together whites, sugar, and vanilla until combined well and stir in flour and coconut. Sprinkle chocolate chips evenly over hot shortbread.

Let chips melt and spread evenly over shortbread. Drop small spoonfuls of coconut mixture onto chocolate and with a fork spread evenly. Bake in middle of oven until top is golden, about 30 minutes. Cool completely in pan and cut into 24 bars.

Cooks' note:
• Bar cookies keep in an airtight container at room temperature 5 days.

DOUBLE-CHOCOLATE ALMOND BROWNIES

Serves 2

⅓ cup sliced almonds (about 1 oz)
¼ cup all-purpose flour
½ teaspoon baking powder
2 oz unsweetened chocolate
½ stick unsalted butter
½ cup sugar
½ teaspoon vanilla
1 large egg
⅓ cup semisweet chocolate chips

Preheat oven to 375°F and line bottom and sides of an 8- by 4- by 3-inch loaf pan with foil, leaving a ½-inch overhang all around.

On a baking sheet toast almonds in middle of oven until golden, about 7 minutes. Into a small bowl sift together flour, baking powder, and a pinch salt.

In a double boiler or a metal bowl set over a pan of simmering water melt unsweetened chocolate and butter, stirring until smooth. Remove top of double boiler or bowl from heat and stir in sugar and vanilla until combined well. Whisk in egg until combined well and stir in almonds, flour mixture, and chocolate chips until just combined. Pour batter into loaf pan and bake in middle of oven until a tester inserted 1 inch from side of pan comes out clean, 20 to 25 minutes. (Center will be fudge-like.)

Cool brownies in pan on a rack 5 minutes and lift out foil with brownies onto rack.

Cooks' note:
• Brownies keep in an airtight container 3 days or frozen 2 weeks.

TOASTED-COCONUT COOKIES

Makes about 100

1½ cups sweetened flaked coconut
1¼ cups all-purpose flour
1 teaspoon baking soda
½ teaspoon salt
1¼ sticks unsalted butter, softened
½ cup packed light brown sugar
¼ cup granulated sugar
1 large egg
1 teaspoon vanilla

Preheat oven to 375°F.

In a shallow baking pan spread coconut evenly and lightly toast in middle of oven, stirring once, until pale golden, 4 to 5 minutes. Cool coconut.

Into a small bowl sift together flour, baking soda, and salt. In a large bowl with an electric mixer beat together butter and sugars until light and fluffy. Beat in egg and vanilla and stir in flour mixture and coconut until combined well.

Drop teaspoons of dough about 1½ inches apart on ungreased baking sheets and bake in batches in middle of oven until golden, 8 to 10 minutes. Cool cookies on sheets 1 minute and with a metal spatula transfer to racks to cool.

Cooks' note:
• Cookies keep in an airtight container at room temperature 1 week.

CHOCOLATE-SESAME CUPS ⊙+

Makes 18 petits fours

Vegetable-oil cooking spray
½ cup currants
1 cup boiling-hot water
8 oz fine-quality semisweet chocolate
    (preferably Callebaut or Valrhona),
    finely chopped
3½ tablespoons tahini (Middle Eastern
    sesame paste)

Lightly spray 18 (1-inch) candy/petit-four cup liners with cooking spray.

Soak currants in boiling-hot water 5 minutes. Drain and pat dry with paper towels. Melt chocolate with 3 tablespoons tahini in a metal bowl set over a saucepan of simmering water, stirring until smooth, and stir in currants. Spoon chocolate mixture into cup liners and cool 5 minutes.

Decorate candies by dipping tip of a skewer or toothpick into remaining ½ tablespoon tahini and swirling over tops. Chill cups until set.

Cooks' notes:
• If using foil cups, line with paper liners before spraying with vegetable-oil cooking spray.
• Petits fours keep, covered and chilled, 1 week.

PHOTO ON PAGE 74

VANILLA-BEAN SUGAR COOKIES

Makes about 36

If you bake these cookies a couple of days ahead, the vanilla flavor will become more pronounced.

¾ stick unsalted butter, softened
2 tablespoons cold vegetable shortening
1 cup sugar
2 vanilla beans
1 large egg
1 teaspoon vanilla extract
1¼ cups all-purpose flour
1 teaspoon baking powder
½ teaspoon salt

In a bowl with an electric mixer beat together butter, shortening, and ¾ cup sugar until light and fluffy. With a knife halve vanilla beans lengthwise. Scrape seeds into butter mixture and beat in egg and vanilla extract until combined well. Sift flour, baking powder, and salt into mixture and beat until just combined.

On a large sheet of wax paper form dough into a 10-by 2-inch log and roll up in wax paper. Chill dough until firm, at least 4 hours.

Preheat oven to 375°F.

Put remaining ¼ cup sugar on a platter. Remove wax paper and roll log in sugar (not all sugar will adhere to log). Cut log crosswise into ¼-inch-thick slices and dip cut sides of slices in sugar on platter. Arrange cookies ½ inch apart on ungreased baking sheets and bake in batches in middle of oven 10 to 12 minutes, or until edges are pale golden. With a metal spatula transfer cookies to a rack to cool.

Cooks' notes:
• Dough keeps, chilled, up to 3 days wrapped in wax paper and foil.
• Cookies may be made 2 days ahead and kept between sheets of wax paper in an airtight container.

PIES, TARTS, AND PASTRIES

APPLE AND PRUNE TART

Serves 8 to 10

For pastry dough
1⅔ cups all-purpose flour
1½ teaspoons sugar
¾ teaspoon salt
1¼ sticks cold unsalted butter, cut into pieces
4 to 5 tablespoons ice water
For filling
⅓ cup water
2 tablespoons Calvados
1 cup packed pitted prunes (7 oz), halved
1 teaspoon cinnamon
Pinch of ground cloves
5 tablespoons all-purpose flour
¾ cup sugar

2 lb tart green apples (5)
1½ tablespoons fresh lemon juice
½ cup walnut pieces, toasted

1 tablespoon whole milk
1 tablespoon sugar

Make dough:

Pulse together flour, sugar, and salt in a food processor. Add butter and pulse until mixture resembles coarse meal. Sprinkle in 4 tablespoons ice water and pulse until pastry starts to hold together, adding remaining tablespoon ice water if needed. Turn dough out onto a very lightly floured surface and knead 4 or 5 times. Form dough into a disk and chill, wrapped in plastic wrap, 30 minutes.

Make filling:

Simmer water, Calvados, and prunes, uncovered, until most of liquid is absorbed, about 10 minutes. Remove from heat and cool.

Preheat oven to 400°F.

Stir together cinnamon, cloves, 2 tablespoons flour, and ½ cup sugar.

Peel and core apples and cut into ½-inch wedges. Halve wedges crosswise and toss with cinnamon mixture. Add lemon juice and toss to coat.

Finely grind walnuts with remaining 3 tablespoons flour and remaining ¼ cup sugar in a food processor.

Assemble and bake tart:

Roll out dough on a lightly floured surface into a 14- by 18-inch oval. Roll dough loosely onto floured rolling pin and unroll onto a large buttered baking sheet. Sprinkle walnut mixture over pastry, leaving a 2½- to 3-inch border.

Stir stewed prunes into apple mixture and spoon over walnut mixture, evenly tucking prunes between apple pieces. Turn edge of dough over fruit to form pleats. Brush top of dough with milk and sprinkle with sugar.

Bake tart, loosely covered with foil, in middle of oven 30 minutes. Remove foil and bake until crust and fruit are golden and juices are bubbling, about 30 minutes more. Cool tart on baking sheet on a rack at least 20 minutes before serving.

Cooks' note:
• Pastry dough may be made 2 days ahead and chilled.

PHOTO ON PAGE 65

LEMON MOLASSES CHESS PIE

Serves 8 to 10

Pastry dough (page 190)
2 lemons
½ stick unsalted butter
4 large eggs
1¼ cups sugar
¼ cup unsulfured molasses
¼ cup heavy cream
2 tablespoons yellow cornmeal
⅛ teaspoon salt

Special equipment: pie weights or raw rice for weighting shell

Accompaniment: lightly sweetened whipped cream

On a lightly floured surface with a floured rolling pin roll out dough ⅛ inch thick (about a 12-inch round). Fit dough into a 9-inch (1-quart) glass pie plate and trim edge. Crimp edge of shell decoratively and with a fork prick bottom of shell in several places. Chill shell 30 minutes, or until firm.

Preheat oven to 375°F.

Line shell with foil and fill with pie weights or raw rice. Bake shell in middle of oven 25 minutes. Transfer shell to a rack and carefully remove weights or rice and foil. Cool shell.

Increase temperature to 450°F.

Finely grate enough zest from lemons to measure 1 tablespoon and squeeze enough juice from lemons to measure 3 tablespoons. Melt butter and cool. In a bowl with an electric mixer beat together eggs and sugar until thick and pale and on medium speed beat in butter, zest, lemon juice, and all remaining ingredients until combined. (Custard will be thin.) Pour custard into shell.

Put pie in middle of oven and reduce temperature to 325°F. Bake pie until just set in center, 35 to 40 minutes, and cool completely on rack. Serve pie at room temperature with whipped cream.

Cooks' note:
• Pie may be made 6 hours ahead and kept, uncovered, at cool room temperature.

PHOTO ON PAGE 17

PASTRY DOUGH ◐+

Makes enough dough for a single-crust 9-inch pie or
a 10- to 11-inch tart

¾ stick cold unsalted butter
1¼ cups all-purpose flour
2 tablespoons cold vegetable shortening
¼ teaspoon salt
2 to 4 tablespoons ice water

Cut butter into ½-inch cubes.

To blend by hand:

Blend together flour, butter, shortening, and salt in a bowl with your fingertips or a pastry blender until most of mixture resembles coarse meal, with rest in small (roughly pea-size) lumps. Drizzle 2 tablespoons ice water evenly over mixture and gently stir with a fork until incorporated.

To blend in a food processor:

Pulse together flour, butter, shortening, and salt in a food processor until most of mixture resembles coarse meal, with rest in small (roughly pea-size) lumps. Add 2 tablespoons ice water and pulse 2 or 3 times, or just until incorporated.

Test mixture:

Gently squeeze a small handful: It should hold together without crumbling apart. If it doesn't, add more ice water, 1 tablespoon at a time, stirring or pulsing 2 or 3 times after each addition until incorporated (keep testing). (If you overwork mixture or add too much water, pastry will be tough.)

Form dough:

Turn out onto a work surface and divide into 4 portions. With heel of your hand, smear each portion once in a forward motion to help distribute fat. Gather dough together and form it, rotating it on work surface, into a disk. Chill dough, wrapped in plastic wrap, until firm, at least 1 hour.

Cooks' note:
• Dough can be chilled up to 1 day.

PUMPKIN PIE

Serves 8

Pastry dough (recipe precedes)
15-oz can canned solid-pack pumpkin
   (about 2 cups)
1 cup heavy cream
½ cup whole milk
2 large eggs
¾ cup packed light brown sugar
1 teaspoon ground cinnamon
1 teaspoon ground ginger
Pinch of ground cloves
¼ teaspoon salt

Special equipment: pie weights or raw rice
Accompaniment: lightly whipped cream

Make pastry dough. Roll out dough into a 14-inch round on a lightly floured surface and fit into a 9-inch glass pie plate (4-cup capacity). Crimp edge decoratively and prick bottom all over. Chill 30 minutes.

Preheat oven to 375°F.

Line shell with foil and fill with pie weights. Bake in middle of oven 20 minutes. Remove weights and foil and bake shell until pale golden, 6 to 10 minutes more. Cool in pan on a rack. Whisk together pumpkin, heavy cream, milk, eggs, brown sugar, spices, and salt, and pour into shell.

Bake pie in middle of oven 45 to 50 minutes, or until filling is set but center still trembles slightly. (Filling will continue to set as pie cools.) Transfer to rack and cool completely.

Cooks' notes:
• If desired, some chopped crystallized ginger (sources on page 252) can be added to the pie filling.
• To prevent overbaking custard, you should start checking the pie's doneness at 45 minutes, as ovens vary.
• Pie may be made 1 day ahead and chilled, covered, but crust will not be as crisp as if made day of serving.

PECAN TART

Serves 8

Pastry dough (page 190)
¾ cup sugar
1 cup light corn syrup
3 large eggs
2 tablespoons unsalted butter
1 teaspoon vanilla
1 teaspoon fresh lemon juice
1¾ cups pecan halves

Special equipment: 10- by 1-inch round fluted tart pan with a removable bottom (sources on page 252) and pie weights or raw rice
Accompaniment: lightly whipped cream

Make pastry dough. Roll out dough into a 15-inch round on a lightly floured surface and fit into tart pan. Roll rolling pin over top of pan to trim dough flush with rim and lightly prick bottom all over with a fork. Chill 30 minutes.

Preheat oven to 375°F.

Line shell with foil and fill with pie weights. Bake in middle of oven 20 minutes. Remove weights and foil and bake shell until pale golden, 6 to 10 minutes more. Cool in pan on a rack.

Cook sugar in a dry heavy saucepan over moderately low heat, stirring slowly with a fork, until melted and pale golden. Cook caramel without stirring, swirling pan, until deep golden. Add corn syrup and simmer, stirring occasionally, until caramel is dissolved (it will harden before dissolving). Remove pan from heat and cool mixture until it stops bubbling.

Whisk eggs with a pinch of salt in a bowl. Whisk caramel mixture into eggs in a slow stream and whisk in butter, vanilla, and lemon juice until butter is melted. Spread pecans in bottom of tart shell and pour in filling, tapping down pecans to coat.

Bake tart in middle of oven until crust is golden and filling is puffed, 20 to 25 minutes, and cool in tart pan on a rack.

Cooks' notes:
• To vary this tart you can spread melted bittersweet chocolate on the bottom crust before filling the shell, and/or add ½ cup chopped dried tart cherries or cranberries to the filling.
• Tart may be made 1 day ahead and chilled, covered. Warm in a preheated 375°F oven to recrisp crust.

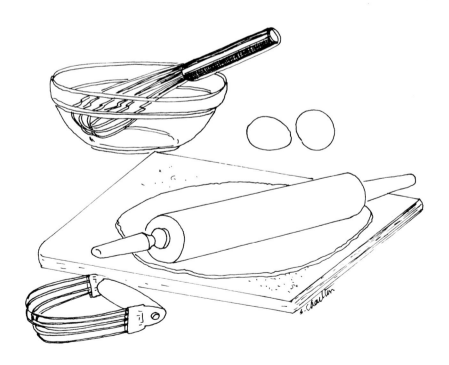

GRAPE TART

Serves 6

Here we used grapes in assorted colors and shapes and halved the larger ones. Taste the grapes before making the pastry cream. Their flavor will determine how much sugar you use—if the grapes are tart, use ⅓ cup sugar; if sweet, use ¼ cup.

For pastry cream
3 large egg yolks
¼ to ⅓ cup sugar, depending on sweetness of grapes
2½ tablespoons all-purpose flour
1 cup whole milk
1 teaspoon vanilla
1½ tablespoons unsalted butter

1 sheet frozen puff pastry (½ lb), thawed
2 teaspoons sugar
4 cups red and green grapes
2 tablespoons red-currant jelly

Make pastry cream:
Whisk together yolks and half of sugar, then whisk in flour and a pinch salt. Stir together milk and remaining sugar in a heavy saucepan and bring just to a boil over moderate heat. Whisk half of hot milk into yolks to temper and whisk yolks into milk remaining in pan. Bring custard to a boil over moderate heat and boil, whisking constantly, until very thick. Remove from heat and stir in vanilla and butter until incorporated. Chill hot pastry cream in a bowl, its surface covered with a buttered round of wax paper, until cold, about 1 hour.

Make tart:
Preheat oven to 425°F while pastry cream chills.

Open puff pastry sheet on a lightly floured surface and roll out to a 14- by 12-inch rectangle. Quarter pastry to form 4 rectangles. Brush ⅓ inch of edges lightly with water and fold in borders. Brush off excess flour and press borders with back of a fork to seal. Brush borders lightly with water and sprinkle with sugar. Prick insides of shells all over with fork. Bake on a large baking sheet in middle of oven until crust is golden brown, 10 to 15 minutes, and transfer to a rack. Gently flatten pastry inside border to deflate, and cool completely.

Halve and seed grapes if necessary. Melt jelly, stirring, and toss with grapes in a bowl.

Spread pastry cream in shells with a spatula and top with grapes.

Cooks' notes:
- Pastry cream may be made 1 day ahead and chilled.
- Pastry shells can be baked 4 hours ahead, then cooled and kept, covered, at room temperature. If not making ahead, you'll want to bake pastry while cream is chilling.

PHOTO ON PAGE 2

PLUM PINE-NUT TART

Serves 8

Sweet pastry dough (recipe follows)
¼ cup plus 2 tablespoons pine nuts
2 lb firm-ripe red or purple plums (about 8)
½ cup confectioners sugar plus additional for dusting
½ teaspoon anise seeds

Special equipment: a 14-inch pizza pan or a large baking sheet

Let dough stand at room temperature until softened and malleable, about 30 minutes to 1 hour.

While dough is standing, preheat oven to 375°F.

In a baking pan toast 2 tablespoons pine nuts in middle of oven until golden, about 5 minutes, and reserve. Cut each plum lengthwise into 12 wedges. In a food processor pulse together remaining ¼ cup pine nuts, ½ cup confectioners sugar, and anise seeds until pine nuts are finely ground.

Knead dough on a lightly floured surface 3 or 4 times to help it roll out smoothly, and form it into a disk. On a work surface overlap 2 pieces of wax paper to make a 17- to 18-inch square and dust with flour. Put dough on wax paper and dust dough lightly with flour. With a floured rolling pin roll out dough into a 17-inch round (about ⅛ inch thick).

To transfer dough to pizza pan, slide a large baking sheet under wax paper and invert pizza pan onto dough. Holding baking sheet and pizza pan together, flip dough onto pizza pan and carefully peel off wax paper. (Use this same method for transferring dough to a baking sheet if you aren't using a pizza pan.)

Sprinkle dough with all but 2 tablespoons nut mixture, leaving a border of about 2 inches. Scatter plums over nut mixture and turn edge of dough over plums. Sprinkle plums with remaining nut mixture and reserved toasted pine nuts.

Bake tart in middle of oven until crust is golden and juices are bubbling, 35 to 40 minutes. Cool tart in pan on a rack at least 20 minutes and transfer to a large wooden board.

Just before serving, lightly dust tart with additional confectioners sugar.

Cooks' note:
• Tart may be made 4 hours ahead and kept, uncovered, at room temperature.

PHOTO ON PAGE 44

SWEET PASTRY DOUGH ◐+

Makes enough dough for a 14-inch tart or double-crust 9-inch pie

1¾ sticks cold unsalted butter
2⅓ cups all-purpose flour
⅓ cup sugar
½ to ¾ teaspoon salt
1 large whole egg
1 large egg yolk
1 teaspoon vanilla
1 teaspoon fresh lemon juice or water

Cut butter into ½-inch cubes. In a bowl whisk together flour, sugar, and salt to taste. With your fingertips or a pastry blender blend together flour mixture and butter until mixture resembles coarse meal. In a small bowl with a fork lightly beat together whole egg, yolk, vanilla, and lemon juice and stir into flour mixture. Toss mixture with fork until egg mixture is absorbed. With your hands gently knead mixture in bowl until it comes together and forms a dough. Turn dough out onto a very lightly floured surface and knead 4 or 5 times. Form dough into a disk. Chill dough, wrapped in plastic wrap, at least 1 hour and up to 1 day.

APRICOT CREAM-CHEESE ICE CREAM

Makes about 1 quart

6 fresh apricots (about 1 lb)
1 cup sugar
8 oz cream cheese, softened
1 cup milk
½ cup heavy cream
2 teaspoons fresh lemon juice

Pit apricots and coarsely chop. In a 2-quart heavy saucepan cook apricots and sugar over moderate heat, stirring, until sugar is dissolved. Cook mixture, stirring occasionally, until apricots are softened, about 5 minutes, and cool. Chill mixture, covered, until cold, and up to 2 days.

In a blender blend cream cheese and milk until smooth. Using a long-handled spoon stir in heavy cream, lemon juice, and apricot mixture (do not blend).

Freeze mixture in an ice-cream maker. Transfer to an airtight container and put in freezer to harden.

CRANBERRY SORBET ◐

Makes about 3 cups

¼ vanilla bean
1 (12-oz) can frozen cranberry juice concentrate
¾ cup water

Scrape seeds from vanilla pod and whisk together with frozen cranberry juice and water. Freeze mixture in an ice-cream maker. Transfer sorbet to an airtight container and freeze to harden.

GINGERSNAP CRUMBLE ICE-CREAM TART WITH CHUNKY PINEAPPLE SAUCE

Serves 6

1 stick unsalted butter
4 cups coarsely broken gingersnaps
⅓ cup sugar
1½ pints super-premium vanilla ice cream
For pineapple sauce
1 ripe pineapple (preferably Del Monte Gold)
½ cup sugar

Special equipment: a 10- by 1-inch round fluted tart pan with a removable bottom (sources on page 252) and 3 cups pie weights or raw rice for weighting shell

Preheat oven to 350°F.

Melt butter. In a food processor grind gingersnaps to fine crumbs and add butter and sugar, pulsing to blend.

Sprinkle 1 cup (not packed) crumb mixture over bottom of tart pan and press with an offset spatula. Sprinkle ½ cup crumb mixture around edge of pan and with your fingers press up side of pan. Carefully line shell with foil, folding over edge to cover crumbs completely, and add pie weights or raw rice. Sprinkle remaining crumb mixture in a shallow baking pan.

Bake crumb mixture in lower third of oven 12 minutes and bake shell in upper third 20 minutes. Cool crumb mixture in baking pan on a rack and, when crumbs are cool enough to handle, with your fingers break up any large clumps. Cool shell in foil in tart pan on another rack 15 minutes. Carefully remove foil and weights or rice and cool shell completely (shell may be soft in center but will firm as it cools). Soften ice cream slightly and fold in half of crumb mixture. Spoon ice-cream mixture into shell, smoothing top, and sprinkle with remaining crumb mixture. Freeze tart until ice cream is firm, about 2 hours.

Make sauce:

Cut rind from pineapple and quarter pineapple lengthwise. Cut off core and cut pineapple quarters crosswise into ¼-inch-thick slices. In a dry 2- to 3-quart heavy saucepan cook sugar over moderately low heat, stirring slowly with a fork (to help sugar melt evenly), until melted and pale golden. Cook caramel, without stirring and gently swirling pan, until golden. Remove pan from heat and add pineapple (mixture will vigorously steam and caramel will harden). Simmer mixture, stirring, 5 minutes, or until caramel is dissolved, and cool sauce to room temperature. Chill sauce, covered, at least 2 hours.

Serve tart with sauce.

Cooks' notes:
• Tart keeps, frozen and loosely covered, 3 days.
• Sauce keeps, covered and chilled, 5 days.

PHOTO ON PAGE 34

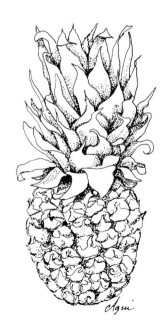

GINGER ALMOND BISCOTTI ICE-CREAM SANDWICHES

Makes 4

½ cup premium low-fat ice cream, softened slightly
8 ginger almond *biscotti* (recipe follows)

Sandwich ⅛ cup ice cream between 2 *biscotti*, pressing them together gently. Put sandwich on a plate in freezer and make 3 more sandwiches in same manner. Freeze sandwiches on plate, covered, just until firm, about 15 minutes.

☛ each ice-cream sandwich about 156 calories and 5 grams fat

GINGER ALMOND BISCOTTI

Makes about 30

¾ cup whole almonds with skins
½ cup crystallized ginger (sources on page 252)
1 cup unbleached all-purpose flour
½ cup sugar
1½ teaspoons ground ginger
½ teaspoon salt
¼ teaspoon baking soda
1 large egg
1 large egg white
½ teaspoon vanilla

Special equipment: 1 (11- by 4-inch) loaf pan
  (see note, below)

Preheat oven to 300°F. Butter loaf pan and line bottom with wax paper.

In a shallow baking pan toast almonds in middle of oven until a shade darker, about 10 minutes. Cool nuts and very coarsely chop. Finely chop crystallized ginger. Into a bowl sift together flour, sugar, ground ginger, salt, and baking soda. In another bowl with an electric mixer beat together whole egg, egg white, and vanilla. Stir in flour mixture and beat until combined well. Stir in almonds and crystallized ginger.

Press dough into loaf pan and bake in middle of oven until pale golden, about 45 minutes. Turn loaf out onto a rack and cool 10 minutes. On a cutting board with a serrated knife cut loaf crosswise into ⅛-inch-thick slices.

Arrange *biscotti* on a baking sheet and bake in middle of oven until crisp, about 15 minutes. Cool on rack.

Cooks' notes:
• These *biscotti* can be baked in different size pans—even free form on a baking sheet—depending on what shape you'd like them to be. We used an 11- by 4-inch pan for a square shape. A 9- by 5- by 3-inch pan yields a long, narrow rectangle. The cooking time will not be affected by the pan you use.
• *Biscotti* keep in an airtight container at cool room temperature 2 weeks.

☛ each serving of 2 biscotti about 113 calories and 4 grams fat

LIME-VANILLA FROZEN YOGURT ☽+

Makes about 1 quart
This recipe requires some advance preparation: The yogurt needs to drain for 12 hours.

2 (32-oz) containers whole-milk plain yogurt
  (sources on page 252)
1 vanilla bean
1 teaspoon finely grated fresh lime zest
6 tablespoons fresh lime juice
½ cup light corn syrup
¾ cup superfine granulated sugar

In a cheesecloth-lined large sieve or colander set over a bowl drain yogurt, covered and chilled, 12 hours. Discard liquid in bowl.

With a knife halve vanilla bean lengthwise and scrape out seeds. In a blender purée vanilla seeds, half of drained yogurt, and remaining ingredients. In a bowl stir together vanilla mixture and remaining yogurt.

Freeze mixture in an ice-cream maker. Transfer frozen yogurt to an airtight container and put in freezer to harden.

Cooks' note:
• Frozen yogurt keeps 1 week.

PHOTO ON PAGE 43

BROWN-SUGAR PECAN ICE CREAM

Makes about 7 cups

This recipe yields about ¾ cup ice cream per person if serving 8 to 10. If you want to make a larger quantity, we recommend making 2 batches rather than simply doubling the recipe.

2 cups pecans (about ½ lb)
1 cup packed light brown sugar
1 tablespoon cornstarch
⅛ teaspoon salt
3 large eggs
2 cups whole milk
2 teaspoons vanilla
2 cups well-chilled heavy cream

Preheat oven to 350°F.

In a shallow baking pan spread pecans evenly and toast in middle of oven until fragrant and a shade darker, 5 to 6 minutes. Cool pecans and finely chop.

In a bowl combine well brown sugar, cornstarch, and salt and whisk in eggs until combined. In a 2½- to 3-quart heavy saucepan bring milk just to a boil. Add hot milk to egg mixture in a slow stream, whisking, and pour into pan. Bring custard to a boil over moderate heat, whisking constantly, and boil, whisking, 1 minute. Stir in vanilla. (Custard will appear curdled.)

Chill custard until cold and stir in cream. Freeze custard, in batches if necessary, in an ice-cream maker. Transfer ice cream to a large bowl and stir in pecans. Transfer ice cream to an airtight container and put in freezer to harden.

Cooks' note:
• Ice cream may be made 1 week ahead.

GRAPEFRUIT TARRAGON SORBET

Makes about 1 quart

4 large red or pink grapefruits
1 cup water
1 cup sugar
1 teaspoon dried tarragon, crumbled

Garnish: 2 tablespoons candied grapefruit strips
 (recipe follows)

Squeeze enough juice from grapefruits to measure 2½ cups and pour through a sieve into a large bowl. In a small saucepan bring water, sugar, and tarragon to a boil, stirring until sugar is dissolved, and simmer 5 minutes. Whisk syrup into grapefruit juice.

Freeze mixture in an ice-cream maker. Transfer sorbet to an airtight container and put in freezer to harden.

Serve sorbet garnished with candied strips.

Cooks' note:
• Sorbet keeps 1 week.

☞ each serving, including garnish, about 182 calories
and less than 1 gram fat

CANDIED GRAPEFRUIT STRIPS ☉

Makes about ½ cup

This recipe also works with oranges and tangerines: Substitute 2 oranges or 3 tangerines for the grapefruit.

1 large grapefruit
⅔ cup water
⅓ cup sugar
1 tablespoon light corn syrup

With a vegetable peeler remove zest from grapefruit in long pieces. With a sharp knife remove any white pith from pieces if necessary. Stack 3 or 4 pieces and cut pieces lengthwise into julienne strips. Make more strips in same manner.

To a 3-quart saucepan half filled with cold water add strips and bring to a boil. Simmer strips 10 minutes and drain in a sieve. In a small heavy saucepan bring ⅔ cup water, sugar, and corn syrup to a boil, stirring until sugar is dissolved. Add strips and simmer gently over low heat until strips are translucent and syrup is thickened, 15 to 20 minutes. Cool strips in syrup.

Cooks' note:
• Candied strips keep, covered and chilled, 2 weeks.

☞ each 1-tablespoon serving about 40 calories
and less than 1 gram fat

RICH CHOCOLATE SAUCE

Makes about 1 cup

We love this velvety sauce as a topping for ice cream and for fruits such as strawberries and bananas.

6 oz fine-quality bittersweet chocolate
  (not unsweetened)
½ cup heavy cream
1 tablespoon sugar

Chop chocolate and transfer to a bowl. In a small saucepan bring cream with sugar just to a simmer, stirring until sugar is dissolved, and pour over chocolate. Stir mixture until chocolate is completely melted. If desired, reheat sauce in a metal bowl, stirring occasionally, over a saucepan of simmering water. Serve sauce hot or at room temperature.

Cooks' note:
• Sauce may be kept, chilled in an airtight container, 1 week.

BLOOD ORANGES WITH GRAND MARNIER SABAYON

Serves 4

When blood oranges are out of season, you can use any type of seedless orange.

6 blood oranges
2 egg yolks
½ teaspoon lemon juice, or to taste
2½ tablespoons sugar
1½ tablespoons Grand Marnier or other
  orange-flavored liqueur

Garnish: 3 tablespoons coarsely chopped pistachios

Finely grate enough zest from 1 orange to measure ½ teaspoon. With a sharp knife cut peel from oranges, including all white pith, and cut sections free from membranes. Squeeze enough juice from membranes to measure 2 tablespoons. Divide sections among 4 stemmed glasses.

Have ready an instant-read thermometer in a measuring cup of hot water. In a metal bowl whisk together zest, yolks, orange and lemon juices, sugar, and liqueur until combined well. Set bowl over a saucepan of simmering water and cook mixture, whisking constantly, until tripled in volume and thermometer registers 140°F, 3 to 5 minutes. Cook sabayon, whisking, 3 minutes more, or until thickened enough so that strokes leave a clear path.

Spoon sabayon over orange sections and garnish with pistachios.

each serving, including garnish,
about 200 calories and 6 grams fat

MANGO IN GINGER-MINT SYRUP ◗+

Serves 4

1 (2-inch) piece fresh ginger
1 cup water
⅓ cup sugar
⅓ cup fresh mint
1 firm-ripe mango (about 1 lb)

Garnish: fresh mint sprigs

Thinly slice ginger and in a saucepan bring to a boil with water and sugar. Simmer mixture 5 minutes and remove pan from heat. Stir in mint and let steep 5 minutes. Pour syrup through a sieve into a bowl and cool completely.

Peel mango and thinly slice. Stir mango into syrup. Chill mixture 30 minutes.

Garnish mango with mint. Serves 4.

🍃 each serving about 119 calories and less than 1 gram fat

PHOTO ON PAGE 80

APRICOT CRISP ◗

Serves 2

4 firm-ripe apricots
4 tablespoons packed light brown sugar
3 tablespoons cold unsalted butter
3 tablespoons all-purpose flour
3 tablespoons old-fashioned rolled oats
¼ teaspoon salt
⅛ teaspoon cinnamon

Preheat oven to 425°F.

Pit apricots and cut into ½-inch-thick wedges. In a bowl toss with 1 tablespoon brown sugar. Divide apricots between two 1-cup ramekins or gratin dishes.

Cut butter into small pieces and in a large bowl with your fingertips or a pastry blender blend into flour until mixture resembles coarse meal. Stir in remaining 3 tablespoons brown sugar, oats, salt, and cinnamon. Mound oat mixture on top of apricots and bake in middle of oven until topping is golden and apricots are tender, about 25 minutes.

APRICOT LEATHER

This fruit leather makes a satisfying energy snack and is delicious in place of chutney on a sandwich.

6 fresh apricots (about 1 lb)
¾ cup sugar

Preheat oven to 200°F. Oil a 13- by 9-inch baking pan.

Pit apricots and coarsely chop. In a 3-quart heavy saucepan cook apricots and sugar over moderate heat, stirring, until sugar is dissolved, about 5 minutes. Cook mixture at a bare simmer, stirring frequently, until thickened, about 40 minutes more. In a blender purée mixture until smooth (use caution when blending hot liquids). Transfer purée to baking pan and spread evenly over bottom.

Dry purée in middle of oven until it feels dry but slightly tacky, about 1 hour. Cool leather completely in pan on a rack.

Peel leather out of pan and roll up in wax paper.

Cooks' notes:
• Leather keeps, wrapped in plastic wrap, at cool room temperature, 1 month.
• For an easy hors d'oeuvre, spread 4 tablespoons softened mild goat cheese onto an 8-inch square of leather. Sprinkle the cheese with 1 tablespoon chopped pistachios and tightly roll up leather into a log. Chill the log and slice it into ¼-inch-thick rounds.

FIG, APRICOT, AND RASPBERRY BRÛLÉE

Serves 6

½ teaspoon finely grated fresh orange zest
¾ cup fresh orange juice
½ teaspoon fresh lemon juice
¼ teaspoon vanilla
6 tablespoons mint sugar (recipe follows)
12 large firm-ripe figs (about 1½ lb)
6 ripe apricots (about 10 oz)
1¼ cups raspberries
6 tablespoons turbinado sugar, such as Sugar in the
　　Raw, or packed light brown sugar

Accompaniment: crème fraîche
Special equipment: blowtorch (sources on page 252)

In a small bowl stir together zest, citrus juices, vanilla, and mint sugar.

Butter 6 (1-cup) shallow flameproof gratin dishes or bowls. Quarter figs. Halve and pit apricots. Divide figs, apricots, raspberries, and juice mixture among dishes.

Just before serving, sprinkle sugar evenly over fruit and caramelize with blowtorch, moving flame evenly back and forth just over sugar until most of sugar is melted and deep golden in places.

Serve *brûlées* immediately with *crème fraîche*.

Cooks' note:
• You can also caramelize *brûlées* under a preheated broiler.

PHOTO ON PAGE 49

MINT SUGAR ☺

Makes about ¾ cup

This sweetener is also delicious sprinkled over fresh fruit or stirred into iced tea.

¼ cup packed fresh mint
½ cup sugar

In an electric coffee/spice grinder finely grind mint with sugar.

Cooks' note:
• Mint sugar may be made 1 hour ahead and kept in an airtight container.

BAKED SABRA ORANGES WITH ORANGE SORBET

Serves 6

For baked oranges
5 thin-skinned juice oranges
1½ cups sugar
¼ cup Sabra (chocolate-orange liqueur)
　　(sources on page 252)
For sorbet
½ cup water
¼ cup sugar
2 cups fresh orange juice
1 teaspoon finely grated fresh orange zest
3 tablespoons Sabra (chocolate-orange liqueur)

Make baked oranges:
Cover oranges with cold water in a medium saucepan. Bring to a boil, then keep at a boil 20 minutes.

Preheat oven to 375°F. Drain oranges and cover with more cold water. Bring to a boil again, then boil 5 minutes more. Drain oranges and cool 15 minutes. Cut each orange (with peel) into 8 wedges and arrange, with a cut side of each down, in a 13- by 9-inch glass baking dish.

Boil 2 cups water with sugar in a 2-quart saucepan, stirring, until sugar is dissolved. Pour syrup over oranges and bake in middle of oven, turning wedges over in syrup halfway through baking, 1 hour total. Pour liqueur over wedges and cool. Chill wedges, covered, at least 3 hours.

Make sorbet:
Boil water and sugar in a 1-quart saucepan, stirring, until sugar is dissolved, then stir in juice, zest, and liqueur. Chill, covered, until cold. (To quick-chill, set in a bowl of ice and cold water.) Freeze in an ice-cream maker. Transfer sorbet to an airtight container and harden in freezer.

Cooks' notes:
• Baked oranges can be made 1 week ahead and chilled, covered.
• Sorbet can be made 2 days ahead.

PHOTO ON PAGE 74

PASSION-FRUIT MERINGUES

Serves 2

Even though you'll only need 4 meringue layers, this recipe calls for 6—thus allowing for the possibility of breakage...or snacks!

For meringue layers
2 large egg whites
⅛ teaspoon cream of tartar
½ cup sugar
For filling and garnish
4 passion fruits
⅓ cup well-chilled heavy cream
1½ teaspoons sugar
1 small pomegranate (optional)

Special equipment: parchment paper pastry
   bag with a ½-inch plain tip

Make meringue layers:
Preheat oven to 200°F and oil a baking sheet. On a sheet of parchment paper, using a 3- or 4-inch heart-shaped cutter as a guide, draw 6 hearts. Turn parchment over and put on baking sheet.

In a large bowl with an electric mixer beat whites with cream of tartar and a pinch salt until they just hold soft peaks. Gradually beat in sugar and beat until meringue just holds stiff, glossy peaks.

Transfer meringue to a pastry bag fitted with a ½-inch plain tip and pipe evenly onto parchment hearts, filling them in.

Bake meringue layers in middle of oven 45 minutes, or until crisp and firm. (If weather is humid, cooking time may be longer.) Cool meringue layers completely on baking sheet in turned-off oven and carefully peel off parchment.

Make filling:
Halve 3 passion fruits and scoop out pulp (including seeds and juice) into a sieve set over a bowl. Force pulp through sieve, pressing hard on seeds, and discard seeds. In a bowl beat cream until it holds soft peaks and fold in passion-fruit juice and sugar until just combined.

Make garnish:
Halve remaining passion fruit and scoop out seeds, reserving them. Halve pomegranate. Bending back rinds, dislodge some seeds from membranes, reserving them, and reserve some juice.

Arrange a meringue heart on each of 2 plates. Top hearts with whipped cream and garnish with some reserved passion-fruit and pomegranate seeds. Top each dessert with 1 more meringue heart.

Garnish desserts with more passion-fruit and pomegranate seeds and some reserved juice.

Cooks' notes:
• If you don't have a pastry bag, you can divide meringue among parchment hearts, spreading with a small spatula to fill in.
• Meringue layers may be kept, layered between sheets of parchment paper, in an airtight container in a cool, dry place 1 week.
• Desserts may be made 2 hours ahead and chilled, loosely covered. Bring to room temperature before serving.

PHOTO ON PAGE 23

PEACHES IN CARAMEL OVER VANILLA ICE CREAM ◔

Serves 2

2 large ripe peaches
1 tablespoon fresh lemon juice
½ cup sugar
2 tablespoons heavy cream
½ pint vanilla ice cream

Have ready a bowl of ice and cold water. Cut an X in blossom end of peaches. In a saucepan of boiling water blanch peaches 15 seconds and with a slotted spoon transfer to ice water to stop cooking. Peel peaches and cut each into 8 wedges. In a small bowl toss peaches with lemon juice.

In an 8- to 9-inch heavy skillet cook sugar over moderately low heat, stirring slowly with a fork (to help sugar melt evenly), until melted and pale golden. Cook caramel, without stirring, swirling skillet, until deep golden, 5 to 6 minutes. Carefully add peaches and cream (mixture will vigorously steam and caramel will harden). Cook mixture, stirring frequently, until caramel is dissolved and peaches are tender, about 5 minutes.

Cool peaches to warm and serve over ice cream.

PEACH COBBLER

Serves 4

6 large peaches, cut into thin wedges
¼ cup sugar
1 tablespoon fresh lemon juice
1 teaspoon cornstarch
For biscuit topping
1 cup all-purpose flour
½ cup sugar
1 teaspoon baking powder
½ teaspoon salt
¾ stick cold unsalted butter, cut into
    small pieces
¼ cup boiling water

Cook peaches:
Preheat oven to 425°F.
Toss peaches with sugar, lemon juice, and cornstarch in a 2-quart nonreactive baking dish and bake in middle of oven 10 minutes.
Make topping while peaches bake:
Stir together flour, sugar, baking powder, and salt. Blend in butter with your fingertips or a pastry blender until mixture resembles coarse meal. Stir in water until just combined.

Remove peaches from oven and drop spoonfuls of topping over them. Bake in middle of oven until topping is golden, about 25 minutes.

GRILLED PINEAPPLE

Serves 8

Be sure to give the grate a good cleaning before putting the pineapple on the fire.

1 pineapple

Accompaniments: super-premium vanilla ice cream
    and rum *dulce de leche* (page 202)

Prepare grill. Cut pineapple lengthwise through leaves, keeping leaves attached, into 8 wedges. Grill pineapple wedges, a cut side down, on a lightly oiled rack set 5 to 6 inches over glowing coals until just charred, about 2 minutes on each cut side.
Serve pineapple with ice cream and *dulce de leche*.

PHOTO ON PAGE 53

RUM DULCE DE LECHE

Makes about 2 cups

Throughout the Spanish-speaking world, thickened sweetened milk is a regular feature at dessert time. Though not difficult to make from scratch on top of the stove, the use of condensed milk eliminates the need for constant stirring. Be sure to check the water level in the pan about halfway through cooking; if it's low, carefully add a little more.

2 (14-oz) cans sweetened condensed milk
⅓ cup dark rum
¼ teaspoon vanilla
⅛ teaspoon salt

Preheat oven to 425°F.

Pour condensed milk into a 9-inch deep-dish pie plate and cover with foil. Put pie plate in a roasting pan and add enough hot water to pan to reach halfway up side of pie plate. Bake milk in middle of oven until thick and golden, about 1½ hours. Carefully remove pie plate from pan and cool completely.

Add remaining ingredients to baked milk and whisk until smooth.

Cooks' note:
· Sauce may be made 2 days ahead and chilled, covered.

PHOTO ON PAGE 53

PLUMS WITH ORANGE AND MINT ◐+

Serves 4

1 lb plums (about 4)
¼ cup fresh orange juice
1 tablespoon finely shredded fresh mint
½ tablespoon sugar

Halve and pit plums. Cut plums into thin wedges and in a bowl toss with remaining ingredients. Chill plum mixture, covered, stirring occasionally, at least 2 hours.

Cooks' note:
· Plum mixture may be made up to 8 hours ahead and chilled, covered.

 each serving about 84 calories and less than 1 gram fat

RED WINE-MACERATED WINTER FRUIT ◐+

Serves 6

1 lemon
3 cups water
1½ cups dry red wine
2 tablespoons sugar
1 cinnamon stick
½ large firm-ripe pineapple
1¼ lb mixed dried fruit such as prunes, apricots, figs, and cranberries

Accompaniments: mascarpone cheese or crème fraîche and cashew orange biscotti (page 186)

Remove zest from lemon with a vegetable peeler and squeeze juice from lemon. In a saucepan bring water to a boil with zest, lemon juice, wine, sugar, and cinnamon stick, stirring until sugar is dissolved. Simmer mixture 15 minutes.

While mixture is simmering, peel and core pineapple and cut into bite-size pieces. Halve figs if using. Pour hot syrup through a sieve into a bowl. Stir pineapple and dried fruit into syrup and cool. Chill fruit, covered, at least 8 hours.

Serve fruit with *mascarpone* or *crème fraîche* and *biscotti*.

Cooks' note:
· Fruit in syrup may be chilled, covered, up to 2 days.

PHOTO ON PAGE 29

RHUBARB CRÈME BRÛLÉE

Serves 6

For filling
2 lb trimmed rhubarb
6 tablespoons granulated sugar,
    or to taste
For custard
5 large egg yolks
½ cup granulated sugar
1¾ cups heavy cream
1 teaspoon minced peeled fresh ginger
2 tablespoons turbinado sugar, such as
    Sugar in the Raw

Special equipment: blowtorch (sources on page 252)

Preheat oven to 375°F and butter a 13- by 9-inch glass baking dish.
    Make filling:
    Cut enough rhubarb crosswise into ¼-inch slices to measure 6 cups and arrange in one layer in baking dish. Bake rhubarb, uncovered, in middle of oven, 1¼ hours. Transfer hot rhubarb to a bowl and stir in sugar until combined well. Cool filling.
    Reduce temperature to 325°F.
    Make custard:
    In a bowl whisk together yolks and granulated sugar. In a small heavy saucepan heat cream with ginger over moderately high heat until it just comes to a simmer. Add cream mixture to egg mixture in a stream, whisking, and skim off any froth.
    Divide rhubarb filling among 6 (¾-cup) flameproof ramekins and divide custard over filling. Put ramekins in a roasting pan and add enough hot water to pan to reach halfway up sides of ramekins. Loosely cover pan with foil and bake custards in middle of oven until just set but still trembling slightly, about 50 minutes. Remove ramekins from pan and cool custards on a rack. Chill custards, loosely covered with plastic wrap, until cold, at least 4 hours.
    Just before serving, sprinkle 1 teaspoon turbinado sugar evenly over each custard and caramelize with blowtorch, moving flame evenly back and forth just over sugar until sugar is evenly melted and deep golden.

Cooks' notes:
• Filling may be made 2 days ahead and chilled, covered. Bring to room temperature before proceeding.
• Custards can be chilled (before caramelizing), loosely covered with plastic wrap, up to 2 days.
• You can also caramelize custards under a preheated broiler set 2 to 3 inches from heat.

HOT BANANA CRÈME BRÛLÉE ◑

Serves 2

2 medium firm-ripe bananas
2 teaspoons fresh lemon juice
2 tablespoons granulated sugar
2 large egg yolks
½ cup heavy cream
1 tablespoon turbinado sugar, such as
    Sugar in the Raw brand

Preheat oven to 350°F.
    Break 1 banana into pieces and purée in a blender with lemon juice, granulated sugar, and yolks until smooth. In a very small saucepan heat cream over moderate heat until hot and add banana mixture, stirring until combined well. Divide mixture between 2 (⅔-cup) ramekins. Put ramekins in a metal baking pan and fill pan with enough boiling-hot water to reach halfway up sides of ramekins. Put pan in middle of oven and lay a sheet of foil over each ramekin. Bake custards until set, about 30 minutes.
    Set broiler rack so that custard tops will be 1½ to 2 inches from heat and change oven setting to broil.
    Just before serving, very thinly slice remaining banana and arrange slices, overlapping them, over custards. Sprinkle turbinado sugar evenly over bananas and heat under broiler until sugar is melted and caramelized.

Cooks' note:
• Brûlée can also be caramelized with a blowtorch (sources on page 252). Move flame evenly back and forth over sugar.

PUMPKIN FLAN WITH PUMPKIN-SEED PRALINE

Serves 8 to 10

2 cups sugar
1 cup whole milk
2 (5-oz) cans evaporated milk (1⅓ cups)
5 large eggs
¼ teaspoon salt
15-oz can solid-pack pumpkin (1¾ cups)
2 tablespoons premium golden 100% agave tequila
    such as Herradura Reposado, or bourbon
2 teaspoons ground cinnamon
1 teaspoon ground ginger
¼ teaspoon ground allspice
¼ teaspoon ground nutmeg

Accompaniment: pumpkin-seed praline
    (recipe follows)

Preheat oven to 375°F.

Heat a 2-quart soufflé dish or round ceramic casserole in middle of oven.

Cook 1 cup sugar in a dry 2-quart heavy saucepan over moderately low heat, stirring slowly with a fork, until melted and pale golden. Cook caramel without stirring, swirling pan, until deep golden, about 5 minutes. Quickly and carefully remove hot dish from oven and immediately pour caramel into dish, tilting it to cover bottom and sides. (Leave oven on.) Keep tilting as caramel cools and thickens enough to stay in place.

Scald whole milk with evaporated milk in a saucepan and remove from heat. Beat eggs and remaining cup sugar with an electric mixer until smooth and creamy. Beat in salt, pumpkin, tequila, and spices. Pour milk mixture through a sieve into a bowl and beat into pumpkin mixture in a slow stream until combined well.

Pour custard over caramel in dish and set in a water bath of 1 inch hot water. Put pan in middle of oven and lower temperature to 350°F. Bake until golden brown on top and a knife inserted in center comes out clean, about 1¼ hours, possibly longer. Remove dish from water bath and transfer to a rack to cool. Chill flan, covered, until cold, at least 6 hours.

To unmold flan, run a thin knife around flan to loosen from sides of dish. Wiggle dish from side to side and, when flan moves freely in dish, invert a large serving platter with a lip over dish. Holding dish and platter securely together, quickly invert and turn out flan onto platter. Caramel will pour out over and around it.

Cut flan into wedges and serve with caramel spooned over and with shards of praline.

PHOTO ON PAGE 65

PUMPKIN-SEED PRALINE ◐+

Serves 8 to 10

1 cup sugar
½ cup water
1 cup hulled (green) pumpkin seeds, toasted
    (sources on page 252)

Preheat oven to 250°F. Lightly oil a large sheet of foil on a baking sheet and keep warm in oven.

Cook sugar, water, and a pinch of salt in a deep 2-quart heavy saucepan over moderately low heat, stirring slowly with a fork, until melted and pale golden. Cook caramel without stirring, swirling pan, until deep golden. Immediately stir in pumpkin seeds and quickly pour onto foil, spreading into a thin sheet before it hardens. If caramel hardens and is difficult to spread, put in a 400°F oven until warm enough to spread, 1 to 2 minutes.

Cool praline on baking sheet on a rack until completely hardened, then break into large pieces.

RHUBARB RICE PUDDING

Serves 6 to 8

Cooking rhubarb to the right consistency is trickier than you might think—it changes from barely tender to falling apart in a matter of seconds. Watch it carefully while it's poaching.

¾ cup white *basmati* rice
1 vanilla bean
3 cups whole milk
1½ cups heavy cream
½ cup plus 1 tablespoon sugar
1 tablespoon unsalted butter
¼ teaspoon freshly grated nutmeg
1 teaspoon unflavored gelatin (less than
    1 envelope)
1 tablespoon cold water
For rhubarb topping
1½ lb rhubarb
1½ cups water
2¼ cups sugar

In a bowl soak rice in cold water to cover 30 minutes. In a sieve drain rice and rinse under cold water.

With a knife halve vanilla bean lengthwise and scrape seeds into a 3-quart heavy saucepan. Add pod, rice, milk, cream, sugar, butter, nutmeg, and a pinch salt. Bring mixture to a boil, stirring occasionally, and simmer, partially covered, over moderately low heat, stirring occasionally, 25 minutes, or until rice is tender and mixture is creamy but still loose. Remove pan from heat and discard pod. In a small cup sprinkle gelatin over 1 tablespoon cold water and let soften 1 minute. Stir gelatin mixture into hot rice mixture until gelatin is dissolved.

Lightly oil a 9-inch springform pan and line with plastic wrap. Pour pudding into pan and cool on a rack. Chill pudding, covered, until firm, at least 3 hours.

Make topping:
Have ready a tray lined with wax paper. Trim rhubarb and cut stalks crosswise into 1-inch pieces. In a 12-inch heavy skillet bring water and sugar to a boil, stirring until sugar is dissolved, and boil 1 minute. Add rhubarb and poach at a bare simmer, without stirring, until just tender but not falling apart, about 10 minutes. With a slotted spoon transfer rhubarb pieces as cooked to tray. Pour syrup through a sieve into a bowl and return to skillet. Boil syrup until it reaches soft-ball

stage (see note, below; 238°F), about 10 minutes (syrup will be reduced to 1 cup), and keep warm, covered.

Remove side from springform pan and invert a serving plate over rice pudding. Invert pudding onto plate and remove bottom of pan and plastic wrap. Arrange rhubarb decoratively on top of pudding and brush with warm syrup. Chill rhubarb rice pudding, uncovered, until cold, at least 1 hour, and up to 3. Serve rhubarb rice pudding chilled.

Cooks' notes:
· Before topping with rhubarb, pudding can be chilled, covered, up to 1 day.
· You'll need to boil the rhubarb syrup to the "soft-ball stage." To determine this, just drop a small amount of syrup into a cup of cold water. If you can form it into a sticky lump that flattens when pressed, it has reached the right consistency. This technique is especially useful with small amounts of syrup, from which it can be difficult to obtain an accurate temperature reading with a thermometer.

PHOTO ON PAGE 38

CLASSIC ZABAGLIONE ☉

Serves 4

This foamy custard is a traditional Italian dessert. Delicious with no accompaniment at all, it's even better spooned over fresh fruit or served with biscotti. Be sure to have anything else you plan to serve with the zabaglione ready to go, as it really is best eaten just seconds off the stove.

3 large egg yolks
¼ cup sugar
2 tablespoons dry Marsala

Have ready an instant-read thermometer in a cup of hot water. In a metal bowl with a whisk or a hand-held electric mixer beat together all ingredients. Set bowl over a saucepan of barely simmering water and beat mixture until tripled in volume and thermometer registers 140°F, about 5 minutes. To ensure that eggs are cooked, beat mixture 3 minutes more.

Serve *zabaglione* immediately.

BREAD-AND-BUTTER PUDDING

Serves 6

1 baguette
½ stick unsalted butter
1 cup whole milk
1¾ cups heavy cream
4 large eggs
¾ cup sugar
1 teaspoon vanilla

Preheat oven to 350°F.

Cut enough baguette into 1-inch cubes to measure 4 cups and in a shallow baking pan toast bread in middle of oven until crisp but not golden, about 5 minutes. Melt butter and in an 8-inch square baking pan toss with toasted bread.

In a bowl whisk together milk, cream, eggs, sugar, vanilla, and a pinch salt and pour over bread, stirring to coat. Chill pudding, covered, 1 hour.

Bake pudding in middle of oven until just set but still trembles slightly, about 50 minutes. Serve pudding warm or at room temperature.

CHEESECAKE MOUSSE WITH RUM-POACHED PLUMS ◯

Serves 2

1 cup water
⅓ cup granulated sugar
2 tablespoons dark rum
2 plums
½ cup whipped cream cheese (about 3 oz)
3 tablespoons confectioners sugar
½ teaspoon vanilla
½ cup well-chilled heavy cream

Have ready a bowl of ice and cold water. In a small saucepan simmer 1 cup water, granulated sugar, and rum, stirring occasionally, 10 minutes. Pit plums and cut each plum into 12 wedges. Simmer plums in syrup until tender, 2 to 3 minutes. Transfer plum mixture to a bowl and set it in bowl of ice water. Let plum mixture stand, stirring occasionally, until chilled.

In a bowl whisk together cream cheese, confectioners sugar, vanilla, and a pinch salt until smooth. In another bowl beat heavy cream until it holds soft peaks and whisk into cream-cheese mixture. Divide mixture between 2 goblets and chill, covered, 15 minutes.

Serve mousse topped with plums and some syrup.

BEVERAGES

ALCOHOLIC

COSMOPOLITAN CHAMPAGNE COCKTAIL ◔+

Makes 10

We thought we would update the popular Cosmopolitan by sub-stituting Champagne for the usual lemon vodka. We garnished the drinks with skewers of sugar-coated fresh cranberries (thawed frozen ones will work just fine, too).

1¼ cups Cointreau or Grand Marnier
1¼ cups cranberry juice cocktail
½ cup plus 2 tablespoons fresh lime juice
3 tablespoons superfine granulated sugar
   (sources on page 252)
4 cups chilled Champagne or other sparkling wine

Stir together Cointreau, juices, and sugar and chill, covered, 2 to 6 hours. Just before serving, divide among 10 Champagne flutes and top off with Champagne.

PHOTO ON PAGE 77

SUNRISE ◔

Makes 1

2 oz (¼ cup) Reserva del Dueño Añejo Tequila
½ oz (1 tablespoon) triple sec
¼ cup bottled whiskey-sour mix
a splash chilled 7-Up
a splash grenadine

Garnish: maraschino cherry and lime slice

In a cocktail shaker filled halfway with ice combine Tequila, triple sec, and whiskey-sour mix and shake well. Strain mixture into a chilled tall glass filled with ice. Top off mixture with 7-Up and grenadine and garnish with cherry and lime.

NELSON SPECIAL ◔

Makes 1

1 oz (2 tablespoons) Smirnoff vodka
1 teaspoon Rose's lime juice
¼ cup chilled lemonade
a splash blue Curaçao
chilled sparkling water

Garnish: fresh mint sprig

In a chilled tall glass filled halfway with crushed ice combine vodka and lime juice. Top off mixture with lemonade, Curaçao, and sparkling water and garnish with mint.

MARTINIS ◉

Makes 2

3 oz (6 tablespoons) gin
Splash of dry vermouth

Garnish: lemon twists

In a cocktail shaker filled halfway with ice combine gin and vermouth and shake well. Strain drink into 2 chilled Martini glasses and garnish with lemon twists.

SUMMERTIME ◉

Makes 1

¾ oz (1½ tablespoons) Absolut vodka
½ tablespoon strawberry syrup
½ tablespoon coconut syrup
½ tablespoon chilled heavy cream
chilled pineapple juice

In a blender blend vodka, syrups, and cream until frothy. Pour mixture into a chilled tall glass filled with ice and top off with pineapple juice.

CAIPIRINHAS ◉

Makes 8

Considered the national drink of Brazil, the caipirinha's main ingredient, cachaça, like rum, is made from sugarcane. Cachaça, however, has the bite and flavor of a rough-edged tequila.

15 limes
½ cup superfine granulated sugar
1½ cups *cachaça*

Garnish: lime wedges and/or sugarcane sticks

Squeeze enough juice from limes to measure 2 cups.
In a pitcher stir together lime juice and sugar until sugar is dissolved. Add ice cubes and *cachaça,* stirring until combined well.
Serve drinks garnished with lime wedges and/or sugarcane sticks.

TURTLE BOAT ◉

Makes 1

⅓ cup fresh chilled orange juice
1½ oz (3 tablespoons) dark rum
¾ oz (1½ tablespoons) Di Saronno Amaretto
¾ oz (1½ tablespoons) coconut-flavored rum
a generous splash chilled 7-Up
¾ oz (1½ tablespoons) grenadine

In a chilled glass filled with ice stir together all ingredients.

TIMES SQUARE COCKTAIL ◉+

Makes 10

1¼ cups Southern Comfort
¼ cup sweet vermouth
½ cup grenadine
5 cups chilled Champagne or other sparkling wine

Stir together Southern Comfort, vermouth, and grenadine. Chill, covered, 2 to 6 hours. Just before serving, divide among 10 Champagne flutes and slowly add enough Champagne to top off.

PHOTO ON PAGE 76

PINK·LEMONADE ☺

Makes 1

2 tablespoons simple syrup, or to taste
  (recipe follows)
¾ oz (1½ tablespoons) Absolut Kurant vodka
¾ oz (1½ tablespoons) Absolut Citron vodka
a splash Key lime juice or regular fresh lime juice
a splash chilled cranberry juice
a splash chilled Sprite

In a chilled tall glass filled with ice stir together all ingredients.

SIMPLE SYRUP ☺

Makes about 2 cups

No well-stocked bar should be without this fabulously versatile sweetener—in the summer, keep some on hand for iced tea, too.

1¼ cups sugar
1¼ cups water

In a small saucepan bring sugar and water to a boil, stirring, and boil until sugar is completely dissolved. Cool syrup.

Cooks' note:
• Cooled syrup keeps, covered and chilled, 2 weeks.

NONALCOHOLIC

GRAPEFRUIT COOLERS ☺

Makes 12 cups

9 cups (2¼ qt) fresh red grapefruit juice
  (from about 6 grapefruits)
3 cups seltzer or club soda

Garnish: fresh mint sprigs

In a pitcher half-filled with ice cubes stir together juice and seltzer or soda and garnish with mint.

GREEN GRAPE JUICE ☺

Makes about 2 cups

4 cups green grapes (about 1¼ lb; preferably
  seedless)
1 teaspoon fresh lemon juice

In a blender blend grapes and lemon juice until very smooth, about 1 minute. Pour mixture through a sieve into a bowl, pressing hard on solids.
  Serve grape juice over ice in tall glasses.

PHOTO ON PAGE 18

CUISINES OF
THE WORLD

Beach on Kho Phi Phi

THAILAND

. . .

From sturdy teak forests in the northern mountains, to lush emerald-green rice fields quilting the Central Plains, to pristine southern beaches lined with graceful coconut palms, the remarkable kingdom of Thailand offers a visual magnificence unique in the world. Profound beauty suffuses the landscape, weaving threads of loveliness into the tapestry of everyday life. A cascade of hot pink bougainvillea spills over a school-yard wall. Glimpsed from a train hurtling through the countryside, a dazzling Buddhist temple seems to float serenely in the distance, glowing green and orange, white and gold. A roadway meanders between liquid fields of ethereal pink lotus blossoms rising triumphantly up and out of the water, their gigantic emerald leaves hovering beneath them like little parasols.

Perhaps Thailand's extraordinary, everyday beauty helps account for the brilliance of its traditional cuisine. Lavish in its use of aromatic herbs and pungent spices, and playful in its juxtapositions of contrasting flavors and textures, Thai cooking reflects its creators, the countless generations of generous and pleasure-loving people whose hands and hearts have brought it to life. In its interweaving of dishes both simple and elaborate, rustic and elegant, into an ever-evolving yet harmonious whole, the cuisine of Thailand is an art form, dazzling and yet accessible, inviting the visitor to come in, sit down, relax, and eat rice in the company of family and friends.

Thailand's culinary heritage includes strong legacies from both China and southern India. Chinese influence is strong, due both to the original migration of the Thai people from southwestern China and the continuing immigration of Chinese-speaking peoples over time. Legacies include the techniques of stir-frying and steaming; the concept of plain rice anchoring a meal of sweet, sour, salty, and spicy-hot flavors; and the prominence of noodle dishes and soups. Indian influences appeared in Thailand well before its cultural flowering around the thirteenth century, via trade in spices and other goods. The spread of Hinduism, Buddhism, and Islam throughout the region over subsequent centuries furthered Thailand's exposure to Indian culinary practices, particularly the technique of grinding fragrant spices and lively herbs into seasoning pastes used in curries. The onset of Western contact in the sixteenth century provided Thailand with hot chile peppers among other New World ingredients, providing an additional source of heat and complexity to the native peppercorns already beloved in Thai kitchens.

The modern nation of Thailand consists of four geographical regions, each with a distinct character, reflected in both its language and its food. The **Central Plains** are the prosperous heart of Thailand, blessed with a temperate climate and fertile soil. Three rice crops are often possible within a year, tropical fruits abound, and numerous waterways lacing the region supply fresh fish, free for the taking. With this abundance central Thai cuisine celebrates fresh and varied ingredients, from a simple *gaeng kiow wahn gai*, green chicken curry with two kinds of Thai eggplant, *kaffir* lime leaves, and Asian basil, to the elegant *kanome jeen sao nahm*, delicate nests of fresh rice noodles topped with fresh ginger, garlic, pineapple, and a coconut sauce. The proximity of **North Thailand** to Burma and Laos is reflected in its traditional cuisine. Both *kao soi*, the signature curry noodle dish of Chiang Mai, and *gaeng hahng ley*, a pork curry bright with tamarind and ginger, show clear Burmese roots. Like their neighbors in Laos, northern Thais eat *kao niow*, sticky rice, a long-grain variety that steams up into a perfect finger food, and *ook gai*, a curry of lemongrass and chicken made without coconut milk. **Northeast Thailand**, known as Issahn, is a vast plateau bordering Laos along the Mekong River and Cambodia along the Dangrek mountain range. Plagued by drought and poor soil, the Northeast is home to intense, rustic dishes, robustly flavored and often volcanically hot, enjoyed Lao-style, with baskets of sticky rice. Issahn classics, such as *lahp*, a hot, tangy dish of minced beef, pork, or catfish; *gai yahng*, garlicky grilled chicken; and spicy *som tum*, green papaya salad, are popular throughout Thailand. The **South** is a postcard paradise of tropical beauty, with gorgeous beaches along both coasts of the Malay peninsula giving way to rubber plantations and lush rain forests inland. Even fiery food-loving Thais consider southern food hot, from *gaeng luang*, a clear and tangy yellow curry of fish and bamboo, to *gaeng dai plah*, a pungent dipping sauce with a bouquet of fresh vegetables and herbs to temper its fire. Culturally the South is complex: The three southernmost provinces are predominantly Muslim; the larger cities are home to large Chinese communities; and Malay, Southern Thai, and several Chinese dialects are widely spoken. Consequently the hungry traveler can enjoy breakfast at a small Chinese dim sum parlor, lunch at a *kanome jeen* noodle stall by the train depot, and supper at a Muslim rice shop in the night market. Spectacular seafood from the waters of the Gulf of Siam and the Andaman Sea can be enjoyed *alfresco* in seaside cafes all along the Thai coastline or in the finest Bangkok restaurants.

In Thailand, where even people of diminutive stature may pack away two or three full plates of rice in the course of a meal, eating rice is synonymous with eating. Rinsed well and then cooked in unseasoned water over charcoal, on gas stoves, and in barrel-sized electric rice cookers, rice is served—morning, noon, and night—as the heart of the meal.

Today, Thais may gather around dining tables in chic restaurants or elegant suburban homes, but many country people still spread out soft reed mats on the kitchen floor and gather the household in a circle around an array of serving dishes. Each place is marked with a plate mounded high with steaming jasmine rice, or sticky rice in the North and Northeast. All the dishes are presented together, with the exceptions of soup and whole fish, which are preferred piping hot and may, therefore, appear a few minutes into the meal. Diners serve themselves bite by bite, mixing spoonfuls of curries and soups into their rice as well as eating them directly.

A typical Thai meal consists of several substantial dishes such as curries, stews, and vegetable stir-fries containing meat, an omelet or savory steamed custard, a mild, clear soup to cleanse the palate throughout the meal, and a pungent spicy sauce called *nahm prik* served with cucumbers, cabbage, and other raw vegetables. All the dishes, except the soup, are intensely seasoned, providing vibrant and varied flavor to the abundant rice. Incendiary chile heat is characteristic of many Thai dishes, but by no means all of them. Thais seek a variety of tastes within one meal, from puckeringly sour to candy sweet, from sharply salty to the legendary spicy-hot—all mediated by mouthfuls of rice.

Unlike their East Asian neightbors, Thais eat rice from a plate, rather than a rice bowl, using a large spoon and a fork rather than chopsticks. The spoon is for scooping up the rice bite by bite, while the fork helps mix in sauces and maneuver morsels onto the spoon. Serving dishes are placed within arm's reach of each diner, and dishes are repeated as needed, so that each person can easily reach everything. This eliminates the need to pass food around, to ask for more, and to serve out one's intended portion in advance. When eating alone, Thais often choose a big bowl of Chinese-style soup noodles, a plate of the stir-fried noodle classic, *paht thai*, or a platter of fried rice with a lacy fried egg on top and a squeeze of lime on the side.

On the following pages we offer a traditional Thai dinner menu for eight, which provides variety and contrast in flavors, textures, and ingredients. We've also included a collection of *ahahn wahng*, a category of dishes that Thais refer to as "leisure-time food," that is found in small cafes, noodle shops, streetside stalls, even from small wooden boats in the floating market. These snacks can be prepared as a grand *hors d'oeuvre* party or a few can be made for a simple supper for two. Two primers follow, one with a look at the traditional Thai kitchen, and the other providing an introduction to Thai ingredients. As you will see, for all its exotic flavors, Thai cooking relies mostly on simple techniques and brilliant combinations of fresh ingredients, with some unusual ones and some as familiar as garlic and ginger, cilantro and mint, chiles and lime. We invite you to prepare a dish or two, or to fill your kitchen with friends and family to help create a complete Thai meal. Either way, do it Thai-style, finding pleasure all along the way, in the shopping and the prepping, the cooking and the feast.

A Thai Dinner

Clockwise from rice: Hot-and-Sour Shrimp Soup with Thai Herbs; Sweet-and-Sour Cucumber Salad; Stir-Fried Water Spinach with Garlic; Green Curried Pork; Grilled Beef Salad

TOME YUM GOONG
HOT-AND-SOUR SHRIMP SOUP WITH THAI HERBS

Makes 8 cups

Fresh lemongrass gives this soup lovely flavor and aroma. For authentic presentation, serve large pieces in the soup; however, do not attempt to eat them as they are hard and fibrous. In Thailand, this soup is served with rice and the other dishes of the meal. If you prefer, serve it as a first course.

4 fresh lemongrass stalks*, dry outer leaves
   discarded and root ends trimmed
8 cups Thai chicken stock (recipe follows)
4 fresh *kaffir* lime leaves* (*bai makroot*)
1 lb medium shrimp (about 40), shelled
   and deveined
8 button mushrooms, thinly sliced
4 tablespoons fresh lime juice
4 tablespoons Asian fish sauce* (*naam pla*)
3 to 4 fresh *kii noo** or *serrano* chiles, minced

Garnish: thinly sliced *chee fah** or red jalapeño
   chiles and fresh cilantro leaves

*sources on page 239

Cut lower 6 inches of lemongrass into 1½-inch pieces. Simmer stock, lemongrass, and lime leaves 5 minutes. Add shrimp and mushrooms and simmer until shrimp are just cooked through, 1 to 2 minutes. Remove from heat and stir in lime juice, fish sauce, and chiles.

Cooks' notes:
• Frozen *kaffir* lime leaves may be substituted for fresh;
  however, do not thaw them.
• When shelling the shrimp, leave the tail and last segment of
  shell intact. Shrimp may be shelled and deveined 1 day ahead
  and chilled, covered.
• Stock will become opaque when lime juice is added.

THAI CHICKEN STOCK

Makes about 9½ cups

4 lb chicken wings
1 lb pork neck bones or other meaty pork bones
1 onion, quartered
1½ teaspoons coriander seeds
1½ teaspoons salt
10 cups water

Simmer all ingredients in a 4-quart pot, skimming foam if necessary, 1 hour. Cool, then pour through a fine sieve into a bowl.

Cooks' note:
• Stock may be made 3 days ahead and chilled, covered.

GAENG KIOW WAHN MOO
GREEN CURRIED PORK

Serves 8 as part of a Thai menu

Kaffir lime leaves are added to Thai soups and stews to impart an herbal lemon-lime flavor. Here they are used whole as both a seasoning and a garnish and are not meant to be eaten.

3 (14½-oz) cans unsweetened coconut milk*
   such as Chao Koh or Goya
¼ cup Thai green curry paste* (recipe follows)
2½ lb boneless pork shoulder, cut into 1-inch pieces
6 fresh *kaffir* lime leaves* (*bai makroot*)
¼ cup Asian fish sauce* (*naam pla*)
2 tablespoons packed palm sugar or brown sugar

Garnish: 6 fresh *kaffir* lime leaves* (*bai makroot*),
   1 cup fresh Asian basil sprigs such as *bai
   horapah**, and 2 thickly sliced *chee fah**
   or red jalapeño chiles

*sources on page 239

Scoop 1 cup coconut cream from 2 cans coconut milk, reserving remainder, and simmer coconut cream in a wok or large heavy skillet, stirring occasionally, until thickened and fragrant, 6 to 8 minutes. Stir in green curry paste and cook over moderate heat until fragrant, 1 to 2 minutes.

Stir in pork until coated and cook, stirring, 2 minutes. Put coconut milk from open cans in a large measuring cup and add enough coconut milk to total 3 cups. Add coconut milk to pork with lime leaves, fish sauce, and sugar and simmer, uncovered, stirring occasionally, until pork is tender, 15 to 20 minutes. If sauce is too thin, transfer pork with slotted spoon to a bowl and simmer sauce until thickened. Return pork to sauce and discard lime leaves.

Cooks' notes:
- Frozen *kaffir* lime leaves may be substituted for fresh; however, do not thaw them.
- Prepared curry paste may be substituted if you do not have time to make it from scratch.
- Curry may be made 1 day ahead and chilled, covered. Reheat before serving.

KRUENG GAENG KIOW WAHN
THAI GREEN CURRY PASTE

Makes about ½ cup

2 teaspoons coriander seeds
1 teaspoon cumin seeds
5 white peppercorns
2 fresh lemongrass stalks*, dry outer leaves
  discarded and root ends trimmed
¼ cup finely chopped fresh cilantro roots or stems
8 fresh *kii noo** or *serrano* chiles, finely chopped
6 garlic cloves, finely chopped
2 tablespoons finely chopped shallot
1 tablespoon finely chopped peeled fresh or
  thawed frozen *galangal** (*kha*)
1 teaspoon finely grated *kaffir* lime zest* or
  regular lime zest
1 teaspoon shrimp paste* (*ga-pi*)
1 teaspoon salt
2 tablespoons water if necessary (see note below)

*sources on page 239

Toast coriander and cumin seeds in a dry heavy skillet over moderate heat, shaking skillet, until fragrant, 3 to 4 minutes. Cool seeds and grind with peppercorns in an electric coffee/spice grinder.

Thinly slice lower 6 inches from lemongrass and in a mini-processor or with a mortar and pestle grind lemongrass with remaining ingredients. Stir in spice mixture.

Cooks' notes:
- If using a mini-processor to grind the curry paste, you may need water to move the blades. This will make a soft paste, but will not change the flavor or cooking properties of the paste.
- If using a mortar and pestle to grind the final paste, you will need the heavy-duty Thai variety made of granite or clay or an extremely large stone/marble Italian one. This heavy duty mortar and pestle may also be used instead of an electric coffee/spice grinder to grind the toasted spices earlier in the recipe.
- Thai curry paste may be made 1 week ahead and chilled, covered.

PLAH NOONG
STEAMED RED SNAPPER WITH GINGER

Serves 8 as part of a Thai menu

1 large banana leaf*, thawed if frozen, or
    parchment paper
1 (1½- to 2-lb) whole red snapper, cleaned with
    head and tail intact
3 tablespoons julienne strips peeled fresh ginger
2 tablespoons fresh lime juice
2 tablespoons Asian fish sauce* (*naam pla*)
1 teaspoon packed palm sugar or brown sugar

Garnish: julienne strips of scallion and peeled
    fresh ginger

*sources on page 239

Put banana leaf on a large steamer rack. Lay snapper
in center of banana leaf and trim excess leaf, leaving
enough to fold over fish. Season fish with salt and
pepper and scatter ginger over top. Fold leaf over fish,
forming a packet, and steam over boiling water until just
cooked through, about 10 minutes. (Check thickest part
of fish with a knife; flesh should just flake.)

While fish is steaming, stir together lime juice, fish
sauce, and sugar until sugar is dissolved. Transfer fish in
leaf with 2 spatulas to a platter and unfold leaf. Pour lime
sauce over fish and sprinkle with scallion and ginger.

Cooks' notes:
• Banana leaf imparts a lovely flavor to the fish, which you will
  not get with the parchment.
• The banana leaf will turn dark during steaming. For a more
  colorful presentation, you may want to transfer the cooked
  fish to another banana leaf.

NEUA YAHNG NAHM TOKE
GRILLED BEEF SALAD

Serves 8 as part of a Thai menu

1 tablespoon plus 1 teaspoon sugar
⅓ cup soy sauce
2 lb 1-inch-thick beef rib-eye or shell steaks
¼ cup fresh lime juice
¼ cup Asian fish sauce* (*naam pla*)
1 to 2 teaspoons coarsely ground dried red chiles
¼ cup finely chopped fresh cilantro
¼ cup finely chopped fresh mint
¼ cup minced shallot
1 tablespoon toasted rice powder (recipe follows)
2 scallions, finely chopped

Garnish: fresh mint sprigs
Accompaniment: soft lettuce leaves such as Bibb
    or red-leaf

*sources on page 239

Dissolve 1 tablespoon sugar in soy sauce in a large resealable plastic bag and add steaks, pressing out excess air. Marinate, turning once, chilled, at least 1 hour.

Prepare grill.

Drain steaks, discarding marinade, and grill on an oiled rack set 4 to 6 inches over glowing coals about 4 minutes on each side for medium-rare. Let stand 5 minutes on a cutting board before cutting into ¼-inch-thick slices (about 2 inches long). Toss steak with remaining teaspoon sugar and remaining ingredients.

Cooks' notes:
- You can marinate steaks up to 3 hours.
- Steaks may be grilled 1 day ahead and chilled (unsliced), covered. Reheat in a 350°F oven until warm, about 5 minutes. This will result in cooked-through meat.
- Steak can be grilled in a hot well-seasoned ridged grill pan but will not have the same flavor as charcoal-grilled steak.

Kao Kua
Toasted Rice Powder

¼ cup raw sticky or jasmine rice*

*sources on page 239

Toast rice in a dry small heavy skillet over moderate heat, shaking skillet, until golden, 4 to 6 minutes. Cool rice and grind to a coarse powder with a mortar and pestle or in an electric coffee/spice grinder.

Cooks' notes:
- Rice powder is best when ground just before using to preserve the nutty flavor and aroma. Toasted whole rice keeps in an airtight container 3 weeks; once it is ground it keeps 4 days.

Taeng Kwa Dong
Sweet-and-Sour Cucumber Salad

Serves 8 as part of a Thai menu

½ cup distilled white or cider vinegar
¼ cup water
¼ cup sugar
1 teaspoon salt

1 English cucumber (¾ lb), peeled, halved lengthwise and cut crosswise into ¼-inch-thick slices
½ cup thinly sliced shallot
1 teaspoon finely chopped fresh *chee fah** or *serrano* chile

Garnish: finely chopped roasted peanuts, fresh cilantro leaves, and thinly sliced red onion

*sources on page 239

Stir together vinegar, water, sugar, and salt until sugar is dissolved. Stir in cucumber, shallot, and chile.

Garnish salad with little mounds of peanuts and cilantro and top with a little mound of red onion.

Cooks' notes:
- If cucumbers are very pale, leave some peel for color.
- Salad may be made 1 hour ahead and chilled, covered.

Pahk Boong Fai Daeng
Stir-Fried Water Spinach with Garlic

Serves 8 as part of a Thai menu

2 lb water spinach* (*paak boong*)
3 tablespoons vegetable oil
6 garlic cloves, finely chopped
3 tablespoons Asian fish sauce* (*naam pla*)

*sources on page 239

Remove bottom 2 inches from water spinach stems. Separately cut remaining stems and leafy tops into 1½-inch pieces, transferring stems and leafy tops to separate bowls.

Heat oil in a wok or large deep heavy skillet over moderately high heat until it just begins to smoke. Stir-fry garlic until golden, about 1 minute. Add stems and stir-fry until crisp-tender, 2 to 3 minutes. Add leafy tops and stir-fry until leaves are wilted and stems are just tender, about 1½ minutes. Stir in fish sauce.

Cooks' notes:
- Substitute regular spinach for water spinach if it is difficult to find.

PAHT PEHT MAKEUA YAO
EGGPLANT WITH CHILES AND BASIL

Serves 8 as part of a Thai menu

¼ cup vegetable oil
1½ tablespoons Thai red curry paste*
2 lb long slender Asian* or globe eggplant, cut
 into 1-inch chunks
¾ cup chicken broth
¼ cup water
2 tablespoons packed palm sugar or brown sugar
2 teaspoons salt
1 teaspoon soy sauce
½ cup fresh Asian basil such as *bai horapah*,
 finely chopped
1 fresh *ki noo** or *serrano* chile, minced

*sources on page 239

Heat oil in a wok or large deep heavy skillet over moderate heat until hot but not smoking and cook curry paste, stirring and mashing paste into oil, 1½ minutes. Add eggplant and stir until coated well. Add broth, water, sugar, salt, and soy sauce and simmer, covered, stirring occasionally, 5 minutes. Remove lid and simmer until eggplant is tender and sauce is thickened, 1 to 2 minutes. Remove wok or skillet from heat and stir in basil and chile.

Cook's note:
• The round golf-ball-sized Thai eggplants may be used in this recipe; however, the pea-sized variety is not appropriate.

KAO HOHM MALI
THAI JASMINE RICE

Serves 8 as part of a Thai menu

3 cups jasmine rice*
3½ cups water

*sources on page 239

Rinse rice in several changes of water (to remove excess starch), swirling, until water is clear and drain well in a large sieve.
 Boil rice and water in a 4-quart heavy saucepan, uncovered, until water is evaporated and steam holes appear on surface. Cover rice and reduce heat to very low. Cook, undisturbed, 15 minutes and let stand off heat, undisturbed, 5 minutes. Turn rice gently or fluff with a fork and keep covered until serving.

Cooks' note:
• Cooked rice may be kept, off heat in covered pan, 1 hour.

NAHM PRIK GOONG HAENG
THAI HOT SAUCE WITH DRIED SHRIMP AND LIME

Makes about ½ cup

1 teaspoon to 1 tablespoon dried shrimp*, chopped
4 garlic cloves, chopped
9 fresh *kii noo** or *serrano* chiles
3 tablespoons Asian fish sauce* (*naam pla*)
1 teaspoon palm sugar* or brown sugar
2 to 3 tablespoons fresh lime juice

*sources page 239

Pound shrimp to taste, garlic, and chiles with a mortar and pestle or pulse in a mini-processor until finely chopped. Stir in remaining ingredients until palm sugar is dissolved.

Cooks' note:
• Sauce keeps, covered and chilled, up to 1 week. Let sauce stand at room temperature 20 minutes before serving.

AI-TEEM GA-TI

COCONUT ICE CREAM

Makes about 1½ quarts

Serve our luxurious version of this Thai classic with fresh fruit.

1 tablespoon cornstarch
1 cup whole milk
4 large eggs
1 cup heavy cream
1½ cups packed palm sugar* or brown sugar
2 cups fresh or canned unsweetened coconut milk*
   such as Chao Koh or Goya, chilled
1 cup sweetened flaked coconut, toasted until
   golden (procedure on page 230) and cooled

*sources on page 239

Dissolve cornstarch in 2 tablespoons milk in a large bowl and whisk in eggs until combined well. Bring remaining milk, cream, and sugar just to a boil in a 3-quart heavy saucepan, stirring occasionally, and whisk half into egg mixture in a slow stream. Whisk egg mixture into milk mixture in pan and cook over moderate heat, whisking, until it comes to a gentle boil. Gently boil, whisking, 1 minute and cool. Chill until cold and stir in coconut milk.

Freeze custard in an ice-cream maker and stir in toasted coconut. Transfer to an airtight container and freeze to harden.

Cooks' note:
• The custard may appear curdled; however, after it is frozen it will smooth out.

Below: Pomelo Salad. Opposite, clockwise from upper left: Spicy Green Papaya Salad; Grilled Chicken Wings with Sweet Garlic Sauce; Squid with Red Curry Sauce; Kabocha Squash Dumplings

BOH BIAH TOTE
FRIED THAI SPRING ROLLS

Makes 36 spring rolls

Thai spring rolls are the Southeast Asian version of the Chinese snack. The thin, delicate wrappers imported from Asia are found in the freezer section in Asian markets. However, the larger, heavier ones, found in supermarkets, can be substituted.

4 oz bean-thread (cellophane) noodles*
2 tablespoons vegetable oil plus additional for frying
¼ cup minced shallots
3 large garlic cloves, minced
½ lb ground pork
½ lb shrimp, shelled, deveined, and minced
¼ cup Asian fish sauce* (*naam pla*)
2 tablespoons palm sugar* or brown sugar
1 teaspoon black pepper
3 tablespoons chopped fresh cilantro
2 cups mung bean sprouts
about 36 square spring-roll wrappers* (from a 1-lb package), thawed if frozen

Accompaniment: sweet garlic sauce (page 231)

*sources on page 239

Soak bean-thread noodles in warm water to cover 10 minutes. Drain and cut into 2-inch pieces.

Heat 2 tablespoons oil in a large nonstick skillet over moderate heat and cook shallots and garlic, stirring, until softened. Add pork and shrimp and cook, stirring to break up pork into small pieces, just until pork is no longer pink, about 5 minutes. Stir in noodles. Add fish sauce, sugar, and pepper and simmer, stirring occasionally, until most of liquid is evaporated. Transfer to a bowl and stir in cilantro and bean sprouts.

Arrange 1 spring-roll wrapper on a work surface with a corner facing you and keep remaining wrappers covered with a damp cloth. Put a slightly heaping tablespoon of filling in center of wrapper, forming it into a horizontal 2- by 1-inch pile, and fold corner closest to you tightly over filling. Fold left and right sides over filling, and, rolling away from you, roll up filling tightly in wrapper. Moisten corner with a finger dipped in water to seal. Transfer spring roll to a baking sheet and cover with plastic wrap. Make more spring rolls in same manner, transferring them to baking sheet and covering.

Heat 2 inches oil to 350°F. Fry spring rolls, 3 at a time, until golden, about 5 minutes, then transfer to paper towels. Return oil to 350°F between batches.

Cooks' note:
• Filling may be made 1 day ahead and chilled, covered.

TODE MUN PLAH
THAI FISH CAKES WITH LONG BEANS AND KAFFIR LIME

Makes 24 fish cakes (hors d'oeuvre)

Although these fish cakes are delicious on their own, they are classically served with a cucumber salad, such as the one in our Thai dinner (page 221).

1 lb halibut or tilapia fillets, cut into 1-inch pieces
¼ cup finely chopped long beans* or green beans
1 teaspoon Thai red curry paste*
½ teaspoon finely chopped fresh *kaffir* lime leaves* (*bai makroot*) or ¼ teaspoon finely grated fresh lime zest
1 large egg
2 tablespoons vegetable oil

*sources on page 239

Pulse fish with beans, curry paste, and lime leaves in a food processor until coarsely chopped, and transfer to a bowl. Stir in egg and salt and pepper to taste until combined well. Form into 24 (1½-inch) cakes and chill, loosely covered, 30 minutes.

Heat 1 tablespoon oil in a large nonstick skillet over moderately high heat until hot but not smoking, then cook half of cakes until golden brown and cooked through, about 2 minutes on each side. Cook remaining cakes in same manner.

Cooks' notes:
- Fish cakes may be cooked 1 hour ahead and reheated in a low oven until just warmed through.
- Remove ribs from *kaffir* lime leaves before chopping leaves. Frozen *kaffir* lime leaves may be substituted; however, do not thaw them.

KANOME JEEP JEY GAENG KIOW WAHN
KABOCHA SQUASH DUMPLINGS WITH GREEN CURRY DIPPING SAUCE

Makes 48 dumplings

These dumplings are our version of the pork dumpling, kanome jeep, with green curry used as a lively dipping sauce rather than an accompaniment to rice.

1 small Kabocha squash* (about 2 lb)
2 teaspoons finely grated fresh ginger, or to taste
1½ to 2 tablespoons finely chopped fresh Asian basil
    such as *bai horapah**
2 large garlic cloves, minced
1 small fresh *kii noo** or *serrano* chile,
    finely chopped
cornstarch for dusting
48 won ton skins or *gyoza* wrappers*, thawed
    if frozen
1½ teaspoons Thai green curry paste*
2½ tablespoons vegetable oil
1 cup canned unsweetened coconut milk*
    such as Chao Koh or Goya
2 tablespoons finely chopped scallion greens
1 teaspoon fresh lime juice
¼ teaspoon Asian fish sauce* (*naam pla*)

Garnish: small fresh basil leaves

*sources on page 239

Preheat oven to 425°F.

Cut squash in half and roast, cut sides down, in an oiled shallow baking pan in middle of oven until tender, about 30 minutes. Cool squash slightly and discard seeds. Scoop out enough flesh to measure about 2 cups. Mash squash with a fork and stir together with ginger, basil to taste, garlic, chile, and salt and pepper to taste.

Lightly dust a platter with cornstarch. Cut won ton wrappers with a 2½-inch round cookie cutter and put 8 on a dry surface, keeping remainder wrapped in plastic wrap. Put a heaping teaspoon filling in center of each wrapper and with a finger dipped in water dampen exposed wrapper. Gather each wrapper up to hug filling, forming a waist (filling should be exposed and level with top of wrapper), and tap on bottom to flatten base so dumpling can stand up. Transfer to platter. Make more dumplings in same manner.

Cook curry paste in ½ tablespoon oil in a small saucepan over moderate heat, stirring, until fragrant and hot. Gradually whisk in coconut milk and bring to a simmer. Remove from heat and keep warm, covered.

Heat 1 tablespoon oil in a large nonstick skillet over moderately high heat until hot but not smoking, then fry half of dumplings, filling sides up, until undersides are golden, about 1 minute. Add ¼ cup water down side of skillet. Cover skillet and steam dumplings over moderately low heat until wrappers are tender and filling is hot, about 2 minutes. Remove lid and cook dumplings until water is evaporated. Transfer to paper towels to drain. Cook remaining dumplings in same manner.

While second batch of dumplings is cooking, stir scallion greens, lime juice, and fish sauce into warm green curry sauce.

Garnish dipping sauce with basil leaves.

YUM SOM-OH
POMELO SALAD

Serves 6 to 8 (hors d'oeuvre)

¼ cup vegetable oil
1 small red onion, thinly sliced
4 large garlic cloves, thinly sliced
1 tablespoon plus 1 teaspoon palm sugar*
    or brown sugar
1 tablespoon plus 1 teaspoon fresh lime juice
1 tablespoon Asian fish sauce* (*naam pla*),
    or to taste
8 pomelos* or grapefruits
1 lb cooked, shelled, and deveined large shrimp,
    thinly sliced
⅓ cup sweetened flaked coconut, toasted
    (recipe follows)
¼ cup chopped fresh cilantro
3 tablespoons chopped fresh mint
2 tablespoons chopped salted roasted peanuts

Accompaniment: Bibb lettuce or cabbage leaves,
    separated

*sources on page 239

Heat oil in a 10-inch nonstick skillet over moderately high heat until hot but not smoking and sauté onion, stirring frequently, until golden brown, about 4 minutes. Add garlic and sauté, stirring, until golden, about 1 minute. Transfer onion mixture to paper towels to drain.

Whisk together sugar, lime juice, and fish sauce until sugar is dissolved.

Cut rind and white pith from pomelos. Working over a bowl, segment pomelos with a sharp small knife.

Just before serving, toss pomelos with lime juice mixture, onion mixture, and remaining ingredients and season with salt and pepper.

Serve pomelo salad with lettuce leaves on the side or spoon about 2 tablespoons salad onto center of each leaf.

MAPRAO KUA
TOASTED SWEETENED COCONUT

Sweetened flaked coconut burns easily, so be sure to give it your full attention. In Thailand, both rice and coconut are gently dry-fried until beautifully browned, fragrant, and heightened in flavor.

Toast coconut in a dry small heavy skillet over moderate heat, shaking skillet, until golden. Alternatively, roast coconut in a shallow baking pan in a preheated 375°F oven, stirring occasionally, until golden, 5 to 6 minutes.

Cooks' note:
• Toasted and cooled coconut may be kept in an airtight
  container at room temperature 5 days.

KWAYTIOW NAHM MOO
RICE NOODLE SOUP WITH ROASTED CHILE PASTE

Serves 6 (starter)

2 (14½ oz) cans chicken broth
3 cups water
8 oz dried rice noodles*
¼ cup Thai roasted chile paste* (*nahm prik pao*)
¼ cup Asian fish sauce (*naam pla*)
2 to 3 fresh *serrano* chiles, seeded and minced
½ lb ground pork
2 scallions, thinly sliced
¼ cup fresh Asian basil such as *bai grapao** or *bai
    horapah**, thinly sliced
10 cherry tomatoes, quartered
¼ cup fresh lime juice

*sources on page 239

Bring broth and water to a boil in a 4-quart pot over high heat.

Cook rice noodles in a large pot of boiling water until just tender and drain.

Stir together chile paste, fish sauce, and chiles. Crumble pork into boiling broth mixture and simmer, 3 minutes until meat is no longer pink. Add chile mixture and noodles and heat through. Remove pot from heat and add remaining ingredients and salt to taste.

PAHT PEHT PLAH MEUK
SQUID WITH RED CURRY SAUCE

Serves 6 (starter)

This dish also can be prepared with shrimp, scallops, small mussels, or Manila clams.

2 lb cleaned squid
1 (14½-oz) can unsweetened coconut milk*
    such as Chao Koh or Goya, chilled
2 tablespoons Thai red curry paste*
1 tablespoon minced peeled fresh ginger
2 tablespoons Asian fish sauce* (*naam pla*)
1 tablespoon palm sugar* or brown sugar
10 fresh *kaffir* lime leaves* (*bai makroot*)
2 tablespoons chopped fresh cilantro

*sources on page 239

Cut squid bodies lengthwise and open flat on a work surface. Score with a knife in a diamond pattern and cut into 1½-inch pieces.

Scoop ¼ cup coconut cream from can of coconut milk and simmer in a 12-inch heavy skillet until it is slightly thickened, 2 to 3 minutes (it may begin to separate). Add curry paste and ginger and cook over moderately low heat, stirring constantly, 3 minutes. Add squid and sauté over moderately high heat, stirring constantly, until squid is opaque, 5 to 7 minutes. Transfer squid to a bowl with a slotted spoon. Add fish sauce, sugar, whole lime leaves, and ½ cup coconut milk to curry sauce and boil, stirring, until thickened, about 5 minutes. Return squid to sauce, tossing to coat, and sprinkle with cilantro.

Cooks' notes:
• To remove coconut cream from a can of coconut milk, scoop out the cream that has separated out from the milk at the top of the can with a spoon, but also look for clumps of the cream in the milk itself.
• Frozen *kaffir* lime leaves may be substituted for fresh; however, do not thaw them.

> *Note: The remaining three dishes, Grilled Chicken Wings with Sweet Garlic Sauce, Spicy Green Papaya Salad, and Sticky Rice are a classic Northeastern Thai combination. All three are served as finger food in Thailand.*

BEEK GAI YAHNG GUP NAHM JEEM WAHN
GRILLED CHICKEN WINGS WITH SWEET GARLIC SAUCE

Serves 6 to 8 (hors d'oeuvre)

3 lb chicken wings
¼ cup vegetable oil
½ cup chopped fresh cilantro
3 tablespoons fresh lime juice
1 tablespoon soy sauce

Accompaniment: sweet garlic sauce (recipe follows)

Cut off wing tips, reserving them for another use, and halve wings at joint. Whisk together oil, cilantro, lime juice, and soy sauce in a large bowl. Add wings and stir to coat. Marinate, covered and chilled, 1 hour.
Prepare grill.
Grill wings on an oiled rack set 5 to 6 inches over glowing coals until cooked through and golden brown, 10 to 12 minutes on each side.

Cooks' note:
• Wings may be grilled 1 day ahead, cooled completely, and chilled, covered. Reheat in a 400°F oven.

NAHM JEEM WAHN
SWEET GARLIC SAUCE

Makes about 1 cup

This sauce is an accompaniment to our spring rolls and our grilled chicken wings—one recipe makes enough for both.

4 garlic cloves, minced
1 shallot, finely chopped
¾ cup sugar
½ cup water
⅓ cup white-wine vinegar
1 teaspoon chile garlic sauce*, or to taste

*sources on page 239

Simmer all ingredients, uncovered, stirring occasionally, 10 minutes. Serve at room temperature.

Cooks' note:
• Sauce may be made 3 days ahead and chilled, covered.

SOM TUM

SPICY GREEN PAPAYA SALAD

Serves 6

6 fresh *kii noo** or 3 *serrano* chiles, seeded
  and chopped
4 garlic cloves, chopped
1 tablespoon dried shrimp*
6 long beans* (optional)
1 (1 lb) green papaya*
¼ cup fresh lime juice
2 tablespoons Asian fish sauce* (*naam pla*)
4 teaspoons palm sugar* or brown sugar
4 cherry tomatoes, quartered

Garnish: fresh herb sprigs (Asian basil such as
  *bai horapah**, cilantro, and/or mint)

*sources on page 239

Pound chiles, garlic, dried shrimp, and a pinch of salt
to a paste with a mortar and pestle. Cut beans into 1-inch
pieces and add to chile mixture, pounding until they are
crushed but not broken apart. Peel papaya. Lay a 4-sided
grater on its side with handle toward you and large
teardrop-shaped holes facing up, then grate papaya
lengthwise to get long thin shreds. Combine papaya,
bean mixture, and remaining ingredients in a bowl and
pound salad with pestle to crush it slightly. Let salad
stand 10 minutes to blend flavors.

Cooks' note:
• If you want a spicier salad, add the seeds from 1 or 2 of
  the chiles.

KAO NIOW

THAI STICKY RICE

Serves 6

*If there's a Thai, Lao, or Vietnamese market near you, chances
are it will carry the large, conical baskets used for cooking
sticky rice, as well as the lightweight pot the basket rests in as
the rice steams. Otherwise, use a large sieve lined with cheesecloth or muslin and put it over a large kettle of water.*

*In Thailand, cooked sticky rice is kept warm and moist dur-
ing the meal by serving it in covered baskets, which also can be
found in some Southeast Asian markets.*

3 cups Thai long-grain sticky (glutinous) rice*

*for sources see page 239

Cover rice with cold water by 2 to 3 inches in a large
bowl (large enough to hold at least twice the volume of
rice, about 6 cups). Soak rice 8 to 24 hours. Alternatively, soak rice in warm water (about 110°F) 2 hours.
The longer soak allows more flavor to develop.

Drain rice and transfer to a Southeast Asian rice-
steamer basket or lined sieve. Set steamer basket over
several inches of boiling water in a large pot or deep kettle. It is important that rice *does not touch* boiling water.
Cover pot with lid. Steam rice, checking water level
occasionally and adding more boiling water if necessary,
25 minutes, or until shiny and tender.

Transfer rice to a basket or bowl, breaking it into
smaller lumps, and immediately cover with a lid or clean
kitchen towel. (Rice dries out if exposed to air as it
cools, so keep covered until serving.)

Cooks' note:
• Sticky rice is also known as sweet, glutinous, or waxy rice and
  may be either short- or long-grain. However, the long-grain
  rice from Thailand must be used here. Do not confuse it with
  Japanese sweet rice which is short-grain and will not cook up
  in same manner.

THE THAI KITCHEN

The simplicity of a traditional Thai kitchen belies the complex cuisine created there. From wooden houses raised on stilts to avoid monsoon flooding come memorable meals, produced with passion and imagination from a low-tech *batterie de cuisine*. Such food sings with flavor.

The ideal traditional kitchen is a modest building separate from the main house, where wooden shutters and doors open on all sides to invite breezes in and to let smoke escape. With a lush bird's-eye view of mango, tamarind, and banana trees and a kitchen garden of chiles, vegetables, and herbs, the cook starts a charcoal fire in two sturdy bucket-shaped stoves raised on a waist-high platform. While the fire catches, the cook and helpers begin to chop garlic, shallots, chiles, and greens, using a heavy Chinese-style cleaver and an assortment of paring and utility knives, on a thick round of hard tamarind wood, 3 to 4 inches high, set on a work table. Alongside is a *kroke*, a mighty mortar and pestle made of granite, or a heavy glazed ceramic mortar with a weighty wooden pestle. Used for pounding curry pastes, intensely flavored *nahm prik* sauces, roasted rice or spices, as well as the simple perennial seasoning mixture of garlic, cilantro root, and peppercorns, the mortar and pestle make rhythmic music, a comforting signal that good things are being prepared to flavor the rice. Any lengthy task, such as trimming lemongrass or pounding an array of herbs and spices into a paste, is carried off on a platter to a pleasant spot where the cook can sit while she works.

Since rice takes time to cook, it is always the first thing to go on the stove in a large pot, called a *maw gaeng*. These tin or stainless-steel pots, ranging from standard saucepan to large dutch oven in size, hang on the wooden walls until needed to prepare not only rice, but curries, soups, stews, and sweets. On the other burner goes a *gra-tah*, a lightweight, shallow wok that resembles a *karhai*, the basic pan of the traditional Indian kitchen. This vessel is used for stir-fries and deep-fried dishes. Steamed dishes are prepared either in a large Chinese-style metal steaming set, or in a *gra-tah* with a steamer basket inserted, or with chopsticks placed over the water in an x-pattern, onto which the dish is balanced. To regulate the heat the cook uses a large bamboo fan to increase the temperature, and heavy tongs to decrease it, by removing hot coals to an airtight metal container.

On one wall is a *dtoo*, a close cousin to an American pie safe, with screen mesh over the doors rather than perforated tin or copper. On its shelves are prepared dishes, perishable dishes, and snacks—all safe from winged creatures via the screen and earthbound creatures via small water-filled ceramic cups that ring the legs of the cabinet. With a daily trip or two to the local fresh market and no means to keep things cold over time, the traditional Thai cook requires little storage space. One corner of the kitchen is reserved for two enormous glazed ceramic jars; one holds rain water for drinking and cooking, while the other keeps 50 or so pounds of jasmine rice at hand. Spatulas, wok scrapers, cooking chopsticks, long-handled wire mesh baskets for deep-frying, and a smattering of other tools hang on the walls. A set of soft reed mats to spread out on the floor when the meal is almost ready is kept nearby, along with a broom made of rice straw to sweep the floor beforehand.

Today's modern Thai kitchens often are gleaming stainless-steel wonders with electric rice cookers, blenders, popcorn poppers, espresso makers, ovens, toasters, and refrigerators galore. The traditional kitchen, however, teaches us that this cuisine can come from any kitchen: simple or sophisticated, Eastern or Western. With a sense of Thai flavors and a spirit of adventure and pleasure in cooking, the home cook can create excellent traditional Thai dishes almost any time, any place.

BASIC INGREDIENTS

The ancient Thai inscription, "In the water there are fish, in the fields there is rice" is as true today as it was some 700 years ago. Certainly, the waters of the Gulf of Thailand and the Andaman Sea, as well as inland ponds and rivers, are still teeming with fish. And rice—jasmine rice in the Central Plains and South and sticky rice in the North and Northeast—is the mainstay of every meal. Other essential ingredients provide the four flavors—salty, sour, hot, and sweet—that appear in equal measure. Fish sauce, dried shrimp, and shrimp paste add saltiness; lime juice, tamarind, and vinegar offer sourness; chiles and peppercorns give heat; and palm sugar, granulated sugar, and coconut milk add sweetness. An extra squeeze of lime, a pinch of sugar, or a dash of fish sauce often are added to dishes at the last moment to adjust the seasoning, and more condiments are available on the table to accommodate personal tastes.

As you cook Thai food in your own kitchen, you'll need to assess the potency of your ingredients and make adjustments accordingly. As you can imagine, Thai ingredients found in America vary greatly depending on where and how they are grown, how they are stored, and other conditions. In general, our recipes aren't particularly fiery or pungent. If you plan on eating them Thai style, with lots of rice, you may wish to intensify some of the flavorings. Below is a list of Thai ingredients that we used in our menus; most items are readily available at Asian markets and specialty foods stores, and supermarkets now carry some items. For mail order sources, see page 239.

VEGETABLES & FRUITS

Thai eggplant (*makeuah*): Thailand has many varieties of small eggplants. The small, round, golf-ball-sized variety (*makeuah poh*) readily thickens sauces and takes on the flavors of other ingredients. This seedy eggplant is dark green at the top, graduating to light green at the bottom, or it is solid purple or white. Smaller, pea-sized varieties (*makeuah puang*) are bitter, but they are simmered in curries for their unique, herbaceous aroma and flavor. Long, slender Asian eggplants (*makeuah yao*) are sweet and tender, with a soft, absorbent texture and often appear grilled in Thai dishes.

Kabocha squash (*fahk tong*): A small, squat winter squash with tough, mottled dull-green skin, Kabocha squash has sweet, smooth golden-orange flesh, beloved in both curries and sweets. This squash is a favorite throughout Southeast Asia and in Japan; it often can be found in supermarkets as well as in farmers markets.

Long beans (*tua fahk yao*): Also known as snake beans, yard-long beans, or asparagus beans, long beans (usually about 18 inches) can be pale or dark green, depending on variety. They are denser, drier, and somewhat crunchier than green beans, and, while they hold up during long cooking, Thais also eat them raw with *nahm prik* sauces. Long beans are sold in loose coils or knots; look for flexible, fresh-looking beans, without any dark spots.

Mung bean sprouts (*tua ngoh*): These tiny, crisp, white-stemmed sprouts, 2 to 4 inches long, have a pale yellow seed attached to one end and a small hairlike, trailing root on the other. You can purchase bean sprouts at the supermarket, but make sure they are fresh, crunchy, and dry, and that the root and head aren't beginning to brown.

Green papaya (*malakaw dip*): Hard, dark-green unripe papayas are peeled, shredded, and used raw as a vegetable in Southeast Asian salads. Smaller ones may be bulbous, while larger ones, sometimes more than 18 inches long, are shaped like elongated footballs. The pale and translucent shreds look similar to cucumber, but they are tougher, with a slightly sour taste. Green papayas are available at Asian and Latino markets.

Water spinach (*pahk boong*): Also known as morning glory, empty-hearted vegetable, water convolvulus, and swamp cabbage, water spinach—a reedlike green with hollow, thin stems and long, arrow shaped leaves—has a delicate, almost sweet flavor. This is a highly perishable green that must be used quickly. Trim away two inches at the base and wash it just before cooking since its hollow stems can be muddy.

Tropical fruits (*polamai*): Thailand's tropical climate sustains myriad fruits--exotic durians, sweet pineapples, juicy mangoes, fragrant melons, luscious papayas, and delicate lychees, among others. A platter of seasonal fruits, the most typical ending to a Thai meal, is refreshing after spicy foods. Citrus is also plentiful. Thai limes (*manow*) are small and juicy with thin yellow-green skin, while large round pomelos (*som-oh*), a close cousin to grapefruit, have a thick yellow-green rind enclosing crisp, sweet-tart pink-tinged fruit. Pomelos are available from November to January at Asian markets.

Coconut (*maprao*): The white meat of mature coconuts is grated to make coconut milk and cream, essential ingredients for many Thai curries, soups, and desserts. In traditional Thai homes, fresh coconut milk and cream (*nahm ga-ti*) are made daily. (To make your own, see Nancie McDermott's book, *Real Thai: The Best of Thailand's Regional Cooking*.) Alternatively, fine quality canned coconut milk is now widely available—we recommend Chao Koh, a Thai brand, or Goya, from Latin America. Never substitute cream of coconut, a highly sweetened and processed drink ingredient. When a recipe calls for coconut cream, use the coconut solids at the top of the can as well as the solids that can be scooped out of the milk. When a recipe calls for coconut milk, shake the can and use the contents.

FLAVORINGS

Chiles: Tiny Thai chiles (*prik kee noo*), sometimes called bird or bird's-eye chiles, are fiery and aromatic. Small (usually about an inch long), slender, pointed, and thin-skinned, they are green and turn red as they ripen. *Serrano* chiles can be substituted. *Chee fa* chiles (*prik* *chee fa*), dark green or bright red, are larger, milder, and more meaty, though still quite hot.

Curry paste, Roasted chile paste, Chile garlic sauce: In Thailand, many cooks make fresh pastes daily by pounding aromatic ingredients together in stone mortars. **Red curry paste** (*krueng gaeng peht*), often scorchingly hot, gets its brick red color from dried red chiles, and its sour, tangy flavor from an abundance of lemongrass and lime peel. **Green curry paste** (*krueng gaeng kiow wahn*) is made with fresh hot green chiles. **Roasted chile paste** (*naam prik pao*) is a smooth, dark red paste made from dried chiles, shallots, garlic cloves, and other aromatic ingredients that have been roasted over a charcoal fire, pounded, and then fried gently in oil. **Chile garlic sauce** (*saus prik/tuong ot toi*) is a coarse thick puree of fresh red chiles with visible seeds. Excellent store-bought pastes and sauces are widely available in small cans, glass jars, or in small plastic tubs. If using a canned paste, transfer leftovers to a small glass jar. It will keep, covered and chilled, for several months.

Galangal (*kah*): Sometimes called Thai ginger, *galangal* is widely used in Thailand, much more extensively than its close relative, fresh ginger. This rhizome resembles ginger, but it is larger and each branching section is encircled with thin, dark ridged lines. Mature *galangal* is golden yellow and when raw, tastes hot, sharp, and peppery with a hint of lemon. Young, ivory-colored rhizomes often have pale pink shoots and are more moist and a bit less fiery. Fresh *galangal* occasionally can be found in Southeast Asian stores, where both dried slices and frozen chunks from Thailand often are available. (With frozen *galangal*, slice off the amount needed and quickly refreeze the remaining chunks to preserve maximum flavor.)

Lemongrass (*takrai*): A few pieces of fresh lemongrass add a lemony aroma and taste to many Thai dishes. A fresh stalk is about 2 feet long and looks like a pale, silvery green scallion with dry, woody outer leaves and a bulblike base. After trimming the hard root end, only the bottom 6 to 8 inches of stalk are used, since the flavor is concentrated there. If using large pieces, cut stalks on the diagonal to expose more of the pale purple interior and extract more flavor. The inner portion can also be finely minced or pounded into a paste with other ingredients.

Wild lime leaves: Sometimes called *kaffir* or *keffir* lime, the dark green, glossy leaves (*bai makroot*) and the bumpy dark green zest (*piuw makroot*) of this citrus fruit are used to impart a strong herbal lemon-lime note with an aroma that is similar to fresh lemon verbena. The leaves are used like bay leaves, and added, whole or crushed, to soups and stews. The leaves can also be finely slivered or ground into pastes, but they should have their tough central rib removed first. Wild limes are grown in California and Florida, so both fresh and frozen leaves often are available in Southeast Asian stores. (If using frozen leaves, do not thaw them.) The whole limes are more difficult to find, but dried wild lime zest or the zest of domestic lime can be substituted.

Thai fish sauce (*naam pla*): Pungent fish sauce is as essential to the cooking of Thailand as salt is to western palates. Small anchovylike fish are fermented in salt in huge stone jars and the accumulated golden brown liquid is extracted and bottled. Fish sauce has a strong fishy taste and smell, but it mellows with cooking. It is best to buy fish sauce in glass bottles; it keeps indefinitely and does not require refrigeration.

Dried shrimp (*goong haeng*), **Thai shrimp paste** (*ga-pi*): Most Thai pastes and many sauces get saltiness and a hint of fish flavor from dried shrimp or shrimp paste. Bright pink-orange crescents with a pungent, briny aroma, **dried shrimp** are tiny shelled shrimp that have been boiled in salt water, then sun-dried. They are usually sold in small plastic packets that are refrigerated, keeping them pliable and moist with a pleasantly oceanic scent. Although they have been dried, the shrimp are still fragile and somewhat perishable (they turn pale gray-brown and brittle as they age). Transfer any unused dried shrimp to a covered container and keep them refrigerated for up to 1 month. Pungent **shrimp paste**, made by pounding dried shrimp, is an important Asian ingredient with varying styles—in southern China, the Philippines, and Indonesia. The Thai version is grayish brown and thick, with the consistency of mud. It is sold in small plastic containers (the ingredients list should simply read shrimp and salt with no added ingredients), and keeps indefinitely on the pantry shelf.

Palm sugar (*nahm tahn beep*): Used in many savory as well as sweet Thai dishes, palm sugar mellows chile heat and balances sour flavors. A moist, sticky, unrefined sugar, it is made by boiling down the sap of palm or coconut palm trees until concentrated and thickened. Sometimes labeled coconut sugar or even coconut candy, it can range in color from creamy tan to mocha brown. In Thailand, the sugar is soft, creamy, and easy to scoop; imported palm sugar varies considerably from moist to rock hard. Look for salad plate-sized cakes, wrapped in plastic, which are easy to break into chunks. If the sugar has hardened, it can be hand chopped or grated or pulsed in a food processor to break it into smaller granules. Brown sugar can be substituted.

Herbs: In Thailand, **mint**, **cilantro**, **and basil** often are added to dishes during the last few minutes of cooking for a burst of fresh, aromatic flavor; generous sprigs of these herbs also are used for garnish. Thais prefer a small-leafed peppermint variety (*bai salaney*) for salads, but any fresh mint will do. And when it comes to **cilantro** (*pahk chee*), also known as fresh coriander or Chinese parsley, the leaves, stems, and roots appear in myriad dishes. If possible, buy cilantro with the roots attached and wash them well. There are three varieties of basil in Thailand, but only **Thai basil** (*bai horapah*), also known as sweet basil, is widely available in the West. It has small, green, shiny leaves, bronzed purple stems, and purple flowers. When added at the last moment, it imbues a dish with a delicate anise flavor and perfume. Italian basil can be substituted. You may also find **holy basil** (*bai grapao*) at some Southeast Asian markets. It has purple or dark green matte leaves with serrated edges and a wonderful spicy taste that is released when it is added to a warm dish.

MAIL ORDER SOURCES

Most Thai ingredients are available at Asian markets and specialty foods stores; a few may be available at local supermarkets. For items that are difficult to find, use the following mail-order sources:

Uwajimaya
519 6th Avenue
Seattle, WA 98104
tel: (800) 889-1928
fax: (206) 624-6915
web: www.uwajimaya.com

The Spice Merchant
PO Box 524
Jackson Hole, WY 83001
tel: (800) 551-5999
fax: (307) 733-6343
web: www.emall.com/spice

Adriana's Caravan
321 Grand Central Terminal
New York, NY 10017
tel: (800) 316-0820
fax: (212) 972-8849
web: www.adrianascaravan.com

Thai Kitchen
229 Castro Street
Oakland, CA 94607
tel: (800) 967-8424
fax: (510) 834-3102
web: www.Thaikitchen.com

The Oriental Pantry
423 Great Road
Acton, MA 01720
tel: (800) 828-0368
fax: (781) 275-4506
web: www.orientalpantry.com

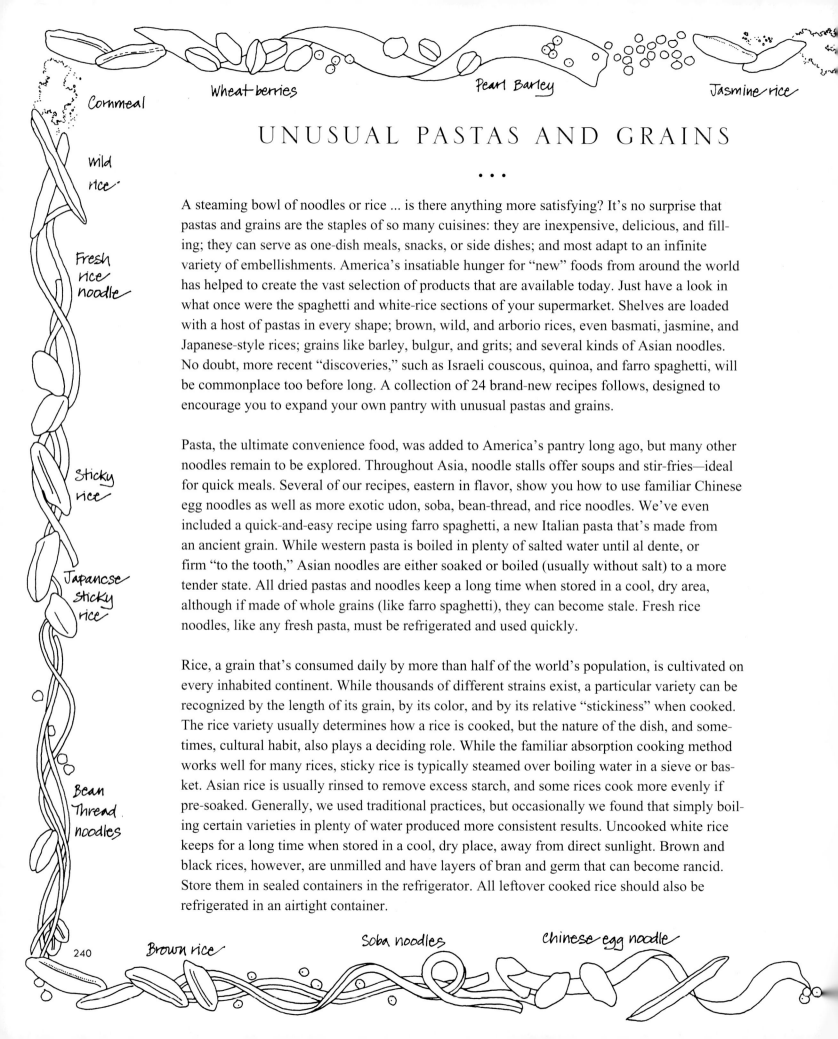

Cornmeal

Wheat berries

Pearl Barley

Jasmine rice

Wild rice

Fresh rice noodle

Sticky rice

Japanese sticky rice

Bean Thread noodles

UNUSUAL PASTAS AND GRAINS

. . .

A steaming bowl of noodles or rice ... is there anything more satisfying? It's no surprise that pastas and grains are the staples of so many cuisines: they are inexpensive, delicious, and filling; they can serve as one-dish meals, snacks, or side dishes; and most adapt to an infinite variety of embellishments. America's insatiable hunger for "new" foods from around the world has helped to create the vast selection of products that are available today. Just have a look in what once were the spaghetti and white-rice sections of your supermarket. Shelves are loaded with a host of pastas in every shape; brown, wild, and arborio rices, even basmati, jasmine, and Japanese-style rices; grains like barley, bulgur, and grits; and several kinds of Asian noodles. No doubt, more recent "discoveries," such as Israeli couscous, quinoa, and farro spaghetti, will be commonplace too before long. A collection of 24 brand-new recipes follows, designed to encourage you to expand your own pantry with unusual pastas and grains.

Pasta, the ultimate convenience food, was added to America's pantry long ago, but many other noodles remain to be explored. Throughout Asia, noodle stalls offer soups and stir-fries—ideal for quick meals. Several of our recipes, eastern in flavor, show you how to use familiar Chinese egg noodles as well as more exotic udon, soba, bean-thread, and rice noodles. We've even included a quick-and-easy recipe using farro spaghetti, a new Italian pasta that's made from an ancient grain. While western pasta is boiled in plenty of salted water until al dente, or firm "to the tooth," Asian noodles are either soaked or boiled (usually without salt) to a more tender state. All dried pastas and noodles keep a long time when stored in a cool, dry area, although if made of whole grains (like farro spaghetti), they can become stale. Fresh rice noodles, like any fresh pasta, must be refrigerated and used quickly.

Rice, a grain that's consumed daily by more than half of the world's population, is cultivated on every inhabited continent. While thousands of different strains exist, a particular variety can be recognized by the length of its grain, by its color, and by its relative "stickiness" when cooked. The rice variety usually determines how a rice is cooked, but the nature of the dish, and sometimes, cultural habit, also plays a deciding role. While the familiar absorption cooking method works well for many rices, sticky rice is typically steamed over boiling water in a sieve or basket. Asian rice is usually rinsed to remove excess starch, and some rices cook more evenly if pre-soaked. Generally, we used traditional practices, but occasionally we found that simply boiling certain varieties in plenty of water produced more consistent results. Uncooked white rice keeps for a long time when stored in a cool, dry place, away from direct sunlight. Brown and black rices, however, are unmilled and have layers of bran and germ that can become rancid. Store them in sealed containers in the refrigerator. All leftover cooked rice should also be refrigerated in an airtight container.

Brown rice

Soba noodles

Chinese egg noodle

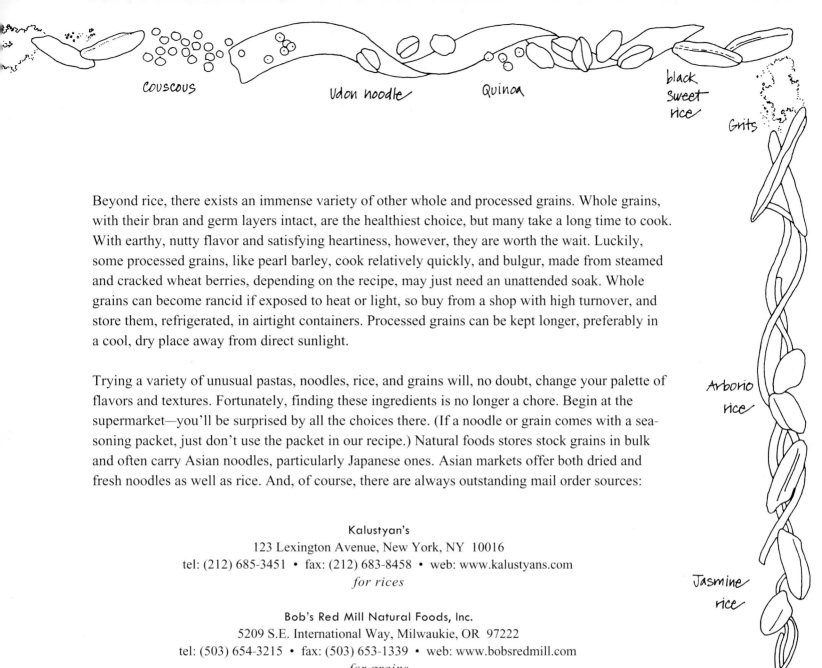

Beyond rice, there exists an immense variety of other whole and processed grains. Whole grains, with their bran and germ layers intact, are the healthiest choice, but many take a long time to cook. With earthy, nutty flavor and satisfying heartiness, however, they are worth the wait. Luckily, some processed grains, like pearl barley, cook relatively quickly, and bulgur, made from steamed and cracked wheat berries, depending on the recipe, may just need an unattended soak. Whole grains can become rancid if exposed to heat or light, so buy from a shop with high turnover, and store them, refrigerated, in airtight containers. Processed grains can be kept longer, preferably in a cool, dry place away from direct sunlight.

Trying a variety of unusual pastas, noodles, rice, and grains will, no doubt, change your palette of flavors and textures. Fortunately, finding these ingredients is no longer a chore. Begin at the supermarket—you'll be surprised by all the choices there. (If a noodle or grain comes with a seasoning packet, just don't use the packet in our recipe.) Natural foods stores stock grains in bulk and often carry Asian noodles, particularly Japanese ones. Asian markets offer both dried and fresh noodles as well as rice. And, of course, there are always outstanding mail order sources:

Kalustyan's
123 Lexington Avenue, New York, NY 10016
tel: (212) 685-3451 • fax: (212) 683-8458 • web: www.kalustyans.com
for rices

Bob's Red Mill Natural Foods, Inc.
5209 S.E. International Way, Milwaukie, OR 97222
tel: (503) 654-3215 • fax: (503) 653-1339 • web: www.bobsredmill.com
for grains

Adriana's Caravan
409 Vanderbilt Street, Brooklyn, NY 11218
tel: (800) 316-0820 • fax: (212) 972-8849 • web: www.adrianascaravan.com
for Chinese, Japanese, and Thai dry ingredients;
Israeli couscous and various grains

Hoppin' John's
Charleston, SC
tel: (800) 828-4412 • fax: (843) 763-5652 • web: www.hoppinjohns.com
for cornmeal and corn grits

Pasta with Peas and Ricotta Salata ◯

Serves 4 to 6 (main course)

1 lb dried pasta
2 (10-oz) boxes frozen baby peas
1 cup fresh basil, cut into julienne strips
½ cup drained dried tomatoes in oil, cut into
   julienne strips
¼ cup extra-virgin olive oil
5 oz *ricotta salata* cheese or feta

Cook pasta in a 6-quart pot of boiling salted water until just al dente. Add peas and cook with pasta until just tender, about 1 minute. Ladle out and reserve 1 cup pasta water and drain pasta and peas. Toss pasta and peas with basil, tomatoes, oil, and ½ cup pasta water. Crumble cheese over pasta and toss, adding more pasta water if mixture is dry.

Farro spaghetti

Farro, also known as emmer, is an ancient grain that fed the Roman army and appeared on rustic Tuscan tables for centuries. As with many once-humble foods, it has become popular in trendy restaurants throughout northern Italy and in a few North American cities. Farro pasta, made with ground farro flour, has an earthy, nutty taste that is complemented by assertive flavors—here we've used rosemary and garlic.

Farro Spaghetti with Rosemary ◯

Serves 6 (first course or side dish)

3 garlic cloves, minced
3 tablespoons extra-virgin olive oil
1½ tablespoons finely chopped fresh rosemary,
   or to taste
1 lb *farro* spaghetti

Accompaniment: grated Parmesan

Combine garlic, oil, and rosemary in a large bowl. Cook spaghetti in a 6-quart pot of boiling salted water

until al dente and ladle out and reserve ½ cup pasta water. Drain spaghetti and add to garlic mixture with ¼ cup pasta water, gently tossing (and adding more pasta water if mixture is dry) until combined well. Season with salt and pepper.

Israeli couscous

Israeli couscous is neither a true grain nor a traditional couscous made from rolled semolina dough. This pea-sized pasta is made from a hard wheat dough that is extruded into tiny balls, then toasted to give it more flavor and color. It requires longer cooking than couscous, but is still quick and easy to prepare. You may find it in the supermarket packaged as pearl pasta or grande couscous (with a flavor packet that shouldn't be used in our recipe).

Israeli Couscous with Exotic Mushrooms ◯

Serves 4 (main course); 8 (side dish)

3 tablespoons unsalted butter
1 tablespoon olive oil
2 large shallots, finely chopped
1 lb mixed exotic mushrooms such as porcini,
   morel, and shiitake, cut into ¼-inch-thick slices
2 teaspoons soy sauce
1 teaspoon sugar
12 oz (2 cups) Israeli couscous
½ cup fresh flat-leaf parsley, chopped

Heat 2 tablespoons butter and oil in a large non-stick skillet over moderately high heat until foam subsides and sauté shallots, stirring, 2 minutes. Add mushrooms, soy sauce, and sugar and sauté until liquid mushrooms give off has evaporated and mushrooms begin to brown. Season with salt and pepper.

Cook couscous in a 6-quart pot of boiling salted water until just tender, 10 to 12 minutes, and drain. Toss couscous with mushrooms, parsley, and remaining tablespoon butter. Serve couscous warm or at room temperature.

Chinese egg noodles

In Chinese tradition, long noodles symbolize long life and are eaten for good luck. Dried Chinese egg noodles, made simply of wheat flour, egg, and water, range in color from pale to neon yellow. They can be thick or thread-thin, and come in nests or compressed round cakes. Just be sure to look at the ingredients list—"imitation" noodles are artificially colored and contain no eggs at all. Some dried Chinese egg noodles have been precooked and require very little boiling time, so check them frequently. Although egg noodles have a rich and distinctively eggy taste, Italian pasta such as angel's hair or spaghettini can be substituted.

Udon noodles

Udon noodles are thick, white Japanese noodles that may be square or flat. In many dishes they are used interchangeably with soba noodles, though udon are made of regular wheat flour rather than buckwheat, and have a more slippery texture when cooked. Udon noodles are the noodle of choice in western Japan, while soba noodles are preferred in the east. Dried udon noodles may be found, sometimes divided into portions by paper bands, in plastic packages; they may also be available fresh, in the refrigerator case, either uncooked or precooked.

CHINESE EGG NOODLES WITH CHICKEN AND SNOW PEAS ⊙

Serves 6 (main course)

¾ lb dried Chinese egg noodles
2 tablespoons Asian sesame oil
2½ tablespoons vegetable oil
8 garlic cloves, thinly sliced
1 tablespoon minced peeled fresh ginger
4 whole chicken legs (¾ lb), skinned, boned, and cut into ¼-inch-thick strips
2 tablespoons hoisin sauce, or to taste
2 tablespoons soy sauce
2 teaspoons Asian chili sauce
¾ lb snow peas, cut into julienne strips

Cook noodles in a 4-quart pot of boiling water until just tender and drain. Toss noodles with sesame oil in a large bowl.

Heat vegetable oil in a large nonstick skillet over moderately high heat until hot but not smoking and sauté garlic and ginger, stirring, until garlic just begins to turn golden, about 1 minute. Add chicken, hoisin sauce, soy sauce, and chili sauce and sauté, stirring frequently, until chicken is just cooked through, about 7 minutes. Add snow peas and sauté, stirring, until just crisp-tender, about 2 minutes. Toss chicken mixture with noodles.

UDON NOODLES WITH STAR ANISE BRAISED BEEF

Serves 4 (main course)

2 tablespoons vegetable oil
1½ lb beef chuck, cut into 1½-inch cubes
1 tablespoon chopped garlic
2 tablespoons grated peeled fresh ginger
2 whole star anise
½ teaspoon hot red pepper flakes
⅓ cup soy sauce
6 cups water
½ lb dried *udon* noodles
3 cups spinach leaves, coarsely chopped

Heat oil in a large heavy saucepan over moderately high heat until hot but not smoking and brown beef, stirring frequently. Add garlic, ginger, anise, and pepper flakes and cook, stirring constantly, until fragrant, about 30 seconds. Add soy sauce and water and simmer, covered, until beef is very tender, 1½ to 2 hours.

When beef is tender, cook noodles in a 6-quart pot of boiling salted water 3 minutes. Stir in 1 cup cold water and return to a boil. Simmer noodles until tender, about 5 minutes, and drain.

Divide noodles and spinach among 4 soup bowls. Skim fat from beef broth and divide beef and broth among bowls.

Soba noodles

Soba noodles—a favorite in Japan for their nutty flavor, slightly chewy texture, and high protein value—are made of buckwheat flour, sometimes in combination with regular wheat flour. The dried light brown noodles, square in cross section, are often found neatly bundled into portions with a paper band. After the noodles are cooked, they should be rinsed in cold water to remove excess starch.

SOBA NOODLES WITH CLAMS AND SCALLIONS

Serves 4 (main course)

½ lb dried *soba* noodles
1 tablespoon vegetable oil
1 bunch scallions, cut into 1-inch lengths
1 tablespoon minced garlic
1 tablespoon minced peeled fresh ginger
2 (13½-oz) cans chicken broth
¼ cup sake (rice wine)
24 small hard-shelled clams

Stir noodles into a 4-quart pot of boiling salted water. When water returns to a boil, add 1 cup cold water and return to a boil again. Boil noodles 2 to 3 minutes, or until tender, and drain. Divide noodles among 4 shallow bowls.

Heat oil in a 5-quart pot over moderately high heat until hot but not smoking and sauté scallions, garlic, and ginger, stirring, 1 minute. Add broth and sake and bring to a boil. Add clams and simmer until they open, about 5 minutes. (Discard any unopened clams.) Divide clams and broth among bowls.

SOBA NOODLES WITH PEA SHOOTS AND SHIITAKES

Serves 4 (main course)

2 tablespoons vegetable oil
4 carrots, cut into 1½-inch-long julienne sticks
½ lb fresh shiitake mushrooms, stems discarded
  and caps thinly sliced

4 scallions, chopped
¼ lb pea shoots, trimmed
2 tablespoons soy sauce, or to taste
1½ tablespoons rice vinegar, or to taste
1½ teaspoons Asian sesame oil, or to taste
½ lb dried *soba* noodles

Heat vegetable oil in a large nonstick skillet over moderately high heat until hot but not smoking and sauté carrots with salt and pepper, stirring, until barely tender, about 2 minutes. Add mushrooms and cook, stirring, until tender, about 3 minutes. Transfer mixture to a bowl and add scallions, pea shoots, soy sauce, vinegar, and sesame oil.

Cook noodles in a 4-quart pot of boiling salted water according to package directions, or until just tender, about 5 minutes, and drain. Rinse noodles under cold water and drain well. Toss noodles with vegetables and salt and pepper to taste.

Bean-thread noodles

Bean-thread noodles, also known as cellophane noodles, are dried, semi-transparent filaments made from mung bean starch. They should be soaked in water before using. After cooking, they become slippery and translucent. Although these noodles are virtually flavorless, they readily take on the flavors of other ingredients.

CURRIED COCONUT-MILK SOUP WITH BEAN-THREAD NOODLES AND PORK

Serves 4 (main course)

¼ lb bean-thread (cellophane) noodles
¾ lb pork tenderloin, cut into ¼-inch-thick slices
1 tablespoon red or yellow Thai curry paste
1 tablespoon vegetable oil
1½ cups canned unsweetened coconut milk
1 (13½-oz) can chicken broth
3 tablespoons Asian fish sauce
2 teaspoons sugar
2 scallions, chopped
¼ cup cilantro sprigs, chopped

Accompaniment: lime wedges

Soak noodles in water to cover 15 minutes. Drain noodles and cut into 4-inch lengths with scissors.

Cook pork and curry paste in oil in a heavy 4-quart saucepan over moderately high heat, stirring, until pork is opaque. Stir in coconut milk, broth, fish sauce, and sugar and bring to a boil. Stir in noodles and simmer soup 5 minutes, or until tender. Stir in scallions and cilantro.

Fresh rice noodles

If you have access to an Asian market, look for fresh rice noodles. They have a slithery, chewy texture that makes all the difference in this dish. Made of rice flour, these white, gummy noodles can be slender or wide, flat or round. Fresh noodles merely need a brief soak in water to soften before cooking. Dried, semi-transparent, flat rice noodles (sometimes called rice sticks) can be substituted, but the result will be quite different: Use ½ pound dried noodles that are at least ¼ inch wide and boil them in ample amounts of unsalted water just until softened; then toss the drained noodles immediately with a little vegetable oil to prevent excessive sticking.

MALAYSIAN FRIED RICE NOODLES

Serves 4 (main course)

1 lb fresh flat or round rice noodles
2 tablespoons soy sauce (preferably Kikkoman)
1½ teaspoons dark soy sauce
1 tablespoon water
4 bacon slices, chopped
½ lb (about 36) small shrimp, cleaned
2 Chinese sausages (2 oz), thinly sliced
2 garlic cloves, finely chopped
½ lb fresh bean sprouts, tops and tails trimmed
18 fresh garlic chives (¼ bunch), cut crosswise
   into ¼-inch pieces
1 small fresh Thai or *serrano* chile, minced,
   including some seeds (wear protective gloves)

Cover noodles with hot tap water by 1 inch in a large bowl and soak until softened, 10 to 15 minutes.

Gently separate noodles and drain well. Stir together soy sauces and water.

Cook bacon in a wok over moderate heat, stirring, until crisp and transfer with a slotted spoon to paper towels to drain. Pour off all but 1 tablespoon fat. Heat remaining fat over moderately high heat until it just begins to smoke and stir-fry shrimp and sausage until shrimp are just cooked through, 2 to 3 minutes. Transfer with a slotted spoon to a bowl. Stir-fry garlic over moderately high heat until golden. Add soy mixture and shrimp and sausage and stir-fry until coated. Add half of noodles, tossing to coat, then add remaining noodles and toss to coat. Add bean sprouts, chives, chile, and bacon and toss until combined.

Jasmine rice

Thai jasmine rice has translucent, long grains that cook into a fragrant, soft, slightly moist white rice. As long as the cooked rice remains hot, it is seductively aromatic with a nutty flavor similar to that of Indian basmati. Aromatic hybrids like Jasmati rice, grown in North America, cook the same way. If you are unable to find Thai jasmine rice, give Jasmati a try. Though jasmine rice is traditionally steamed, it can also be simply boiled in plenty of water (we found this to be a foolproof method).

JASMINE RICE WITH
CILANTRO AND PEANUTS

Serves 6 (side dish)

1¾ cups (¾ lb) Thai jasmine rice
½ cup salted peanuts, chopped
½ cup fresh cilantro sprigs, chopped
4 scallions, sliced
1 tablespoon peanut oil
2 teaspoons seasoned rice vinegar, or to taste
1 tablespoon fresh lime juice, or to taste

Cook rice in a 4-quart pot of boiling salted water, stirring occasionally, until tender, 10 to 15 minutes and drain. Toss rice with remaining ingredients and salt and pepper to taste.

BROWN RICE AND BEANS WITH CILANTRO

Serves 4 (side dish)

2 tablespoons unsalted butter
1½ teaspoons ground cumin
1 medium onion, chopped
1 cup American short-grain brown rice,
    rinsed and drained
2 cups water
1 (15½-oz) can small red beans, rinsed and drained
2 cups fresh cilantro sprigs, chopped
3 tablespoons fresh orange juice

Heat butter with cumin in a 2-quart heavy saucepan over moderately high heat and sauté onion and rice, stirring, 2 minutes. Add water and simmer, covered, until rice is tender and water is absorbed, 40 to 50 minutes.

Toss rice with beans, cilantro, orange juice, and salt and pepper to taste.

Basmati rice

Grown in India and Pakistan, basmati rice is aged for at least one year to allow its full flavors to develop. The long, thin grains taper to points and when cooked expand to four times their length (instead of plumping) and exude a subtle, buttery aroma. Basmati is available as a white or a brown rice; we've chosen white for a more delicate pudding. American-grown basmati rice, such as Texmati and Calmati, widely available in supermarkets, is not the same, though in a pinch it can be an adequate, if less fragrant, substitute.

BASMATI RICE PUDDING
WITH RASPBERRIES

Serves 6

1 cup white *basmati* rice
3 cups whole milk
½ cup granulated sugar
1 cup well-chilled heavy cream
½ teaspoon vanilla
½ lb raspberries (2½ cups)
¼ cup confectioners sugar

Wash rice well in a sieve. Soak rice in a bowl of cold water 30 minutes and drain.

Bring milk and granulated sugar to a strong simmer in a 3-quart heavy saucepan. Add rice and cook, stirring, 2 minutes. Reduce heat to very low and simmer rice, covered, until rice is tender and almost all milk is absorbed, about 25 minutes. Cool completely.

Whip cream and vanilla into soft peaks and fold into rice. Toss raspberries with confectioners sugar and fold into pudding.

Cooks' note:
• Before adding raspberries, pudding can be made 2 days
  ahead and chilled, covered.

Japanese rice

Everyday Japanese rice (sushi rice) is a short- or medium-grain translucent white rice. When cooked, the rice is slightly moist and clingy. This rice has neutral flavor, so it allows the delicate taste of fresh fish (or paper-thin slices of smoked salmon) to predominate. Good-quality Japanese-style rice is grown in the United States (it is next to impossible to find rice from Japan). Look for Kokuho Rose, CalRose, or Nishiki brands, available at Japanese and other Asian markets.

JUMBO SMOKED-SALMON SUSHI
WITH MUSTARD DILL SAUCE

Serves 6 (first course)

1¼ cups Japanese short-grain white rice (sushi rice)
1 cup plus 2 tablespoons water
2½ tablespoons seasoned rice vinegar plus
    additional for molding rice
1½ tablespoons drained capers, minced
¼ small red onion, minced
¾ lb thinly sliced smoked salmon
For mustard sauce
2½ tablespoons fresh dill, chopped
¼ cup coarse-grained mustard
2 tablespoons seasoned rice vinegar
1 teaspoon sugar
¼ cup vegetable oil

Wash rice in a large bowl in several changes of cold water until water is clear. Drain rice in a sieve and let stand 30 minutes. Bring rice and 1 cup plus 2 tablespoons water to a boil in a 2-quart heavy saucepan covered with a tight-fitting lid over moderate heat. Gently boil rice 6 minutes without removing lid. (Lid will clatter when water boils. If water boils over, lower heat slightly.) Reduce heat to low and cook rice 7 minutes more. Remove pan from heat and let stand, without removing lid, 15 minutes. Transfer rice into a large bowl with a flat wooden spatula and gently separate grains. Sprinkle vinegar over rice and toss with a fork. Add capers, onion, and salt to taste and toss to combine.

Have ready enough additional vinegar in a small bowl to wet fingertips. Lightly oil a ½-cup ramekin and line with plastic wrap. Line ramekin with salmon, cutting and overlapping pieces to fit and leaving a 2-inch overhang. Dip fingers into vinegar and lightly press about ½ cup rice mixture into ramekin. Fold salmon overhang over rice to cover completely. Unmold sushi using plastic wrap as an aid and invert onto a plate. Make five more sushi in same manner.

Make sauce:

Whisk together dill, mustard, vinegar, sugar, and salt to taste and whisk in oil until emulsified.

Serve sushi with sauce.

Cooks' notes:
- Sauce can be made 1 day ahead and chilled, covered.
- Sushi can be made up to 6 hours ahead and chilled, covered. Let sushi stand 15 minutes at room temperature before serving.

Arborio rice

Arborio rice is ideal for making risotto. Turning creamy as it slowly absorbs broth, it nevertheless retains its shape and firm texture while taking on the flavors of any ingredients cooked with it. This medium-grain white rice from northern Italy is readily available; look for the top grade (superfino). Vialone nano and carnaroli, other fine quality Italian rices, may be substituted.

RISOTTO WITH MUSSELS AND FENNEL

Serves 4 (main course)

1 large fennel bulb (sometimes called anise)
3 cups chicken broth
2 cups plus ¼ cup water
1 medium onion, finely chopped
2 tablespoons olive oil
1½ cups Arborio rice
⅓ cup grated Parmesan
2 tablespoons unsalted butter
2 lbs cultivated mussels, scrubbed and
  beards removed
1 tablespoon chopped fresh flat-leaf parsley

Cut enough fennel into ½-inch pieces to measure 2 cups. Bring broth and 2 cups water to a simmer and keep at a bare simmer.

Cook fennel and onion in oil in a 2½- to 3-quart heavy saucepan over moderate heat, stirring occasionally, until softened. Add rice and stir to coat. Add 1 cup simmering broth mixture and cook, stirring constantly and keeping at a simmer, until absorbed. Continue cooking and adding broth mixture, about ½ cup at a time, stirring constantly and letting each addition be absorbed before adding next, until rice is creamy looking but still al dente, about 18 minutes total. Remove pan from heat and stir in Parmesan, butter, and salt and pepper to taste. Cover pan to keep risotto warm.

Bring remaining ¼ cup water to a boil in a 5-quart heavy pot and steam mussels, covered, until shells open, 5 to 8 minutes. (Discard unopened mussels.)

Reheat risotto over low heat if necessary, stirring occasionally, and divide among 4 shallow bowls, mounding in center. Arrange mussels around rice and strain liquid, dividing among bowls. Sprinkle with parsley.

Thai black sweet rice

Thai black sweet rice (also called sticky or glutinous rice) is an unmilled, long-grain rice with an outer layer (bran) that varies from mahogany brown to ebony black. The rice turns a purplish black when cooked and is chewy and hearty, with rich flavor. Throughout Southeast Asia, black rice is usually prepared with coconut milk to make sweets, snacks, and breakfast dishes. Here, it is paired with coconut and shrimp for an entrée that has subtle sweetness. Although this rice is traditionally soaked, then steamed, it also can be boiled.

SPICY COCONUT SHRIMP WITH BLACK SWEET RICE ◐

Serves 4 (main course)

1 cup Thai black sweet rice
1 lb large shrimp (21 to 30), cleaned
1¼ cups sweetened flaked coconut
½ teaspoon cayenne
1 tablespoon vegetable oil
2 small tomatoes (½ lb), cut into ¼-inch dice
4 scallions, chopped

Cook rice in a large saucepan of boiling water until tender, about 25 minutes, and drain. Pat shrimp dry and toss with sweetened coconut, cayenne, and salt and pepper to taste.

Heat oil in a large nonstick skillet over moderately high heat until hot but not smoking and sauté shrimp, stirring, until cooked through and coconut is golden, about 10 minutes. Toss shrimp with rice, tomatoes, and scallions.

Sticky rice

Sticky rice, also known as sweet, glutinous, or waxy rice, may be either short- or long-grain. The long-grain white rice used here is the staple rice of northern and northeast Thailand, Laos, and parts of China and Vietnam, where it is the centerpiece of every meal. When cooked, the rice turns beige and becomes chewy. Aptly named, it is slightly sweet and quite sticky, forming clumps that easily can be picked up with the fingers or chopsticks.

STICKY RICE WITH TOASTED COCONUT AND FRIED SHALLOTS ◐+

Serves 4 (side dish)

Thai, Laotian, and Vietnamese markets usually sell the large, conical baskets used for cooking sticky rice, as well as the lightweight pot the basket rests in as the rice steams. Otherwise, use a large sieve lined with cheesecloth or muslin and put it over a large kettle of water.

1 cup long-grain Thai sticky rice
⅓ cup canned unsweetened coconut milk, stirred well
2 large shallots, cut into thin rings
3 tablespoons vegetable oil
⅓ cup sweetened flaked coconut, toasted
2 tablespoons chopped fresh cilantro sprigs

Rinse rice in a bowl in 2 or 3 changes of cold water, or until water is clear. Soak rice in water to cover at least 1 hour and up to 8.

Drain rice and transfer to a Southeast Asian rice-steamer basket or cheesecloth-lined sieve (see note above). Set steamer basket or sieve over 1 inch boiling water in a large pot. (It is important that rice does not touch boiling water.) Cover rice and steam, checking water level occasionally to make sure pot doesn't boil dry and adding more water if necessary, 20 minutes. Fluff rice with a fork and gradually pour coconut milk over rice. Steam rice, covered, 10 minutes more, or until rice is just tender (rice will be sticky).

While rice is steaming, cook shallots in oil over moderate heat, stirring occasionally, until golden and transfer to paper towels to drain.

Stir coconut and salt to taste into rice and serve sprinkled with shallots and cilantro.

WILD RICE WITH FAVA BEANS AND CORN

Serves 6 (side dish)

6 oz (1 cup) wild rice, rinsed and drained
1½ lbs fava beans in pod, shelled, or ¼ lb (⅔ cup) frozen baby lima beans
2 tablespoons olive oil
1 cup corn (cut from 2 ears) or frozen corn

½ medium red onion, finely chopped
2½ tablespoons fresh lime juice

Cook rice in a large saucepan of boiling water until tender, about 45 minutes, and drain.

While rice is cooking, have ready a bowl of ice and cold water. Cook beans in a saucepan of boiling salted water until just tender, about 2 minutes, and drain. Plunge beans into ice water to stop cooking and drain. Pat dry and, if using favas, gently peel away outer skins. Heat oil in a large nonstick skillet over moderately high heat until hot but not smoking and sauté corn, onion, and beans, stirring, until corn is just tender, about 3 minutes.

Stir wild rice, lime juice, and salt and pepper to taste into corn mixture. Serve dish warm or at room temperature.

Wheat berries

Wheat berries, also called wheat groats, are whole-wheat kernels that have not been milled, polished, or heat-treated. They have a lovely nutty flavor and are well worth the substantial time it takes to cook them. It is very important to cook wheat berries without salt, or they will never soften sufficiently. Wheat berries vary in color from tan to deep red-brown. For even cooking, look for grains that are uniform in color.

WHEAT BERRIES WITH BUTTERNUT SQUASH AND TOASTED PECANS

Serves 4 (main course); 8 (side dish)

1 cup wheat berries
1 medium (1½ lb) butternut squash
3 tablespoons olive oil
1 cup pecan halves
2 large garlic cloves, chopped
4 cups fresh spinach leaves, chopped

Simmer wheat berries in 5 cups water in a large saucepan (do not add salt) until tender, about 1 hour, and drain.

While wheat berries are cooking, peel squash and cut enough into ½-inch cubes to measure 2½ cups.

Heat 2 tablespoons oil in a 12-inch heavy skillet over moderate heat and toast pecans until fragrant and 1 shade darker. Transfer pecans with a slotted spoon to a large bowl. Add remaining tablespoon oil to skillet and sauté squash over moderately high heat until tender, stirring occasionally. Add garlic and sauté 30 seconds, stirring. Add squash mixture to pecans.

Add wheat berries, spinach, and salt to taste to squash and toss to combine.

Bulgur

Bulgur—whole wheat berries that have been steamed, hulled, dried, and cracked into a nutty flavored grain—ranges in texture from fine to coarse, but all is quick-cooking. In fact, in some cases, as in our recipe below, it is simply soaked in hot water. Bulgur is stronger in flavor than cracked wheat, which is simply made from uncooked cracked wheat berries.

BULGUR SALAD WITH RADICCHIO, FETA, AND CUCUMBER ◑+

Serves 4 (main course); 6 (side dish)

1 cup coarse bulgur
1 cup hot water
½ cup pumpkin seeds, toasted
2 teaspoons cumin seeds, toasted
1 medium cucumber, peeled, seeded, and cut into ½-inch pieces
2 cups *radicchio* leaves (from 1 large head), chopped
½ lb feta, crumbled
2 tablespoons chopped fresh flat-leaf parsley
¼ cup olive oil
2 tablespoons red-wine vinegar

Combine bulgur and hot water in a bowl. Chill bulgur, covered, until water is absorbed, about 1 hour.

Toss bulgur with remaining ingredients and salt and pepper to taste until combined.

Quinoa

Quinoa (pronounced KEEN-wah), though not a true cereal grain, comes from a grainlike plant indigenous to the high valleys of the Peruvian Andes. The tiny oval seeds—ranging in color from buff to russet to black—cook up light and somewhat crunchy, with mild, sweet, earthy flavor.

QUINOA AND SMOKED CHICKEN SALAD

Serves 4 (main course)

1½ cups quinoa
1 (¾-lb) smoked chicken breast, cut into ½-inch pieces
2 celery ribs, thinly sliced on the diagonal
1 small apple, such as Granny Smith, peeled and cut into ½-inch pieces
Zest of 1 lime
1½ tablespoons fresh lime juice
½ teaspoon cumin seeds, toasted and ground
¼ cup olive oil
¼ cup finely chopped fresh cilantro sprigs

Wash quinoa in a large bowl in at least 5 changes cold water, gently rubbing grains and letting them settle before pouring off water, until water is clear and drain in a large fine sieve. Cook quinoa in a 3-quart saucepan of salted boiling water 10 minutes. Drain in sieve and rinse under cold water. Set sieve over a saucepan of boiling water (quinoa should not touch water) and steam quinoa, covered with a kitchen towel and lid, until fluffy and dry, about 10 minutes. Toss hot quinoa with remaining ingredients and salt and pepper to taste. Serve at room temperature.

MUSHROOM-BARLEY SALAD WITH GOAT CHEESE

Serves 2 (lunch main course); 4 (side dish)

1 cup (½ lb) pearl barley
6 tablespoons olive oil
½ lb mushrooms, stems coarsely chopped and caps quartered

2 teaspoons Dijon mustard
2 tablespoons red-wine vinegar
1 shallot, finely chopped
½ small head *radicchio*, chopped
2 celery ribs, finely chopped
¼ cup chopped fresh dill
¼ lb (½ cup) soft, mild goat cheese

Cook barley in a 3-quart saucepan of boiling salted water until tender, about 30 minutes.

While barley is cooking, heat 2 tablespoons oil over moderately high heat until hot but not smoking and sauté mushrooms with salt and pepper to taste, stirring, until golden brown, about 5 minutes.

Whisk together mustard, red-wine vinegar, and salt and pepper to taste and whisk in remaining oil until emulsified. Whisk in shallot.

Drain barley and toss with mushrooms, *radicchio*, celery, dill, and vinaigrette, tossing until combined well. Cool to room temperature. Crumble goat cheese over salad and gently toss.

Kasha

"Kasha," Russian for cooked buckwheat groats, is one of the most substantial and strengthening foods, and, not surprisingly, it is a winter staple of Siberia and northern China. Buckwheat, neither a wheat nor a cereal grain, is the vitamin- and calcium-packed seed of a rhubarb relative. Kasha is toasted to a deep brown for a powerful, roasted flavor.

KASHA WITH GREEN BEANS AND DRIED CURRANTS ◔

Serves 4 (main course); 6 (side dish)

¾ lb green beans, cut into ½-inch pieces
1 medium onion, chopped
1½ tablespoons olive oil
1 large egg
1 cup whole kasha
1 (13½-oz) can chicken broth
¼ cup water
⅓ cup dried currants
2 tablespoons chopped fresh flat-leaf parsley

2 teaspoons chopped garlic
2 teaspoons finely grated fresh lemon zest

Cook green beans in boiling salted water until crisp-tender, about 3 minutes, and drain. Cook onion in oil in a 12-inch nonstick skillet over moderate heat, stirring occasionally, until softened.

Lightly beat egg and stir in kasha. Add mixture to skillet and cook over moderate heat, stirring to break up clumps, until egg is cooked, about 2 minutes. Stir in broth and water and simmer, covered, 5 minutes, or until most of liquid is absorbed.

Stir in beans and remaining ingredients and cook, uncovered, stirring occasionally, until heated through and liquid is evaporated. Season with salt.

Sautéed Shrimp and Corn with Creamy Grits

Serves 4 (brunch or dinner main course)

2 cups water
2 tablespoons unsalted butter
½ cup grits (not quick-cooking or instant)
2 teaspoons kosher salt
1½ to 2 cups half-and-half or milk
¼ lb (4 to 6 slices) bacon
20 large shrimp, cleaned
2½ tablespoons olive oil
1 cup corn (cut from 2 ears)
2 garlic cloves, minced
½ lb (¾ pint) cherry tomatoes, quartered
4 scallions, coarsely chopped

Bring water and butter to a boil in a 3-quart heavy saucepan and whisk in grits and salt. Reduce heat to low and cook grits, stirring occasionally, until thick and most of water is absorbed, about 5 minutes. Whisk in ½ cup half-and-half and continue to cook, stirring occasionally, until absorbed. Continue to cook, adding remaining half-and-half ¼ cup at a time, until grits are creamy and moist, at least 45 minutes more.

While grits are cooking, cook bacon in a large non-stick skillet until crisp and transfer to paper towels to drain. Reserve 1 teaspoon bacon fat and wipe skillet clean. Pat shrimp dry and season with salt and pepper. Heat reserved fat and 1 tablespoon oil in skillet over moderately high heat until hot but not smoking and sauté shrimp, stirring, until cooked through and golden brown, about 3 minutes. Transfer shrimp to a plate and keep warm, covered. Add remaining 1½ tablespoons oil to skillet and cook corn with salt and pepper to taste, stirring, until golden and crisp-tender. Add garlic, tomatoes, and scallions and cook, stirring, 1 minute. Crumble bacon and stir into mixture.

Serve grits topped with shrimp and vegetables.

Corn Thins

Makes about 50 (snack)

¾ cup all-purpose flour
¼ cup yellow or white cornmeal
1 teaspoon baking powder
½ teaspoon salt
½ stick unsalted butter, softened
1 tablespoon sugar
1 large egg, at room temperature
1 cup whole milk, at room temperature

Preheat oven to 350°F and butter 2 large shallow baking pans, each about 17 by 12 inches.

Sift together flour, cornmeal, baking powder, and salt into a bowl. Beat butter with an electric mixer in another bowl until soft and creamy and beat in sugar. Beat in egg until combined well and beat in milk. Add flour mixture and beat until just combined (do not overbeat).

Pour 1 cup batter into 1 baking pan and spread, tilting pan back and forth to cover bottom completely. Bake corn thins in middle of oven 5 minutes (leave oven on). Cut corn thins into 2½-inch squares with a sharp knife and bake corn thins 10 to 15 minutes more, transferring them to a rack as they turn golden (edges will turn golden before middle does). Make more corn thins in same manner.

GUIDES TO THE TEXT

SOURCES

Below are sources for the sometimes hard-to-find ingredients and cookware used in the Recipe Compendium.

Asian chile paste is available at Asian markets, many specialty foods shops and supermarkets, and by mail order from Uwajimaya, (800) 889-1928. (Feel free to experiment with different chile pastes—we tried Chinese chile paste and Thai *sambal oelek* and liked both.)

Asian fish sauce is available at Asian markets, many specialty foods shops and supermarkets, and by mail order from Uwajimaya, (800) 889-1928. The fish sauce has an extremely strong aroma, but don't let that put you off—it lends wonderful depth to dishes.

Banon cheese is a soft, rindless French sheep's- or goat's-milk cheese. It comes wrapped in chestnut leaves that have been soaked in eau-de-vie to protect against uninvited mold. (As the cheese ripens, its surface takes on the color and aroma of the leaf.) We like a bourbon-soaked young version made in Indiana by Capriole. Capriole Banon is available at some cheese shops and by mail order from Capriole, Inc., (800) 448-4628 (five-cheese minimum per order, about $38).

Bocconcini, Italian for "morsels," are 1-inch balls of mozzarella. They can be found in Italian markets, specialty foods shops, and some supermarkets.

Blowtorch (miniature) is the first choice of professional chefs for caramelizing the surface of a crème brûlée because it gives greater control than does a broiler. These mini-blowtorches are available by mail order from Williams-Sonoma, (800) 541-1262; regular-size blowtorches can be purchased at most hardware stores.

Buffalo steaks can be found at some butcher shops and supermarkets or ordered from Denver Buffalo Company, (800) 289-2833.

Bulgur (medium or coarse) is available at natural foods stores and specialty foods shops, and at some supermarkets. Supermarket brands are typically a medium grind; if you purchase your bulgur in bulk or at a natural foods store, you'll find the grinds are numbered 1 to 4, with 4 being the coarsest.

Caviar is shipped throughout the U.S. from several sources. One of our favorites is Petrossian, (800) 828-9241.

CHILES

Anchos are actually dried *poblano* chiles. *Anchos* are considered the sweetest of all dried chiles and are said to be the most commonly used in Mexico. You can order them from Chile Today—Hot Tamale, Inc., (800) 468-7377.

Canned chipotles in adobo can be found in Latino markets and specialty foods shops and can be ordered from Chile Today–Hot Tamale, Inc., (800) 468-7377.

Dried chipotles can sometimes be found in supermarkets, usually in the produce section. They are also available at Latino markets and specialty foods shops and can be ordered from Chile Today–Hot Tamale, Inc., (800) 468-7377.

Poblanos are bought fresh but are not traditionally eaten raw. Their thick flesh makes them perfect for stuffing; cooking or broiling brings out their earthy flavor. They're available at specialty foods shops.

Dried Aleppo chile flakes can be ordered from Kalustyan's, (212) 685-3451. New Mexican chile flakes are a good alternative and can be ordered from The Chile Shop, (505) 983-6080.

Chinese five-spice powder—the fragrant combination of star anise, Sichuan peppercorns, fennel, cloves, and cinnamon—is available at Asian markets and most supermarkets. Blends vary, so you may want to sample a few; a supermarket brand we like is Spice Island.

Coconut (unsweetened desiccated) is stocked by many supermarkets (in the baking or the Asian aisle) and natural foods stores. It's also available from Uwajimaya, (800) 889-1928.

Corn husks (dried) are available at Latino markets, specialty foods shops, and some supermarkets, or by mail order from Kitchen Market, (888) 468-4433.

Crystallized ginger, pieces of gingerroot that have been cooked in sugar syrup and coated with granulated sugar, can be purchased at some supermarkets and specialty foods shops and by mail order from Williams-Sonoma, (800) 541-1262.

Cupcake liners are available by mail order from Sweet Celebrations, (800) 328-6722. They are not always well labeled; ask for item #601524 (red) or #502332 (white with gold).

Edamame, soybeans in the pod, are available frozen in the U.S. year-round (keep your eyes peeled for fresh ones at farmers markets during the summer months). They are available in Japanese and other Asian markets, some specialty foods shops, and by mail order from Uwajimaya, (800) 889-1928.

Edible flowers must be unsprayed and organically grown. We ordered ours from Indian Rock Produce, (800) 882-0512, and Diamond Organic, (800) 922-2396; they are also available from some farmers markets, and some specialty produce shops.

Foie gras (raw) may be found at some specialty foods shops and ordered by mail from Citarella, (212) 874-0383.

Frenched racks of lamb have been trimmed down to the bone. They are available by request from butchers.

Garam masala, an all-purpose Indian blend of spices (typically based on coriander seeds, cumin seeds, black peppercorns, cardamom, cloves, and cinnamon) is available at East Indian markets and some specialty foods shops and by mail order from Penzeys Spices, (414) 679-7207.

Israeli couscous has larger grains than regular couscous and is available from Dean & DeLuca, (800) 221-7714 or (212) 226-6800, ext. 269. A good substitute is *acini di pepe*, tiny peppercorn-shaped pasta, available in supermarkets.

Masa harina, sometimes called tortilla flour, is made from dried corn kernels treated with cal (the mineral lime), then dried and powdered. Although it looks similar to fine-ground cornmeal, it's not the same thing at all; one should not be substituted for the other. Look for it at Latino markets, specialty foods shops, and some supermarkets, or by mail order from Kitchen Market, (888-468-4433).

Merguez, a spicy French-Moroccan lamb sausage, is available from D'Artagnan, (800) 327-8246 or (973) 344-0565.

Mirin, or Japanese sweetened rice wine, is a flavoring, not a beverage like sake. Check the Asian aisle of your supermarket (or your local Asian markets) or order from Uwajimaya, (800) 889-1928.

Mizuna, **tatsoi**, and **radish sprouts** can be found at specialty produce markets, farmers markets, and at some supermarkets.

Olive branches make a beautiful and unusual Mediterranean-style garnish for many dishes. We found ours at Zezé, (212) 753-7767.

PEPPERCORNS

Green peppercorns in brine are sold in specialty foods shops.

Pink peppercorns, actually the dried berries of the Baies rose plant, are available at specialty foods shops and by mail order from Kalustyan's, (212) 685-3451.

Sichuan peppercorns are available at Asian markets and by mail order from Kalustyan's, (212) 685-3451.

Porcini mushrooms, also called *cèpes*, are available seasonally at specialty foods shops, specialty produce markets, and by mail order from Urbani, (800) 281-2330 (they also sell them frozen).

Poussins is the French term for young, or spring, chickens. Ask your butcher for them or call D'Artagnan, (800) 327-8246 or (973) 344-0565.

Powdered egg whites can be found in your supermarket's baking aisle. A mail-order source is New York Cake and Baking Distributors, (800) 942-2539. (We used Just Whites brand.) Many supermarkets also carry pasteurized liquid egg whites in the dairy case.

Preserved lemons, indispensable in the Moroccan kitchen, are first pickled in salted lemon juice, then seasoned with spices such as cinnamon and cloves. Their unique flavor and silken texture cannot be duplicated by fresh lemon pulp. They are available from Assouline & Ting, (800) 521-4491.

Pumpkin seeds (hulled green) are available at natural foods stores, Latino markets, specialty foods shops, some supermarkets, and by mail order from Kitchen Market, (888-468-4433).

Red lentils—smaller, rounder, and lacking the seed coat of the green variety—are available at Indian and natural foods stores and at some supermarkets.

Rice noodles are sold dried in Asian markets and many supermarkets, and by mail order from Uwajimaya, (800) 889-1928.

Rosewater, a fragrant distillation of rose petals, can be ordered by mail from Kalustyan's, (212) 685-3451. We liked Cortas brand, from Lebanon, the best.

Sabra is an Israeli chocolate-orange kosher liqueur. It's available at liquor stores.

Smoked peppered mackerel is available at specialty foods shops and by mail order from Ducktrap River Fish Farm, (800) 828-3825.

Smoked whitefish caviar is available by mail order from Collins Caviar Co., (800) 226-0342. The caviar keeps, chilled, opened or unopened, up to 5 days.

Star anise, the dried seed pod of a Chinese evergreen, is available at Asian markets, specialty foods shops, and some natural foods stores and supermarkets, and by mail order from Uwajimaya, (800) 889-1928.

Stove-top smoker/cooker and wood chips are available from Williams-Sonoma, (800) 541-1262.

Superfine granulated sugar dissolves in an instant. Look for it in the supermarket.

Sweet Spanish smoked paprika is sold at some specialty foods shops and by mail order from The Spanish Table, (206) 682-2827; La Tienda, www.tienda.com; and Dean & DeLuca, (800) 221-7714. We like La Chinata brand the best.

Ten- by 1-inch tart pan can be a little difficult to find. A good mail-order source is Sur La Table, (800) 243-0852.

Thai curry paste can be found at Asian markets, some specialty foods shops and supermarkets, and can be ordered by mail from Uwajimaya, (800) 889-1928.

Whole-milk yogurt (most of what you find on your grocer's shelves is low-fat) is available at natural foods stores, specialty foods shops, and some supermarkets.

GENERAL INDEX

Page numbers in *italics* indicate color photographs
☉ indicates recipes that can be prepared in 45 minutes or less
☉+ indicates recipes that can be prepared in 45 minutes but require additional unattended time
🍃 indicates recipes that are leaner/lighter

INDEX OF RECIPE TITLES

Page numbers in *italics* indicate color photographs

TABLE SETTING ACKNOWLEDGMENTS

To avoid duplication below of table setting information within the same menu, the editors have listed all such credits for silverware, plates, linen, and the like under "Table Setting."

Any items in the photograph not credited are privately owned.

Back Jacket
Table Setting: See Table Setting Credits for Easter Brunch.

Frontispiece
Grape Tart (page 2): Basket—Broadway Panhandler, (212) 966-3434.

Table of Contents
Beach Setting (page 6): See Table Setting Credits for A Weekend at the Shore: Breakfast on the Beach.
Buffet Setting (page 7): See Table Setting Credits for Southern Comforts.

The Menu Collection
Backyard Setting (page 10): See Table Setting Credits for Beyond Backyard Basics.

A Ski House Dinner
Table Setting (page 12): Eighteenth-century English Champagne flutes—Bardith, (212) 737-3775. "Highlander Plaid" cotton fabrics (napkins and pillows), available through decorators—Clarence House, (212) 752-2890. Eighteenth- and nineteenth-century English wood candlesticks (table and mantel); vintage plaid tole box—Bob Pryor Antiques, (212) 688-1516.
Roasted Veal Chops with Shallots, Tomatoes, and Olive Jus; Soft Polenta (page 14): "Naturalware" stoneware chargers; "Beekman" crystal wineglasses—for stores call Calvin Klein, (212) 292-9000. Acrylic and stainless-steel flatware by Sabre—Marel Gifts, (800) 261-3501. Vintage sterling-rimmed horn cups—Holland & Holland,

(212) 752-7755. "Highlander Plaid" cotton fabric (place mats), available through decorators—Clarence House (see above).
Warm Chocolate Raspberry Pudding Cake (page 15): Nineteenth-century creamware plates by Wedgwood—Bardith (see above).

Southern Comforts
Crab Spread with Benne-Seed Wafers (page 16, upper left): "Tapered" stoneware bowls—Simon Pearce, (212) 421-8801.
Buffet Setting (page 17): Hand-thrown and hand-glazed earthenware buffet plates—for stores call Potluck Studios, (914) 626-2300. Plastic-handled stainless-steel flatware by Dubost—Sur La Table, (800) 243-0852. "Lavender Column" wineglasses—Tuscan Square, (212) 977-7777. Cotton napkins by Shyam Ahuja; stoneware bowl (sweet-potato purée)—Simon Pearce (see above). Wood saltshaker by Peugeot and pepper mill by Perfex—Bridge Kitchenware, (800) 274-3435 or (212) 838-1901.

A Weekend at Home: Breakfast
Breakfast Tray (page 18): "Laura" resin-handled flatware—Villeroy & Boch, for stores call (800) 845-5376. American silver mug (roses), circa 1850—F. Gorevic & Son, (212) 753-9319.
Buttermilk Waffles with Crisp Prosciutto (page 19): "Tsao Mat" stoneware plates designed by Calvin Tsao for Nan Swid—for stores call

(800) 808-7943. Sterling coffeepot with wood handle—F. Gorevic & Son (see above).

A Weekend at Home: Lunch
Table Setting (page 20): "Hunslet" earthenware bowl (salad) designed by Hartley Greens for Leeds Pottery—for stores call Penshurst Trading, (212) 447-5266. "Edme" Wedgwood earthenware plates—for stores call (800) 955-1550. Glass bowl (sauce)—Simon Pearce, (212) 421-8801. Silver-plated ladle, circa 1880—S. Wyler, (212) 879-9848. Sterling knives and forks, London, 1792-1807—F. Gorevic & Son, (212) 753-9319. "Burgundy" crystal wineglasses from the Oenology Collection—Baccarat, (212) 826-4100. "Tabriz" linen place mats—Ad Hoc Softwares, (212) 925-2652.

A Weekend at Home: Dinner
Table Setting (page 22): "Tsao Mat" stoneware dinner plates designed by Calvin Tsao for Nan Swid—for stores call (800) 808-7943.
Passion-Fruit Meringues (page 23, lower): Continental silver dessert spoons, circa 1895-1910—F. Gorevic & Son, (212) 753-9319.

Cocktails in an Artist's Loft
Party Setting (page 24, upper): *Grey Sitting With Me* and *Red Sitting With Me* by Jim Dine—courtesy of Pace Prints, (212) 421-3237. Plates by Maryse Boxer—Barneys New York, (212) 826-8900. Martini glasses—Ad Hoc Softwares, (212) 925-2652.

Orrefors "Vintage" wineglasses by Erika Lagerbielke—for stores call Galleri Orrefors Kosta Boda, (800) 529-4557. Silk cocktail napkins (solid colors)—ABH Design, (212) 688-3764. Grosgrain-ribbon cocktail napkins—for stores call Dransfield and Ross, (212) 741-7278. Arne Jacobsen chairs—Troy, (212) 941-4777. Glass vase—Frank McIntosh Home at Saks Fifth Avenue, (212) 940-2738.

Shredded Chicken Wraps with Avocado, Cucumber, and Cilantro (page 24, lower): Annieglass salad plate—for stores call (800) 347-6133. Linen cocktail napkin—Gracious Home, (212) 517-6300.

Ginger-Hoisin Beef on Crispy Noodle Cakes; Chocolate Caramel Diamonds (page 25, lower): Annieglass salad plate (ginger-hoisin beef) and oval platter (chocolate diamonds)—for stores call (800) 347-6133.

A Vegetarian Italian Dinner

Table Setting (page 27): "World View" porcelain plates—for stores call Sasaki, (212) 686-7440. "Inox" stainless-steel flatware; "Classic" wineglasses (2 sizes); linen place mats and napkins; black glass *sake* bottle—Ad Hoc Softwares, (212) 925-2652. Kjaerholm woven-wood chairs—Troy, (212) 941-4777. Eames wood folding screen—The Museum of Modern Art New York Design Store, (800) 793-3167.

Easter Brunch

Table Setting (pages 32 and 33): "Rendez-Vous" crystal Champagne flutes by Baccarat, (212) 826-4100. Multicolored candy eggs by Burdick Chocolates, (800) 229-2419.

Celebrate Spring

Gingersnap Crumble Ice-Cream Tart (page 34, upper): Handmade pottery cake stand by Frances Palmer, (203) 222-3532. Stainless-steel cake server—Crate & Barrel, (212) 308-0004.

Mushroom, Radish, and Bibb Lettuce Salad with Avocado Dressing (page 34, lower): "Annecy" blue-and-white bowls by French Heritage—Solanée, (800) 717-6526.

Table Setting (page 35): "Annecy" blue-and-white plates by French Heritage; "Provençal" painted-wood side chairs—Solanée (see above). "Pierre Deux Provence" blue and green chargers; "Country French" pewter-handled flatware; "Boutis" and "Indianaire" printed cotton fabric (napkins); "Calendau" printed cotton fabric (tablecloth); "Terre Mêlée" urn—Pierre Deux, (212) 570-9343. "Astoria" wineglasses and water goblets—Crate & Barrel (see above). Yellow vegetable dish by Fiestaware—Bloomingdale's, (212) 355-5900.

A Weekend at the Shore: Breakfast on the Beach

Baked Blueberry-Pecan French Toast with Blueberry Syrup (page 36): Kitchen towel with multicolored stripes—Anthropologie, (212) 343-7070.

Beach Setting (page 37): Steamer chair—Smith & Hawken, (212) 925-0687. "Gio" juice glasses—Zinc Details, (800) 811-4020. "Stone Harbor" bowl—Wedgwood USA, (800) 677-7860. "Basique" plates in celadon and stone—Barneys New York, (212) 826-8900. Raffia-wrapped bottle; striped chambray kitchen towel (on hamper); mug—Ad Hoc Softwares, (212) 925-2652.

A Weekend at the Shore: Lunch Indoors

Composed Salad of Sautéed Chicken Breasts, White Beans, Asparagus, and Roasted Peppers (page 39): "Stone Harbor" plates—Wedgwood USA, (800) 677-7860. "Cambridge" flatware—Mariposa, (800) 788-1304. "Gio" glass tumblers—Zinc Details, (800) 811-4020.

A Weekend at the Shore: Dinner on the Deck

Curry-Marinated Mussels on the Half Shell; Jícama Date Canapés; Farmers Market Green Salad with Fried Shallots (page 41, upper and lower): "Aqua" glass plates (hors d'oeuvres); "Frost" glass bowls by Fossilglass—First Cup, (617) 244-4468.

Grilled Lobsters with Southeast Asian Dipping Sauce; Sautéed Peas and Small Potatoes; Grilled Parsley-Butter Bread (page 42): "Williams Collection" wineglasses—Williams-Sonoma, (800) 541-1262. Raffia-wrapped pitcher (with flowers)—Ad Hoc Softwares (212) 925-2652. Linen napkins—Simon Pearce, (800) 774-5277.

Star Anise and Coriander Spice Cake with Lime Vanilla Frozen Yogurt (page 43): Glass plates—William-Wayne & Co., (800) 318-3435. Napkin rings—Tommy Bahama, (941) 643-7920.

Cooking with Friends Toni Ross and Jeff Salaway

Grilled Butterflied Leg of Lamb with Lemon, Herbs, and Garlic (page 44, lower): Wood platter—Crate & Barrel, (212) 308-0011.

Table Setting (page 45): "Brasilia" ceramic dinner plates and salad bowl—Jonathan Adler, (212) 941-8950. "Recamier Ceruse" wood-handled flatware by SCOF—for stores call Mariposa, (800) 788-1304. "LSA" wineglasses; linen place mats—Bergdorf Goodman, (800) 218-4918. Linen and cotton napkins by Xochi—for stores call Laytner's Linen & Home, (888) 690-7260.

Feta and Marinated Niçoise Olives with Grilled Pitas (page 46): Ceramic platter—Crate & Barrel (see above).

Lamb on Grill (page 47, lower): Glass bottle—Crate & Barrel (see above).

A Vineyard Dinner

Table Setting (page 48): English transfer-printed earthenware plates, circa 1915—STV Productions, (212) 874-5253. "Classique" plates (white)—Crate & Barrel, (800) 323-5461. Green glass chargers—Fishs Eddy, (212) 420-9020. "Blackberry" linen napkins—for stores call Dransfield & Ross, (212) 741-7278. Coach lantern—for stores call Design Ideas, (800) 426-6394. "Round" wineglasses (clear)—Simon Pearce, (212) 421-8801. Eighteenth-century Irish chair with original needlepoint—Mercia Bross Antiques, (212) 355-4422. Eighteenth-century English walnut armchair with original needlepoint upholstery; eighteenth-century English fruitwood bench—Newel Art Galleries, (212) 758-1970.

Fig, Apricot, and Raspberry Brûlée (page 49, lower): English transfer-printed earthenware bowls, circa 1915—STV Productions (see above). Photographed at the vineyards and fruit farm of Mr. Sam Argetsinger.

A Sizzling Summer Fiesta

Chilled Roasted Red Pepper Soup (page 50, upper): "Small Rimmed Bowl" glass bowls—Simon Pearce, (212) 421-8801.

Grilled Steak; Chimichurri Sauce; Avocado and Sweet Onion Salad; Corn Pancakes (page 52): Porcelain plates (steak and salad)—Gordon Foster, (212) 744-4922. "Whiskey" wineglasses—Simon Pearce (see above).

A Wedding in the City

Party Setting (page 54): 24-inch resin bowl (covered in gold foil)—Martha Sturdy Inc., (604) 872-5205. Small gold-leaf vases and votive candle-holders; metal lantern (covered in fabric); pewter vase (near chair)—Bardin Palomo, (212) 989-6113. Aqua beaded silk georgette dress—Susan Lazar, (212) 302-5888. Blue velvet slip dress—Jill Stuart, (212) 343-2300. Men's green angora V-neck sweater—Paul Smith (212) 627-9770.

Smoked Caviar and Hummus on Pita Toasts (page 55, upper): Red resin side plate by Dinosaur Designs—Zeeland Modern Design, (310) 318-6040.

Beet and Jícama on Endive with Yogurt Dressing; Israeli Couscous with Butternut Squash and Preserved Lemon (page 56, upper): Neon purple and pink resin slabs—Martha Sturdy Inc., (604) 872-5205. Antiqued bronze serving set—Pottery Barn, (212) 219-2420.

Plated Dinner (page 56, lower right): Napkins—Kinnu, (212) 334-4775.

Wedding Cake with Blackberries and Roses (page 57): Giorgio Armani Classico cashmere sweater—Giorgio Armani, (212) 988-9191. Tocca embroidered dress (under sweater)—Tocca Store, (212) 343-3912.

Without Ceremony: Wedding Food for an Intimate Dinner

Plated Dinner (page 58, upper): "Moon" porcelain dinner plate by Rosenthal—Ad Hoc Softwares, (212) 925-2652. "Gloria" hand-cut and engraved wineglass—William Yeoward Crystal, (800) 818-8484.

Blossom-Topped Cupcakes (page 59): "Limbo" painted wood coffee table—Rhubarb Home, (212) 533-1817.

Beyond Backyard Basics

Backyard Setting (page 60): Teak bench (weathered by owner)—Kingsley-Bate, (703) 978-7200. Celadon Pottery Bowls—Ad Hoc Softwares, (212) 925-2652. Tumblers—Banana Republic, (888) 277-8953. White bowls and dinner plates by Syracuse—Bloomingdale's, (212) 705-2000. Wineglasses—Williams-Sonoma, (800) 541-2233.

A Vegetarian Thanksgiving with Anna Thomas

Buffet setting (page 62): 9-inch round plates in celadon and linen (on table)—Luna Garcia, (800) 905-9975. Ice bucket—Simon Pearce, (800) 774-5277. Mustard-colored footed compote by Barbara Eigen—Curly Willow, (516) 324-1122.

Risotto Cake; Roasted Wild Mushrooms in Red-Wine Reduction; Cranberry Ginger Sauce; Jícama and Cilantro Relish (page 64): Peach pasta bowl and linen round plate—Luna Garcia (see above). Linen tablecloth and napkins—ABH Design Inc., (212) 688-3764. "Windsor" wineglasses—Simon Pearce (see above).

Squash and Sweet Potato Soup with Chipotle Sauce (page 65, upper right): Square plate (under soup bowl)—Luna Garcia (see above). "Tristan II" stainless flatware in bright finish—Gorham, (800) 635-3669.

Thanksgiving Primer

Table Setting (page 67): "Ruth" goblets—William Yeoward Crystal, (800) 818-8484. Pewter and ceramic oval platter (with turkey) by Arte Italica—Neena's, (877) 877-9292.

Girl's red piqué dress—Spring Flowers, (212) 717-8182.

A Gingerbread Christmas Party

Gingerbread House (page 70, upper right): Gingerbread house kit—Beth's Fine Desserts, (800) 425-BETH. Cutting board; "Stromboli" chair—Crate & Barrel, (800) 996-9960.

Macaroni and Cheese with Garlic Breadcrumbs; Lime, Apricot, and Soy-Sauce Chicken Wings (page 70, lower right): "Pivoine" red oval baker—Emile Henry, (302) 326-4800. "Classique" cream dinner plates—Crate & Barrel (see above).

Man and girl making gingerbread house (page 71, upper): Man's polo sweater—Brooks Brothers, (800) 274-1815. Girl's overalls—Old Navy, (800) 653-6289.

Buffet Setting (page 71, lower): "Prisma" platter and linen napkins—Gracious Home, (800) 338-7809. "Red Hot" pasta bowl and dinner plates—Gaetano America, Inc., (626) 442-2858. Pewter carving set—Arte Italica, (212) 213-4773.

Hanukkah with Rozanne Gold

Table with Candles (page 72): Gelt—Art CoCo, (800) 779-8985. Bowl—Calvin Klein Home Collection, (877) 256-7373. Dreidel—Pavillon Christofle, (212) 308-9390. Vintage tablecloth—Françoise Nunnallé, (212) 246-4281. "Sapphire" goblets—Hoagland's of Greenwich, (203) 869-2127.

Seared Smoked Salmon with Cucumbers Pressé (page 73, upper): "Chinoise Blue" dinner plates—Hoagland's of Greenwich (see above).

Rib-Eye Roast, Gravlaks Style (page 74, upper left): French porcelain platter (ca. 1820)—Bardith, (212) 737-3775.

Baked Sabra Oranges with Orange Sorbet (page 74, upper right): "Firmament" fruit bowl—Cristal Saint Louis, (212) 679-5566.

Chocolate-Sesame Cups (page 74, lower left): Gold plate—Calvin Klein Home Collection (see above).

Plated dinner (page 74, lower right): "Agathon" porcelain dinner plates—Fabergé Collection, (203) 761-8882.

"Horizon Gold Granite" chargers—Devine Corp., (732) 751-0500.

New Year's Eve Cocktail Party

Times Square Cocktail; Panko Scallop with Green Chile Chutney (page 76, upper): Champagne glasses—ABC Carpet & Home, Inc., (212) 473-3000. Napkin—Takashimaya, (800) 753-2038. *Salt-and-Pepper Edamame* (page 77, upper left): Red pedestal plate—Takashimaya (see above).

Cosmopolitan Champagne Cocktail; Jerk Pork and Red Pepper Mayo on Black-Eyed-Pea Cake (page 77, upper right): French *bento* box; glass—Takashimaya (see above).

Low Fat & Delicious: A Hearty Dinner

Roasted Spiced Shrimp on Wilted Spinach; Buffalo Steak and Onion Confit on Garlic Toasts; Roasted Beets with Garlic Beet Purée (pages 78 and 79): "Colorstone Birch" plates—for stores call Sasaki, (212) 686-7440.

Low Fat & Delicious: A Taste of India

Mango in Ginger-Mint Syrup; Cumin Pea Soup; Tandoori Spiced Chicken Breasts; Carrot Salad with Lime and Cilantro (pages 80 and 81): Marble dishes—Jamson Whyte, (212) 965-9405.

Low Fat & Delicious: Midsummer Light

Gazpacho; Grilled Scallops, Zucchini, and Scallions with White Beans (pages 82 and 83): "Craftworks" ceramic plates by Lindt-Stymeist—ABC Carpet & Home, (212) 473-3000. "Corner" embroidered linen napkin—for stores call Area, (212) 924-7084. PN "Carre" French hand-molded terra-cotta tiles (in Rouge)—Country Floors, (212) 627-8300.

A Recipe Compendium

Pappardelle in Lemon Cream Sauce with Asparagus and Smoked Salmon (page 84): Ceramic dinner plates by Aletha Soule—for stores call The Loom Company, (212) 366-7214.

A Thai Dinner

Tablesetting (pages 216 and 217): Flatware, bronze vase; napkins—Pottery Barn, (800) 922-5507. Rectangular cream platter (beef) and celadon bowl (pork)—Ad Hoc Softwares, (212) 925-2652. Placemats—Rustika, (212) 965-0004. Screen; pillows; table; pottery bowl (cucumber salad)—Jacques Carcanagues, (212) 925-8110.

A Collection of Thai Snacks

Grilled Chicken Wings with Sweet Garlic Sauce (page 226, upper right): Square blue plate; light blue pedestal bowl—Global Table, (212) 431-5839. *Squid with Red Curry Sauce* (page 226, lower right): Maroon oval plate (squid)—Global Table (see above). *Pomelo Salad* (front jacket and on page 227): Ceramic turquoise bowl; square plum plate—Global Table (see above).